My Thoughts, My Life:

Institutionalized Racism in Canada

Deneace Green

First Edition - July 2011

Edited by Orville "Picky" Green.

ISBN

978-1-77067-157-7 (Hardcover)

978-1-77067-158-4 (Paperback)

978-1-77067-159-1 (eBook)

Published by:

FriesenPress

Suite 300 - 852 Fort Street

Victoria, BC, Canada V8W 1H8

www.friesenpress.com

For information on bulk orders contact:

info@friesenpress.com or fax 1-888-376-7026

Distributed to the trade by The Ingram Book Company

Table of Contents

Part I

Racism in the Canadian Armed Forces

— Chapter 1 —

Bars at the Gate

Today is Friday, April 09, 2004, and the time is 10:01 a.m. Since I have been thinking about death for the past few days, and since I have no intention of leaving without telling my story, I believe this is as good a time as any to tell you what happened to me—considering that it is a hell of a lot easier to tell my story than it is to sue for damages. I am going to tell you about my experiences in the Canadian Armed Forces.

It started in late 1996. I was working at Coca-Cola Bottling Limited as a customer service representative. The job was boring and debilitating. It was damaging the nerves in my ears, wrists, fingers—which hurt night and day—and my back and neck were in constant pain. I endured it because . . . that is a whole other story.

Every morning and evening, to and from work, I saw the same poster in the bus: The Canadian Armed Forces, "There is no life like it." It appeared to offer a life of adventure and pride, conducted with a sense of urgency, and the acceptance of all Canadians. I considered how my job was affecting my mental state as well as my physical well-being. I noted the phone number for the recruiting office and made the call. I was scheduled for testing in February 1997. No one told me that since I was a university graduate, I could apply as an officer candidate. When I found out, I called the recruiting office to have my application changed from non-commissioned status to commissioned officer status. The woman on the phone told me that my marks fell just a few points below the cut-off mark for an officer. She refused to tell me my test score, and she would not tell me the cut-off score for a commissioned officer candidate. This was my introduction to the lies and deception of the Canadian Armed Forces. Had I realized how much worse the lies would get, I would have withdrawn my application at that point.

Months passed. I came to a point where, physically, I could no longer bear working at Coca-Cola; so, I left and was out of work. As a recent graduate (or so I was told), it was almost impossible to find meaningful work that related to my studies in sociology and political science. I focused on finding employment with social service agencies; however, employers would often say to me, "You don't have experience."

I took on five volunteer jobs at the same time, to get experience: as a *group facilitator* and *telephone counsellor* for the North York Women's Centre; at my Member of Parliament's office; in the City of North York, Ward 4 Councillor's campaign; and as a telephone solicitor at the Liberal Party's office. During this time, I called the Canadian Armed Forces Recruiting three or four times to find out what was happening with my application. The answer each time was the same, "We'll call you once your application has been processed." I wondered what had happened to the sense of urgency that the poster had suggested and, with some urgency of my own, I looked at jobs with Corrections Canada, Canada Customs, and the Royal Canadian Mounted Police (RCMP). My intention was to secure a position as a corrections, customs or police officer. None of these positions required a degree, neither did they require a college diploma; however, since I had earned an Honours Law Enforcement college diploma prior to attending university, I thought the government agencies would welcome me upon passing their entrance exam. In July 1997, I attended an RCMP information seminar. August 1997, I wrote the entrance exam. In September 1997, I received a letter from the RCMP informing me that I passed the test.

Later in September, someone from the Canadian Armed Forces called me to attend an interview and physical testing. The interview came before the physical testing, and I was rather surprised to see that an American Petty-Officer was conducting the interview. He was a Black man, friendly yet professional, in his very early thirties. The White man who conducted the physical testing was not as friendly. He, too, was young—maybe late twenties. The way he treated me was a precursor of what was to come: His demeanour was cold and his words critical; I counted one more sit-up than he had counted. Then, he added, "If your heart rate was slightly higher, you would not be able to join [the army]." He refused to reveal the reading of my heart rate to me. When the testing was over, an army personnel immediately told me that I had passed both the interview and the physical components. This caused me to believe that I would start training within a week, at most. A month later, I called to find out when I could start training. The answer was, "We'll call you once your application has been processed." I kept up my job search and continued volunteering.

Late in October 1997, the executive director of the Ontario Networks of Employment Skills Training Projects (ONESTEP) called me for an interview. I did the interview on a Friday and by the time I got home, there was a phone message stating that I could start working on the Monday. *I need to mention that because of traffic, I was ten minutes late for that interview; yet, I was offered the job as Membership Services Coordinator. I should also mention that Lloyd Davis, my "husband," had made a concerted effort to get me to the interview as quickly as he could maneuver the car through downtown traffic.* It was a one-year contract position, but I felt that it was my first real job. The Conference Coordinator, Lisa, and the Executive Director interviewed me. I mention Lisa because she later became an unexpected source of support for me.

On the Wednesday of my first week on the job, I checked my answering machine messages from a phone booth during my lunch break and there was a message from the Canadian Armed Forces. They wanted me to start picking up the gear for basic training on Thursday, the very next day. I was to be an administrative clerk for 25 Medical Company. No one in the military asked me what job I wanted to do; they just looked at my test score and decided to make me an administrative clerk. Truth be told, I never thought of a soldier as someone behind a desk doing paperwork. I applied with the intention to do what "soldiers" do—train to fight. According to the voice mail, the process would commence at 6:00 p.m. and should take about an hour. I had just started a job but, after all, I had put much more time and energy into the army. *One of my weaknesses is that I don't know when to quit, except for intimate relationships which I tend to quit before giving them a real opportunity to take root—that, too, is another story.*

— Chapter 2 —

Getting My Gear

I arrived at the military base, Moss Park Armoury in Toronto, about 5:45 p.m. At ten o' clock, I was still there filling in paperwork and listening to why joining the army was such a wonderful decision. At the end of the glamour stories, the group of new recruits—mostly university and college students—was told to report again the next Thursday at 6:00 p.m., to pick up gear. Just about all the other recruits for this company were there to be medics of some sort while aspiring to become doctors.

The next Thursday, I did as I was told; however, I got only a few pieces of gear. There was an ice storm in Quebec, and most of the reserve gear and troops were sent to help deal with the natural disaster. Our group was told that we would be finished by 8:00 p.m. At ten o'clock, we were still there.

This night, I really took notice of two teenage Pakistani boys because they were the only ones whose parents came to our first orientation and now they were back, paying as much attention to the speakers and the paperwork as though they were the ones joining the military. They were tired, but proud of their boys and made themselves very visible. It was obvious that the boys were doing what the father would have liked to be doing himself. The smile on this father's face gave him the look of youth; his years seemed to drop away, so that he looked very much the age of his older son. The younger brother was smart, but his older brother did not seem to possess the same level of intellectual ability.

Throughout basic training, the younger one always tried to help the older one without making him feel at all inferior. The older one failed at just about everything, but he was allowed to complete the course because of the presence of his parents. No, the parents did not follow the recruits into the fields for basic training, but they made themselves quite visible in the first few sessions conducted at the armouries. Furthermore, each time they dropped off the boys for training or picked them up, one could see and feel their excitement for their offsprings' participation in the Canadian Armed Forces. I felt sorry for the older brother. I thought that his parents put excessive pressure on him, that he was there because his parents wanted the status back in Pakistan of having their son in the Canadian Armed Forces. It seemed to me that it was the ultimate case of living vicariously through one's children. In fact, the older brother had failed out of York University and was to 'transfer' to a college the next year. Usually, the disgrace of failing out of university would cause someone in that culture to commit suicide (or at least think very strongly of it), but he was now a member of the Canadian Armed Forces. Therefore, everything else was secondary.

At the end of the evening, we recruits were told to go to Fort York Armoury the coming Tuesday evening to get the rest of our gear. The stated objective was for us, recruits, to be fully geared for the next meeting. I went to get my gear, but the personnel at the supply shop turned me away because they had sent more equipment to Quebec to alleviate the effects of the ice storm.

The third Thursday of our induction started out no differently from the first—more paper work and listening to propaganda—except that, by now, several of the recruits had become frustrated and returned their partial gear. Some did not bother to leave properly; they just threw the gear down and walked out. One recruit, upon throwing his gear down, told a warrant officer to go f—k himself. This recruit's display of aggression was in response to the tone the officer used when the recruit said he wanted out. I should have left, too. But again, I didn't know when to quit.

This was the first night of some basic military drills. I am almost embarrassed to tell you that our trainers had me running back and forth in the gym in my high heel shoes and shin-length, pleated skirt. You see, after my regular day job, I went directly to the armoury thinking that we would be exposed to more classroom talk on theories, history, and specialized areas of the Canadian Armed Forces.

We indeed heard theory; however, I got the sense that no one really knew what to do with recruits lacking military gear. Thus, as warm up for drills, two corporals lined up the recruits at one end of the gym and told them to run to the other end. One corporal ran alongside us. When we got to the opposite end of the gym, the corporal who ran with us ordered us to run back to the end at which we started. He stayed put. The two corporals, at each end of the gym, had us running back and forth for a good ten minutes.

Had it not been for a few of the male recruits wearing their business attire, I would have felt that I really messed up this time. Oddly enough, everyone kept looking at my shoes as though I should have known better than to be wearing heels or watching for what they perceived as the inevitable fall. The obvious question was, why not just take them off? The answer was that a corporal, without saying it in such plain language, informed me that the health and safety issues my bare feet posed to others outweighed the risk of injury to myself. The next question: What about taking off the shoes but leaving your knee high stockings on? Answer: Neither the army nor I was willing to risk my running around in nylons on a slippery gymnasium floor. I was quite relieved when we were ordered to stop running and, instead, to start marching—even though it meant that my first experience of marching in the military was in high heel shoes and a shin-length skirt. To begin the march, we were divided into three groups of about fifteen recruits and one corporal to each group. The corporal ordered us to walk behind him and swing our arms as he was swinging his, position our heads as he positioned his, and move our feet in unison with his. I felt like I was in Grade Two again, playing "Simon Says," except that we were saying, "left, right, left, right, left, right. . . ." The bottom line was this: The government was paying the recruits to be present from 6:00 p.m. to 9:30 p.m.; the repetition in military propaganda had grown stale after the first session; the recruits had to "earn" their wage instead of sitting around waiting for the clock to strike 9:30 p.m.; safety was secondary to the government's payment of $7.50 per hour, per recruit.

At the end of this night, the group was told to report to Denison Armouries on Friday (the next day) for training. I still had not been issued any military clothing, so a corporal told me to wear gym clothing. The problem was that the only gym-type clothing I had was a pink track suit.

— Chapter 3 —

Weekend 1: Late November 1997

Drills, Drills, Drills and More Drills

Our group of approximately fifty recruits assembled and was divided into three roughly equal sections, and named accordingly: One Section, Two Section and Three Section. I was in One Section; and by the luck of this selection process, I was now with the people with whom I would be doing the rest of my training.

Approximately half of the recruits were wearing proper military attire. I was in my pink track suit among everyone else with their deep-green attire or some other dark colour. Even though I had not much choice in the matter, it was a big mistake because I was immediately made a target; every second question or reference was made to "Green." The name was easy to remember, and my pink clothing made the situation worse: a Black woman named Green in pink clothes. It could have been a human moment, recognizing that we were all there together in spite of the deficiencies of military management of gear and clothing, but nobody relaxed. Instead, the trainers targeted me as if it was my fault. A warrant officer, Warrant Ross, tried to help me out the next day (Saturday) by lending me his green overalls; but by then it was too late—all the trainers knew "Green" and enjoyed the feeling they got exploiting my unfortunate situation.

The weekend consisted of drills, drills, drills and more drills: drills on proper line formation; drills on how to march; drills on how to turn and when to turn; drills on how to salute; drills on how to come to attention; drills on how to carry your weapon, which was a rifle; drills on how and when to be at ease; drills on how to step in and out of line formation. . . .

Corporal DeGroot felt that he had to give someone a chit, and guess who got it? I think it was for improper line formation. I signed the chit, even though I had the right not to do so. I signed because the situation was new to me. Ultimately, chits are allocated to show one's imperfections; they are negative statements written about recruits to make it easy to show why certain recruits are not suitable to be the Number One Candidate—not suitable to graduate at the top of the class. I knew that my signing pleased DeGroot, because he wrote in his daily report that I had a "good attitude." These reports were read to the recruit at some point during the weekend. It appeared that Corporal DeGroot and Corporal Ludwig were going to be One Section's direct supervisors; they were going to provide the bulk of the actual training.

Actual training meant doing the following: getting up at 6:00 a.m.; using a half hour for ablutions in a bathroom that was shared with about fifteen other females (luckily, some did not feel the need to shower); getting properly dressed, including burning lint from your clothing and picking fur from your beret (I felt lucky that I did not have a uniform from which to burn lint); ensuring that your boots were properly laced and polished (again, I felt lucky that I had no boots to polish); squeezing the air out of your pillow and sleeping bag, rolling them up nice and tight as taught by DeGroot; standing over your sleeping gear and waiting for inspection. All of this was to be accomplished in a half of an hour.

The corporals would then come over to inspect our presentation and berate the recruits for some incompetence or another, mostly imagined; after which they ordered us to put away our sleeping gear and line up for bodily inspection. The corporals had no reservations about pointing out any flaws they noticed before the official inspection; and the master corporals and sergeants would join in to turn inspections into a feast of degradation.

I thought, as an eight-year-old child, coming to Canada from Jamaica in the heart of winter and enduring snow and ice for an hour, during what teachers call "lunch hour," was a culture shock; but this, the army, was the ultimate culture shock.

Next came drills for about an hour; then a catered breakfast; then drills; then classroom training; then drills; then a catered lunch; then drills; then more classroom training; then drills; then training on insignia; then drills; then training on how to salute and whom to salute and whom to call "Sir" and whom to call by rank. *For example, you should never call a non-commissioned officer "Sir." He would yell at the top of his lungs to inform you why: "Do not call me 'Sir'! I work for a living!"* After a catered dinner, the recruits were sure of more drills; there would be time for some sort of physical activity such as volleyball, and plenty of time to polish your boots—or, in my case, review classroom work.

We were informed for the first time that our course of basic training was going to be every other weekend, completely away from home. No one had told the recruits this during all those hours of filling us with propaganda in the first long evenings. This meant that what we thought would be six Saturdays of training, turned out to be twelve weekends away from home. In fact, even after telling us that we would be away from home for twelve weekends, we were away for fourteen weekends. No one in authority bothered to address this discrepancy with the recruits. I guess they figured we would not notice an additional four nights away from home, of not sleeping in our own beds.

— Chapter 4 —

A Few Words about Military Hierarchy

The colonel and the lieutenant colonel, at the top of the heap of command, were, typically, old White men who looked as if they should have retired ages ago. Even after basic training, I still viewed them as distant figures walking around, displaying untold numbers of insignias, bells and shiny buttons pinned to their hats, sleeves, and chests.

In rank immediately below the lieutenant colonel was the major. He was a tall White man in his mid-forties, with dark hair and dark eyes—Major Jensen. A few months into the future, he would tell me that his wife characterized him as an ape. Regardless of her intent, to be characterized as other than human implies that one is of sub-human intelligence. After interacting with him, I was convinced that his wife was correct in her assessment of him.

Our captain also was a White man, a little below average height and size, in his mid-thirties, and he appeared to be an approachable person.

Next down the line was Lieutenant Nguyen, a small-statured man of Vietnamese descent, who looked like he should be in elementary school. He was a commissioned officer.

The warrant officer (WO) was Ross. He was huge, White, and bald-headed. He was a non-commissioned officer (NCO).

The difference between an NCO and a commissioned officer is that a commissioned officer has earned a university degree of some sort and is therefore recognized by the Queen; whereas, an NCO can be totally illiterate and as brave as they come, but is not worthy of the Queen's recognition. Without a degree, an NCO will never move into a commissioned rank; without a degree, an NCO will never become an officer in the true sense; he remains a *common* soldier.

The sergeant was Cherniawski, a White man in his late twenties, average size, handsome, but a creepy aura emanated from him—perhaps because of the way his shoulders hunched up to meet his rather large head which appeared to squinch down to meet his shoulders, and the way he looked at people as though he were looking through them. His choice for a girlfriend (a corporal) said a lot about his self-esteem; he could not tell if she was looking at him or across the room, as her severely misaligned eyes always left everyone to wonder where or at what or at whom she was actually looking—through her long outdated spectacles.

The master corporal responsible for my section was Gardner. He was in his late twenties, average size, dirty looking, smoker; a White man who, as a result of his right side being lower than his left side, wiggled and jiggled like a woman as he walked. *Decent* White people would refer to him as White trash.

Corporal Dennis and Corporal Miller were two average-looking Black women in their early thirties, who helped out where they were needed among the three sections.

Two corporals were directly responsible for my section. They were Corporal DeGroot and Corporal Ludwig, and they were both White. DeGroot was twenty years old and Ludwig was nineteen. DeGroot was about 5'8" tall; his eyes may have been hazel or brown, hair light brown. He had a scrawny body from which his uniform hung much too loosely. His neck was too long for his body, and his under-developed, upside-down triangular head bobbed up and down when he walked. His boots looked too big and heavy for him. Just about every word he said came through clenched teeth: likely a reflection of the frustration he had been going through for the past few weeks, trying to arrange training gear for his recruits. Despite DeGroot's physical appearance, his IQ was notably higher than Ludwig's.

Ludwig was as cute as they came. He would have made a much better fashion magazine model than a soldier. He was 5'5" tall, 130 pounds, with thick (but not too thick) brown hair, beautiful brown eyes, nicely chiseled jawbones, clothing that fit well on his pumped body, and a smile that would encourage his mother to soothe his cheeks and kiss them often. His physical appearance and his calm demeanour drove most of the female recruits nuts, but I saw him as a cute little boy. He had an East Indian girlfriend, a corporal, who was a bitch from hell. She treated him like shit and ensured that the female recruits kept their horny bodies away from her property. She never bothered me because she knew that I was not interested in him; besides, what would he do with me?

Upon successful completion of basic training and two other courses, we would become *privates trained*. We, the recruits, were *privates untrained*—the bottom of the hierarchy. We were taught the chain of command, and we were cautioned that we must never skip any of it when dealing with grievances or other issues related to the army. Thus, whenever you see the word *superior* when referring to people in the army, it has nothing to do with superiority as human beings; rather, it means *higher than one's own rank*. For example, a corporal would refer to a master corporal as his *superior* and a private as his *subordinate*. The phrase *immediate superiors* refers to lower rank soldiers directly responsible for recruit training; while *superiors* is the general term applied to people of higher rank. Privates refer to each other as *peers* or *Private*.

The private aspires to be a corporal; the corporal aspires to be a master corporal, who aspires to be a sergeant; the sergeant aspires to be a warrant officer. Without a degree, the warrant officer's career stops. Assuming the warrant officer earns a degree, he can aspire to be a lieutenant, which is the lowest rank of a true officer. The lieutenant aspires to be a captain, who would like to be a major. A major aspires to be a lieutenant colonel and then colonel; and the colonel looks forward to becoming a corpse. However, by a miracle of some sort, a colonel may become a brigadier, then a general and finally a field marshal.

— Chapter 5 —

Weekend 2: December 1997

More Drills and I Get My Gear

I still did not have military attire, because even more equipment was being sent to Quebec to help with the ice storm emergency.

Between spending so much time getting things sorted out in the army and my day job, I was exhausted. Nonetheless, on the way home from my day job, the next Friday evening of training, I stopped at a Goodwill store. It was really just for the sake of doing something relaxing, but I felt lucky when I came across a pair of army-green track pants. I bought them, along with brand new pairs of elbow pads and kneepads; additionally, I bought a pair of awesome, padded, leather gloves. The pads looked brand new, and the gloves looked like they had never been worn. I did not realize how handy my gloves and pads would be in the months to come. God always, always, takes care of me. I do not believe in coincidences. I believe, even with all the hell that you will come to know about my life's journey, God orchestrates my life according to His will and for my good. He knew exactly what I would need while training in the field, and He structured this Friday evening accordingly.

The events of the day did not allow me to make it to the army base by 7:00 p.m. It felt so good to be home after such a very long week that I decided to stay home and rest; however, I still found time to wash the pair of track pants I had just bought at the Goodwill store.

I was really planning to skip training that weekend, so I had my "husband" call the base to report my illness. The voice on the other end of the phone told him that I should report for training by 8:00 a.m. the next morning. Nonetheless, within an hour, Sergeant Cherniawski called back to find out why I was not present for training. After I reiterated my reason, like the previous voice on the phone, he told me to show up at eight o'clock next morning.

My "husband's" parents named him Lloyd Davis; but considering the extent to which he used and abused me, I find it difficult to call him anything other than the official four-letter word relating to the hole where solid waste matter leaves any mammal's body.

When I arrived at the base on time in the morning, I was greeted with a stern, "Green! Where were you last night?" I told Corporal DeGroot that a call was made to the unit informing them that I was "sick." I might as well have just relaxed instead of bothering to have the call made, because the absence went on my file as a "fail to report." According to my superiors, "No one knew where you were." You will see how my reported absence affected me, and how, a few months later, a White fellow-recruit named Garant was not at all affected by her unreported absence—properly referred to as AWOL (absent without official leave).

Corporal Ludwig ridiculed me for not being more persistent in getting military attire. What was I to do? Raid the garrison supply shop and take what I wanted? More people quit this weekend. On Weekend #1 we had about fifty recruits, and this weekend we were down to about forty. I remember one university student, a Black girl, came by to quit because the army was "interfering" with her studies.

Again, the weekend consisted of drills, drills, drills and more drills; and the chits kept on coming. I was too slow lining up, improperly dressed, in improper line formation. . . ."Too slow lining up" meant I was the last one to stand up *straight* in line—there was no way for me to verify this, considering that my eyes must be straight ahead. "Improper dress" meant there might have been a piece of lint or thread somewhere on my clothing. Yes, DeGroot had no qualms about invading my personal space to zero-in on microscopic lint. When he found a piece of something barely visible to the naked eye, he was as elated as a man who just panned a piece of gold for the first time. In all fairness to DeGroot though, he may have occasionally considered his proximity an invasion of personal space because he would sometimes leave his body at a fair distance and extend his scrawny neck so that his head alone was in my personal space. Other times he would retract his neck and be as close as a dog sniffing its food, nostrils flayed and all. "Improper line formation" meant my back was not straight *enough* or my shoulders were not squared with the shoulders of the two people standing next to me: White recruits. I tried to remain positive, though I noticed that chits were not being given out as generously to White recruits.

WO Ross drew me a map of where I needed to go to get my gear. The man had a talent—he drew the road and the buildings for markers so precisely that I had absolutely no problem finding the garrison. Even though this garrison was only ten minutes away from my training base and fifteen minutes from my home, it was still very inconvenient to be driving around a second time trying to get my military gear after a full day at my regular job.

I managed to get two military combat outfits. At the garrison, two teenage Black boys with teenage attitude, and a mature Black woman, were handing out the supplies. People always have trouble telling my age because I look much younger than I really am, and this situation was no different. That is, the boys treated me as though I were their age mate. When they talked to me, they would blink their eyes slowly, look down and smile at each other sideways. When I shook my head and rolled my eyes, they somewhat smartened up. It amazes and annoys me when little boys try to pick me up.

The supply pickings were quite slim, to say the least. The first pair of pants I tried on were so tight that my bottom was squashed up like an inflated balloon jammed into a too-small container. I did not want to turn around to show it to the boys because I know what my bottom looks like when pants are too tight. Furthermore, I did not want to give them anything more at which to blink and smile at each other. They insisted, and I complied. One responded as he shook his head from left to right: "Take it off. Take it off. Take it off." The look on the other guy's face read, "Now I've got to go look for more pants." The female supplied me with my sleeping bag, water bottle, plate, etc., while the boys went to look for other pants. They returned with two jackets and two pants. The style of one jacket was outdated, but they commented that the choices were limited. One pair of pants was notably too short but; again, those were the only choices. The boots were unbearably tight, and my two big toes suffered a lot as a result. Why was I putting myself through this shit? The army promised a future of adventure; I could see the world through the army; I could have a meaningful career. You know, when I looked around the gymnasium at inspection times, I thought that of all the people in the three groups, I got the worst deal on the military-issued clothing and footwear. This is so typical of my life.

— Chapter 6 —

Weekend 3: December 1997

More Drills, Polishing Boots

The size of the three groups, for one reason or another, kept declining; we were down to about thirty recruits.

In addition to drills, drills, drills and more drills, we were taught First Aid and CPR. I passed both the practical and written with 24/25 on my written test. Additionally, we had training on the Geneva Convention. I was rather surprised to find that WO Ross read below a third-grade level. He was teaching the class one aspect of the Geneva Convention; his part of the lesson lasted less than five minutes, in which he read aloud part of the Convention, but I do not think the class heard any of it because the recruits were shocked by his lack of reading skills. When I looked at my fellow recruit, Private DaCosta, her mouth was wide open; and her eyes were open even wider. She was so stunned at the warrant's inability to read, she did not realize her mouth was open. She was about twenty years old, of Portuguese descent, with short black hair and dark eyes. She made an effort to control her weight but her body still looked slightly too wide for her age and height. All I could think about was the warrant's ability to draw directions. He was a volunteer with the Metropolitan Toronto Police Force, but I don't think he could have passed the written entrance exam for a constable, and he would have had even more difficulty passing the physical. I felt sorry for the gentle, bald-headed, White giant.

The recruits needed to provide a medical form, signed by a physician, indicating that their physical health could withstand the army's physical training. I did not have my form from the army; however, I did have my physician-approved medical form for employment with the Royal Canadian Mounted Police (RCMP)—which had much higher physical standards than the army. I asked if it was okay to use that form. WO Ross said, "Yes." It did not take long for all my superiors and most of my peers to know that I had applied and was being considered for employment with the RCMP, and that was when the claws came out from my immediate superiors. I did not realize that a police force was first choice for just about all of them, and when they did not make it they then turned to the army. This is where the "school of life" really started for me. The chits to discredit me started coming left, right and centre. Corporals Degroot and Ludwig, Master Corporal Gardner, Sergeant Cherniawski and Lieutenant Nguyen were demons without disguise. I thought it was because of my race, but I later found out that race was just one factor. Later still, I came to realize that the RCMP and other government agencies foster this resentment toward minorities by making White society feel that minority recruiting policies actually help minorities get jobs. It is my experience that these policies are there to keep Black people, in particular, from openly rebelling and to remind White people to carefully guard "their place" in society: I will tell you about my experience of this in Part 2, *My Thoughts, My Life: Racism in the Royal Canadian Mounted Police (RCMP).*

The recruits were told to write their biography. Of the thirty-plus recruits, I knew mine was the most comprehensible because WO Ross complimented me on it. He did so after he released the recruits from the classroom and said, "Green. Wait here." His compliments included, "Very little detail was left out." Nonetheless, I had to re-write it because everyone else was required to re-do theirs. I think the warrant said "very little was left out," to influence me to not feel resentful for having to re-write my essay. He further stated, "I am impressed. It takes a lot to impress me, and I am impressed by your life and accomplishments." I felt good about all the compliments; they were genuine.

However, there is a lesson here: By knowing my plans to go to law school, and seeing that the RCMP was in the process of hiring me—something just about all of them strongly desired with one police force or another—the jealousy my immediate superiors felt was evident in the way they started treating me; they targeted me for failure and were successful in sabotaging my life. They targeted me in the army and lied to the RCMP about me. How was I to know that some people's goal in life is to keep you from attaining your goals? I say *some people,* though I want to say *people*; that is, the treatment that I received from my immediate superiors is not limited to people in the army. Again, when I start telling you about other aspects of my life, you will understand why I do not limit my statement regarding people to only those I encountered in the military. If I had not truthfully shared my future plans in that biography, my life would be very different today: In that, I would have been hired by the RCMP; or, they would have had to look for a different reason to reject me—a reason that, perhaps, would have made it more obvious that they do whatever they can to ensure that Black people do not enter into "their domain." Between the medical certificate from the RCMP and the biography that I wrote, my fate was sealed. In truth, the biography was just the icing on the cake; the moment I revealed the certificate, my life was set. Here is some advice for you: Before you reveal anything about yourself to anyone, think about whom the person is and how this person could affect your life. Better yet, do not reveal anything to anyone unless it is absolutely necessary. Trust me; I have seen enough to know what an innocent statement or action can do to a person's life, and this is not limited to White versus Black. Rather, this relates to people whose purpose is to prevent you from achieving yours. You can use my presenting the RCMP's medical certificate as an example of how an innocent action caused me to become a target and changed the course of my life. I cannot count the number of times a Black corporal on the course, Corporal Miller, would remark that the army does not belong to "them," meaning, *Black people belong here, too*. She used the official hair style for women as a reference: "The style they are still teaching in basic training is the same one used in World Wars 1 and 2, where White women twisted their hair into a ponytail, wrapped it into a bun at the back of their heads, and set their berets on top." A White corporal, named Heather, would demonstrate this for *all* female recruits; and that was the lesson on hair for me, with my cornrows, and other women who did not have hair long enough or straight enough to twist into a ponytail.

As if my revelation from my presenting the RCMP certificate and writing of my plans for law school would not suffice to last my lifetime, Corporal Miller further drove the point home in telling me the story of a Black man who went through basic training. When I thought I had seen the worst and that racism could not get more blatant, she told me that my experiences paled in comparison to that Black man's. What became obvious to her was that prior to entering the army, the man had seen enough of the world to know who to let into what aspects of his life. What no one in the army (including her) knew about him was that he was in medical school. When he announced that he was a doctor, leaving the army to practise medicine, the disbelief on the faces of his peers and superiors was more than satisfaction for all he had endured. The gravy for him, however, was the look on those same faces after the initial shock had worn off slightly—which read, "If only I had known."

I was the first female to finish the test consisting of a mile and a half run, and I was the only female to do it in less than the allotted time; all the other female recruits failed this part of the course. Corporal Ludwig was proud of my performance; when I reached the finish line, he said, "Give me some of that," while raising his hands for me to slap a high five; but that didn't matter because I soon learned that the army has its own set of rules that are not written in Queen's Regulations and Orders. I would even venture to say that some of their rules are contrary to the Queen's Regulations and Orders. For example, according to the Queen's Regulations and Orders, no one who failed any test can be Number One Candidate; yet, it was a female not named Deneace Green who became Number One Candidate.

Far too much time was spent on polishing boots. Whenever we were not engaged in official training—i.e., drills, physical activities, or lectures—a corporal, master corporal or a sergeant was quick to remind us not to waste taxpayers' money by sitting idly; so, he or she would order us to polish our boots. I could not understand why, if the army wanted soldiers to have smooth, shiny boots, the army did not purchase boots with a smooth finish. To make things worse, the superiors expected the privates to have their boots looking like theirs by the next weekend of training. I thought Vaseline would do the trick.

The Thursday night before Week #4, I packed my gear, because I knew there would not be time on Friday. I did not see a need to waste time polishing my boots throughout the week because I had confidence that Vaseline would save me hours of polishing. I rubbed my boots with a dry cloth to ensure that any dust not visible to the naked eye was removed. I then spread newspaper on my carpeted bedroom floor, removed the laces from my boots, scooped out a dollop of Vaseline from its plastic container, plopped it on the toe area of one boot and began to spread it over the boot. The leather was not absorbing the Vaseline the way my skin does after my morning showers. I used the dry cloth to wipe away the excess Vaseline. The boot shone all right, but it was a very different shine from that of my superiors'. Theirs had a smooth, sparkling shine like black glass; mine simply looked like it had been greased. There was no point in doing one boot and not the other. I hoped that my superiors would appreciate the obvious effort that I had put into polishing my boots.

— Chapter 7 —

Weekend 4: January 1998

Boots, Guns and Army Food

I was sharing my car with my "husband," Lloyd Davis ("Anus"). We lived in the north end of the city, at Bathurst and Wilson; I worked in the south end, Bathurst and Wellington; Lloyd worked in the west end, the Toronto Airport. He would drop me off at my workplace in the mornings, then drive my car to his job. In the evenings, he would pick me up and drive me home.

The Friday evenings of my weekend training were particularly stressful, because Lloyd had to battle rush hour traffic on the Queen Elizabeth Way (QEW) to pick me up from work; then, he had to battle with rush hour traffic some more to get me home to get dressed for the military and drop me off at Denison Armoury. Even though the armoury was less than a ten-minute drive from home, I needed the use of my car because I had to transport my gear; and Lloyd needed to use the car over the weekend. He got off work at 4:30 p.m. I finished work at 5:00 p.m. and was required to be at the base by 7:00 p.m. Two hours might seem like plenty of time, if you are not sitting in traffic for sometimes ten minutes at a time without moving two car lengths.

This Friday, I walked into the base relieved that I had arrived on time. I assembled with my group to wait for a superior to call us to "A. A. A. A-TEN-N-N-TION!" Instead, I heard, "GREEEEN!" I looked around and saw Corporal DeGroot marching towards me, as if he were about to strangle me, his eyes glaring at my boots, teeth clenched, "Greeeen! What have you done? Your boots look disgusting!" By the time he finished growling through his clenched teeth, his chit book was in his hand, ready to write me up.

Not long after that, Sergeant Cherniawaski decided to give me a chit for a piece of thread that was not burnt from my clothing. He loved to say, "I give them out like parking tickets." Then, he would use a sentence that included the word "discombobulated." Apparently, he had just learned the word and felt it was his duty to teach it to everyone else; or to let people know of his extensive vocabulary. Not to be out-done, Master Corporal Gardner wiggled over to the recruits to yell at them about how to wear their berets: "It should be formed into a peak and pulled down towards the left side of your head. I don't want you pulling them down over your eyes like those fucking Jamaicans in the Caribbean!"

At this point of my training, the statement shocked me because I was taught to be aware of political correctness; I was taught not to make generalizations; I was taught that people in authority should appear to be beyond reproach. As the statement became a regular part of Gardner's speeches, it was apparent that he had a particular hatred for Jamaicans—a hatred that went beyond the usual intolerance of someone whose ethnicity differs from one's own. It was as if Jamaicans had taken something of great value from him. I thought of my visits to Jamaica; I thought of the shows I had seen about Jamaica; I cannot remember seeing anyone wearing their beret the way he described. Moreover, except to attend other military bases in other parts of Ontario, I do not think Gardner had ever left Toronto in all his life. *I promise to tell you how, in a city of over three million people, someone close to me at the time actually encountered Gardner in a totally different environment and came to the same conclusion as I—ultimate White trash.* The fact that not one of his superiors cautioned him about the verbalization of his disdain for Black people—coded in the word Jamaicans—is quite telling of how deep racism runs in this society, where people pretend to be polite and accepting of each other.

Although no one in authority addressed Corporal Gardner's racism, one of the superiors decided to help the recruits by telling us how to easily shape our berets: "Since they are made of felt, wet them; wring them out; and form them on your heads while they are still wet." This tip made our lives easier, in that we did not need to waste precious time fussing over our berets.

When I considered the hell I went through in traffic, trying to get to the armoury on time, the berating over my boots and now this direct attack on Jamaicans, I walked over to DeGroot and told him that I was ready to be discharged. He didn't say a word; however, he breathed in and out heavily through his nostrils while clenching his teeth, pushed back one shoulder while straightening his back, turned and stomped off to the office. Not ten minutes passed before he returned, life in his steps, head bopping towards the ceiling as he moved towards me saying, "Green. How quickly the wheels turn." Before he was within arm's length of me, he extended his hand holding a sheet of paper, "Here! Sign this. It's your release [document]." The look of triumph on his face caused me to look at him politely, blink slowly and, without addressing him by his rank say, "I changed my mind." This time I took pleasure watching him repeat his dance—the teeth and breath, the shoulder and back, and the stomp—back to the office.

Master Corporal Gardner was in charge of conducting the physical exercise this Saturday morning. After marching the recruits around the gymnasium a few times he decided that it was time for push-ups. He ordered the recruits, "Make sure you keep up with me!" I prepared myself for a hundred, because Gardner had made the troops believe that he could do at least that many without breaking much of a sweat. On about the fifteenth push-up, I noticed that the corporal started to slow down; he appeared to be a lot more tired than I. I smiled within myself because I was just getting warmed up. At about the eighteenth push-up he started to rest by pausing a few moments in the up position. I knew he was not going to make it past thirty push-ups. After the twentieth push-up, he ordered us to relax; in my mind, I shook my head. I could have easily done seventy push-ups and then immediately run a mile and a half in less than twelve minutes, because the physical test for the RCMP required that level of fitness; and I surpassed their requirement. Gardner's colleagues and superiors looked at him as if to ask, "*What the hell was that?*" The relief I could see in most of the troops told me they were grateful that the master corporal was in no better shape than they. I looked around and concluded that perhaps three or four of the male recruits (of about thirty) could have made it to thirty push-ups. The master corporal disappointed me, in that my energy level was just starting to rise when he quit. His smoking was getting the better of him.

This was the weekend we started learning about weapons. Of course, we learned first about our weapons on paper, starting with the C7 rifle and ending with the C10. The C7 is the weapon of choice for the Canadian army, and each soldier is issued his or her own. Recruits were not issued a weapon; instead, a weapon belonging to a trained soldier was loaned to a recruit—the same weapon to the same recruit for the entire term of basic training. The corporal whose weapon I used liked me because I took good care of his weapon. When he handed it to me, he always smiled. Not so, for some of the other recruits—their superiors would say, "Make sure you fucking clean it properly this time."

We were taught drills using the C7. We were taught how to take them apart, clean them, and put them back together . . . in the dark. We were instructed to go everywhere with the rifle, our *wifle.* The term *wifle* says a lot about the army. Here I am, a very straight woman, carrying around a *wifle.* What about gay men? Should they be forced to carry around a *wifle*? What was this *wifle* terminology doing psychologically to gay recruits who would rather die than expose their sexual orientation—for fear of how they would be targeted by these higher ranks who totally lacked restraint? I did not expect the military to be a tea party; however, I expected basic respect, fairness, acceptance and civility amongst people who were getting together for a common purpose: to protect their country and each other.

Once I got up to go to the bathroom and then realized I did not have my *wifle* with me. I had taken only about six steps before I realized that I forgot my *wifle*. I ran back to get it. Corporal DeGroot and others saw what happened. The corporal decided to give me a chit for "unsecured weapon." *Wait until you read how this was presented to the RCMP, but let me present it to you as it happened.*

Except for the bathroom area and some classrooms, we basically lived in the gymnasium for the entire weekend: at night, we converted it into a dormitory—laid out our sleeping bag and air pillow, daytime clothing folded and placed on the floor above pillow, boots next to clothing, *wifle* next to us. At 6:00 a.m., we reconverted the gym to a drill training hall. At 7:00 a.m., we converted the gym to a catered cafeteria—lined up for a plate of bacon, egg and toast, moved to the table offering milk and juice, moved on to get an apple or orange, then took a seat on the bleachers off to the side of the gym. After breakfast, at 7:30 a.m., we converted the gym into a weapons training classroom—identifying parts of the C7, disassembling it, cleaning it and re-assembling it. Throughout the day, the gym would be converted many more times: lunch room, drill training hall, First Aid and CPR classroom, physical fitness centre, dinner hall . . . and dorm again, at 11:00 p.m.

When the recruits lined up to eat, they were required to place their weapons in a nearby designated area where our officers congregated. After eating, the recruit was required to pick up his or her weapon before going to the bathroom. I cannot tell you the number of times recruits, who ran off to the bathroom, reached the bathroom only to remember that they had forgotten their weapon; some did not even remember their weapon until they got back from the bathroom. Sometimes, a superior would even say, "Leave it; I am watching them." In my case, the recruits had just finished a weapons cleaning exercise. I packed up my cleaning supplies and got up off the floor to go to the bathroom. I was not six steps from my weapon before I felt something was missing. I turned around and dashed back to my spot to retrieve my *wifle . . .* and DeGroot saw me. Since he did not get the opportunity to call my attention to my weapon being left unattended—it happened too quickly—he whipped out his chit book. Considering that all my peers and immediate superiors were present, the weapon could not have been any safer; in other words, there was no chance of the weapon being stolen or damaged or otherwise. We were being taught to look out for each other; therefore, even if I had forgotten to take my weapon with me, it would have been safe, just as everyone else's was safe when they left theirs behind. Yet, this went into my permanent file, even though its documentation was nonstandard procedure. Have you noticed that I have not mentioned anything about bullets? That is because there were none; we did not have access to bullets until months later, when we had our field training. Nonetheless, DeGroot filed his report as though I had wantonly left my weapon "unsecured."

— Chapter 8 —

A Soldier First

Regardless of the position a person applies for in the army, he/she must attend basic training. You are a soldier first. My job, upon graduation from basic training, was administrative clerk. Thus, I had the opportunity to view many of my colleagues' files. When reading through their files, it was clear that some people who failed miserably at certain tasks were made to look like ideal candidates; and not one included any information about "unsecured weapon," as it should have been. This I knew because Master Corporals Miller and Dennis told me repeatedly, "What happened in the field is not supposed to go on your permanent file!" Furthermore, Warrant Ross told me, "Don't worry about it, Green. It doesn't go on your file." What made my situation different? Sometimes I scream with my mouth shut.

Once, when I observed Sergeant Cherniawaski (White man) give Private Garant (White woman) a chit and then immediately tear it up, I thought, "Something is really fucked up here. So, your "parking tickets," chits, are reserved for particular people?" But when Garant actually had the nerve to brag about it, that's when I stopped signing those fucking chits. Now, every report read, "Green has a bad attitude." In the larger society, this type of racism is no different; it is just a bit more covert. Cherniawaski had this apologetic look on his face as he would write up my chit, and he often verbalized the phrase, "It ain't easy being *green*." Since I have yet to see a green person, I knew exactly what he was really saying, "It is not easy being Black." He actually felt sorry for my being Black, yet he perpetuated racism; obviously, his pity for my being Black was not enough to enable him to overcome his racist practises.

I think the vast majority of White people truly believe that Black people would rather be White. Let me clear up this erroneous thought for you. No, we actually like being Black; however, we hate the fact that we have to fight twice as hard to get half of what they get with no effort at all. Confusing? How about this? All the recruits earned $7.50 per hour. I was constantly reminded of how I was not deserving of my pay, while Garant just needed to exist to be worthy of hers. You can retort, "But you were both getting paid"; and I will answer, "Yes, but the pay was not just in dollar amount; she got to be Number One Candidate with no effort at all." Hell, she was even too good for chits that were not supposed to make it into one's file; chits were supposed to be used as a guideline for giving recruits constructive criticisms during basic training. Because of the constant struggle to survive in any part of the world, some Black people wish they were not Black; not because they would rather be White, but because every facet of their lives is a constant struggle—a struggle that is escaped only via death. So now you know that the self-loathing some Black people harbour has nothing to do with thinking that being White is in and of itself more desirable; it has to do with shedding the constant fight to be treated as a fellow human being.

Did you know that the terms Niger, Nigger, Negro and Nero all came from the Latin word *niger* meaning *black?* The point I am making is this: Niger means *black*, not black *person*. Therefore, when I am referred to as Negro, I am being referred to as *simply black* rather than *black person*. For this reason, I (and other Blacks) get to see people at their core; they (White people) believe we (Blacks) do not understand. Consequently, in general, they treat us as they would treat retarded White children.

We were tested on the steps to firing the C7 rifle. At this time, there were twelve people in my section. Of the twelve people tested only two passed—Private DaCosta and Private Bezchilbuyk; everybody else failed, including Private Garant who later became the Number One Candidate. The Queen's written rule of the army is clear: If a person fails any part of the course, that person cannot be Number One Candidate. Who said the army was a place for discipline and rigidity? In the civilian world, Number One Candidate is equivalent to valedictorian: usually the highest educationally ranked student among those graduating from an educational institution.

I think of this situation, and I remember a sociology professor who taught a course titled Social Change. The course dealt extensively with the European Expansionism. The professor's name was Jean-Louis de Lannoy. He got my undivided attention during a particular lecture as he gave the class an insight into how the world outside of school operates. He said, "When you are in school, you are evaluated and compensated based on your abilities; but in the outside world, you are evaluated and compensated based on your racial identity." This greatly surprised me, coming from a White man. He was partially correct: With a few exceptions, he being one, teachers are no different from employers where racial discrimination is concerned; I guess because he is fair-minded, he believes all teachers are, for the most part, the same as he. He went on to lecture on East Indians and their caste system, but what struck me was when he said, "A lot of well-educated people in that society prefer to remain in their environment with little financial reward and a great deal of respect, rather than immigrate to North America where the financial rewards are great but the sense of being valued is greatly lacking." I was watching the situation with Garant, and it was as though I was sitting in the lecture.

I was remembering Professor de Lannoy and taking comfort in knowing that not all White people wish I did not exist. I know this for a fact. During my last year of university, in the heart of winter, Canada Post had a mail strike. I had asked Professor de Lannoy for a reference regarding law school. Even though I was no longer his student, he wrote the reference and hand delivered it to my home. One might say, "Big deal." Oh, but it was indeed a big deal: You see, despite their hefty salaries, some of those professors do not even want to acknowledge students as people; in their opinion, they are way above us in societal and intellectual status; we are wasting "their" time. We feel it in their reluctance to interact with students during their scheduled office hours; and as a Black woman, I sometimes felt this treatment went far beyond the issue of class. For some, office hours were just a required formality.

It was a big deal because, when the professor got to the entrance of my building, he found the door locked and the intercom not working. Instead of going home, he drove to a public phone booth, called his wife and told her to look for my phone number among his documents; then, called to tell me that he was outside and could not get in. When I looked outside through my bedroom window, he was getting out of his car. By the time I clad myself with something decent to greet him at my apartment door, he had slid the reference letter under my door and was on his way. Someone had let him into the building. I opened my apartment door, thanked him and offered him a cup of tea. In his thick German accent, I believe, he replied, "Oh, no. No thank you. It is no problem. I have been playing mailman to my students all week." In the midst of being treated as "black," I knew there was someone in the "dominant class" who saw me as "person."

That night, WO Ross assigned each recruit a study partner for the next part of the test that was scheduled for the following day: dismantling and then re-assembling the weapon. He sternly said, "You are responsible for your partner; if your partner fails, you fail." Private DaCosta was my partner.

There was a very self-centered recruit in Three Section, Private Stone, who was assigned to partner a private of Middle Eastern descent. Stone, supposedly, had been in the army in Britain. Instead of practicing with his partner, he spent the whole time making a repulsive spectacle of himself; he did so by telling a whole bunch of totally fabricated war stories. He was supposedly in a war zone when he and his partner were on a balcony and enemy soldiers fired shots, barely missing him; but his partner was shot in the face and killed. Another story had to do with a friend of his going home from a party with a woman whom he met at the party. The woman had it set up so that enemy soldiers killed his friend in her apartment. DaCosta's eyes were saying what everyone else was thinking, "Your partner is going to fail." Her mouth opened a few times, but the words just could not find their way out. She slowly closed her mouth and brought her attention back to me. Stone's partner sat as though he had no speech, waiting for Stone to stop exalting himself. When the neglect became too obvious, Stone would quickly interact for a moment with his partner and then get back to a more important issue—his stories or helping other people, White people. No recruit was surprised when Stone's partner miserably failed the test and was ordered to return to his unit.

Stone fitted perfectly with his racist superiors. He was assigned to Three Section along with a Black girl named Dalel. Stone never missed an opportunity to treat her the way my White, immediate, superiors were treating me. Dalel's situation was worse than mine because she was catching hell from her teammates as well as her immediate superiors. Because of Stone's experience in the army, whenever a superior called "fall-in," Stone would quickly find a spot in the gym and come to attention. All the other recruits were expected to form a line using Stone as the "marker"; he was considered the head of the line. As a result, he was expected to "help" his teammates. For him, that was the opportunity to target Dalel who withstood a lot from him.

In years to come, I would work in a treatment centre with boys much younger and somewhat younger (7-17) than Stone (who was twenty-two at the time of basic training); and now I can say from experience that Stone had Attention Deficit Hyperactivity Disorder (ADHD). A treatment centre would have better served him than the army.

Stone might very well have been the most experienced recruit in Three Section; Garant did not even rank in the top three in One Section. Yet she appointed herself as the "marker." In fact, once she offered to "give you [me] a shot" over something to do with line formation—she was taking charge because she was the favourite of the people in charge. I told her to make sure that she got a good one in because it may be her only opportunity. I meant it. During our first week in the army, I heard her telling someone about a relative of hers who just finished the officers' training. Her connections would not have saved her from all the anger I was feeling. Had she given me that shot, I would have had a sweet relief.

Corporal DeGroot was surprised to see that I passed his portion of the test. We had to go from station to station to do various parts of the test. At DeGroot's station, part of my gun barrel was stuck. I knew I was doing the right thing, so I added some muscle power. Things fell into place—snap! Instead of giving me a word of encouragement or allowing me a moment to savour my success, DeGroot demanded to know: "Green, where *is* your socks?"! He was born and raised in Canada, yet he could not even get his singular and plural correct. I could see him getting ready to give me another chit for *improper* dress, this time, for not wearing socks. I dug down into my boots and pulled up my socks. My feet were excessively dry and he, too, noticed the dryness. I didn't care. Now that the more important issue—my socks—was out of the way, he was ready to address the issue of lesser importance: "For a while there I didn't think you were going to make it, but you must have known what you were doing because you got it in there." He was not able to give me a chit, nor was he able to fail me—a small victory for me. The fact that he expected me to fail the test is evidence of how White people typically treat me; as if to say, *she is not intellectually capable*. There is always that *look* they give each other, and that feeling they emanate reeks "incompetent"; but they think we are not intelligent enough to sense *it*—they think *we do not understand*.

There was one guy I was rather happy to see sent back to his unit. He was of Middle Eastern descent. He ate as though there would be no food around tomorrow and he needed to store as much as possible *today*. The worst part was that he chewed with his mouth open. He felt the need to pray just about every half hour, and he prayed with his hands open, palms up. I watched him pray and thought, "You glutton; are you begging for food? Does the Koran not teach you that gluttony is a major sin?" Every time I looked at the ball he carried where his belly should have been, I thought, "*Glutton.*" Had he been a Black person, I would not only have been repulsed by his greed for food; but I would also have been embarrassed for Black people.

That night, we had physical education indoors. During the relay section, I was whipping the other girls' asses. Corporal Heather—the White woman who had given all the female recruits the lesson on how their hair should be worn—could not stand it. She stopped the race and told me to start over. I was shaming the other females with my physical abilities—most notably, my ability to run fast. Heather and her male accomplice stopped the race again and this time told me to wait until my rival started running before I could start. Can you imagine? Yep, Blacks must keep to their place—the back of the bus. Nonetheless, I complied; but you know what happens to me when people challenge me, especially when they hold me back so that White people can maintain the advantage: I ran so fast that when I got to the end, my peers had to move out of my way to avoid being bowled over. As I slid past the finish line, my team members cheered me. Corporal Heather was not happy that her team members were no match for me. Neither she nor her accomplice cheered, but the look on some of their colleagues' faces told me some of them were very happy with the results. In hindsight, I now realize they had a bet on me; it could have been for money, or it could have been for beer. These racist people make me sick. They saw me as a racehorse, and they think I do not understand. They saw me pretty much the way I was taught to see non-human animals, as less-intelligent beings. Yes, I do believe animals are much smarter than people would like to believe; but that fight is for animal activists. As it stands, this life is too short for me to write all I intend to write about racism in terms of skin colour. Yes, the assumption that humans are more intelligent than other mammals is racism: *human race-ism*. No, I am not a vegetarian. Rarely do I eat a meal that does not include meat.

The recruits were quite stressed this weekend. I witnessed something I had never seen before. That is, during the morning inspection, three recruits just fell straight backward like falling trees. I do not remember their knees buckling; I remember seeing them fall flat as if they didn't even know that they had hit the gym floor. There were no apparent head injuries, but I know what I saw. They were not side-by-side in the line formation, but they fell within seconds of each other. This prompted WO Ross to demand that the troops eat earlier, and that each person select a fruit and milk during each meal. He was a gentle giant. God bless him.

This was the weekend when I found a metal coil in my scrambled eggs. Other recruits found foil paper and God knows what else. The food was apparently ordered from a local caterer. The appearance of the servers told it all: a man with most of his teeth gone and the remaining ones badly decayed; and a short, fat, White woman with stringy hair. They desperately needed a bath. There were tongs for picking up the bacon, but somehow the guy's fingers always found their way to the pile of bacon; and after putting the bacon on a private's tray, he would lick his fingers. The look I gave him each time he served me—moving my eyes from the serving utensils to his eyes and then to the food—made him realize that I did not need any of his saliva on my food; therefore, he remembered to use the tongs.

This, too, was the weekend when WO Ross got frustrated with the food. He brought his serving and plopped it on the captain's desk and told the captain that he should eat it, that he was not serving any more of it to his troops.

The next morning, a portable military canteen was set up on base. This military canteen was actually a truck parked out back of the building, but it was like eating from a fine restaurant. As we, the recruits, walked through the canteen, we could choose what we wanted. For example, there were eggs—scrambled, fried, boiled, sunny-side-up; and there was cheese—mild, medium, old, sliced, etc. I did not know people ate like that in the army. The food was prepared by military cooks. Lunch and dinner were basically the same as breakfast, in that we had a good selection of healthy foods, and our meals continued that way until we went out into the field.

I will never forget Private Bezchilbuyk. I was prepared to spend hours putting my military utility belt together using an instruction booklet, when Bezchilbuyk offered to help me. As soon as we were about to start, he shocked me by saying, "Green, you can go to bed. You look tired. I will work on this." He didn't need to tell me twice. There must have been at least forty pieces to attach to the base of the belt. The pieces looked like one complicated jigsaw puzzle that only people who had no life would attempt to solve. To make matters worse, even if a piece would work just as well in one spot, it was "unacceptable" to the army to make modifications; every piece must be in the same spot on every single belt. Understanding the logic behind standardizing the assembly of the belt did nothing to ease the annoyance of putting every piece in a designated spot, and there was a spot on this belt for just about everything: water bottle, bullets, knife, helmet, compass. . . . Obviously, the recruits would not have a need for all those pieces, but the belt had to be assembled to the army's standard.

In the morning, my belt was perfectly assembled. I could just imagine how much time he spent on it, although there was a 1:00 a.m. curfew. People like Bezchilbuyk make it difficult for me to totally hate White people. His step-father was a police officer; and he, too, was aspiring to become one. His quiet confidence and sense of fairness would have been an asset to any police force. Private Dacosta had a desire for Bezchilbuyk. This was easy to understand, considering that his physical appearance was just as appealing as his personality. True to his character though, his eyes did not wander from his girlfriend—who was not in the military.

— Chapter 9 —

Home

My hemorrhoids flared up so badly that my family physician had me see a specialist within two days. The specialist operated immediately to cut and burn them, and gave me Tylenol 3. Not wanting me to take time off work, the executive director at my day job responded to this "inconvenience" by saying, "It can't be all that painful, cause you are not actually sitting on it." It was painful enough for me to go back to the specialist two days after the operation because the Tylenol 3 did nothing to ease my pain; furthermore, the hemorrhoids were now bigger than before the operation. As I left work to go back to the specialist, I thought, *"Imagine, this woman is telling me how much pain I am feeling; she is telling me that I am not sitting on my hemorrhoids. I guess 'black' is not capable of knowing how much pain she is feeling, nor if she is sitting on her own backside."*

The doctor told the nurse present, not me (*because I would not understand, being just a 'black'*), "If I cut them again, they will only get bigger." He prescribed

Tylenol 4. With those pills, I could sit without severe pain dominating my life. The doctor advised me to stay away from the army for at least a month. Of course, this would mean I would miss two weekends of basic training and that would be the end of all my hard work. No way was I going back to my unit. I showed up for training the following Friday evening.

– Chapter 10 –

Weekend 5: January 1998

Human Beings at Their Core

I gave Sergeant Cherniawski the doctor's note, so that I would not be disciplined for "taking pills" in the army. His response upon looking at the note was, "That stuff will bung you up." I popped each pill on schedule and managed to make it through the weekend, feeling pressure in the affected area rather than pain.

We were up by 6:00 a.m., as usual. We packed our sleeping bags, did our ablutions, and prepared for inspection. Dalel, a Black girl, was lined up for inspection. Master Corporal Gardner was doing the usual inspection of Dalel's section. The guy was a smoker. For whatever reason, even though he liked to yell in the recruits' faces, he didn't feel the need to brush his teeth. This particular morning, he just about killed Dalel with his breath. She and I were not friends, but she needed to tell somebody. This was the same guy who, from day one, when teaching us how to wear our berets, would remind us that we were not those ". . . fucking Jamaicans in the Caribbean, so don't be leaning them to the side of your heads." Decent people are embarrassed by their own bad breath, and most smokers I know are particularly concerned about morning breath. But not Gardner; since he did not have the ability to smell his own, he must obviously have believed no one else could smell it. Otherwise, it could be that he had the opportunity to "torture" his subordinates and took it. I am inclined to believe this was his reason for yelling in people's faces with his morning breath. In fact, do you remember those three recruits who fell like falling trees? All three of then were in Three Section, Gardner's group. Coincidence? Guess who was bawling them out when they fell?

I could not understand why Dalel kept asking me for hair conditioner that weekend; but before the weekend was over, she told me. During inspection, the sergeant responsible for her section, Sergeant Mahood, told her, "Your hair is unacceptable!"

In the change room, as she spoke and I handed her my hair grease, my mind went back to an incident in the morning that had caught my attention. I had watched him as he had further ranted, "You need to have hair like mine!" while touching his hair to show "superiority" in quality; and I had thought, "*He actually thinks Dalel is admiring him rather than despising him.*"

Most of the male soldiers were undesirables, in terms of character; but the women soldiers who shared the same characteristics were even worse than the men. I observed Corporal Heather bawling out two female recruits from Two Section for a minor offence—perhaps their attire. When the corporal walked away, one of the recruits made a comment on "the bitchiness of the women in the army." The Corporal overheard, turned around, stomped over to the recruits and bawled out the Asian recruit; she completely ignored the Caucasian recruit, even though it was the Caucasian recruit who made the remark. The Asian girl obviously had integrity, for she stood there meekly absorbing the verbal abuse and embarrassment for her "friend." She took the abuse for a "friend" who said nothing, which also shows the character of her friend: she let the Asian girl take the fall.

Corporal Heather was another person whom "decent" White people would correctly refer to as White trash. She had a habit of belching to bring attention to herself; when she was ignored, while looking at the people around her to ensure they noticed her, she belched repeatedly and as loudly as possible.

This is a good time to point out an unwritten policy of the Canadian army. The government allocates money to the army, based on figures that the army provides; and at a certain time of the year, the army conducts an aggressive recruitment program. Many people join, and the units are then funded based on the numbers. Once a unit receives money for its budget, the administrators try to cut back on staff by failing people out of the training courses. The excess money is not returned to the federal budget but kept within the military's fund. Even without getting this information from two reliable sources—both senior administrative personnel—one does not need to be of superior intelligence to notice the deliberate effort on the part of immediate superiors to have recruits discharged from the army without regard for the time and effort the recruits invest in the process.

Corporal Heather was notorious for trying to fail recruits. Remember that biography I mentioned earlier?

She did the critiques for her group, Two Section. Just about every word in her critique was spelled wrong. My spelling is not good; but hers was atrocious, as I was told by a Black social worker (an African immigrant) whom she sent back to his unit. He told me he could not believe someone of her educational level was critiquing people's written work. On more than one occasion, he complained directly to me that he had great difficulty with her spelling errors when reading the reports she wrote about him. He said, "I am so focused on deciphering the words [she intends to put forth] that I lose track [of the content]."

She was not the only one with spelling and grammar problems; but somehow, I think she wrote the speeches for the corporals and master corporals. For example, I could never get over the way each trainer, when doing a demonstration, would say, "Watch myself," when what they should have been saying was simply, "Watch me." Once, when I could not stand it anymore, and I whispered, "Watch me," DaCosta looked at me and mouthed the words, "I know," as if to say, "It's shameful." This is just one reason why, when a superior would say to me, "Green! You are not an individual!" I would say to myself, "Oh-h-h, yes, I am." If grammar of such sort meant being a part of the unit, I would much rather remain an individual.

Reflecting on Corporal Heather's personal characteristics—the methods she used in attempting to ensure her team won the physical challenges, the poor reaction she displayed when I won, her lack of basic social manners, her lack of restraint when attacking the Asian recruit, her inappropriate body language around males (including recruits), her inadequate educational skills—I confidently conclude that her process for being accepted into the military was vastly different from mine. Her abilities and characteristics speak to the army's reasons for keeping test scores secret, even from the individual who wrote the test. How easy is it to admit or deny applicants entry into the Canadian Armed Forces, if the applicant will never see the result of his/her entrance test?

If I had not seen so much in life, I would not read so deeply into this situation. However, for me, it just reinforces the notion that "we" (non-Whites) are here to serve "them"(White people).

This weekend we had training with the C9 rifle. The training was in basically the same format as was the C7; however, we were not required to take a C9 apart or re-assemble it. Since we were being tested again on the C7, a corporal took me into the basement for extra practise. He told me that he would come back to get me. It seemed to me that about forty minutes had passed: This was an unusual length of time for anyone to be left alone in the army. I waited for what seemed like another twenty minutes, and then I decided to return to the gymnasium. I returned to find that everyone was half-way through eating lunch. I looked at my superiors' faces and saw a look that said "We forgot about you." The corporal who brought me down to the basement had the "Oh shit!" look on his face. I passed the final C7 exam with no complaint; yet, a few months into the future, I would receive my course report and it would read, "Failed C7 Performance Test."

Things were going well with the testing, but this time I overheard Ludwig and another corporal again placing bets on "Green." I did my C9 exactly the way DaCosta did hers, because we practised together. There was a step in the process that was taught by some instructors and not by others. DaCosta and I both did that extra step. Even though I did my test immediately after DaCosta, Ludwig passed her but failed me. This meant he won the bet he had made with his colleague. I complained to Warrant Officer Ross about the extra step. The WO answered, "That's so minor I would've passed you, but it's not up to me." I did not complain about the bet because I knew it would have made things worse. I could kick myself for not making a stink about that bet. I chose not to point out the DaCosta factor because it would have caused tension between DaCosta and me; her feelings mattered to me.

I was dealing with people who were free to expose the very core of their selves. They were in an environment where they were free to be themselves—free to express their pleasure in wrecking other people's lives. Of course, they were selective in whose lives they chose to manipulate to suit their purposes. After all, they do not even see us as full human beings; we are Negroes (*knee grows*); in terms of intellect, we grow to their knee-height only. I believe Ludwig eventually made it onto a police force. Can you imagine? My experiences, in the army as well as my civilian life, were turning me into a being who was finding it difficult to feel anyone's pain. Truth be told, I started to feel a sense of satisfaction when I saw certain people suffering; I felt that they were indirectly feeling the effects of the pain they or their loved ones inflicted on others.

It was time for the unit to do some more pruning, to keep the funding up. Our superiors slapped us with written tests throughout the weekend: a test on the Geneva Convention; a test on the theoretical aspects of firearms; a theoretical test on tear gas attacks; tests on material they never covered or perhaps covered with *certain* recruits; they went on and on with the tests.

In the midst of all the testing, I discovered that Sergeant Cherniawski had been correct—the pills had bunged me up, and now I had no time to lose in getting to the toilet. Instead of spreading toilet paper on the seat to protect myself, I climbed up on the toilet, boots and all, and relieved myself. I must have wiped myself at least six times and could still use more paper. I wiped two or three more times. The toilet looked like it could handle the mound of paper, so I flushed it. It did not make even a half-decent effort to flush, and flushing it again would have caused it to overflow. I thought of the people who would have to clean up the mess, and I left it clogged. After all, if it overflowed and anyone noticed, I might be the one cleaning it up. I fixed my clothing and walked out of the stall to the sink area. I knew that once I got out of the stall without anyone seeing me, I was safe. Thus, I did not need to hurry when washing my hands. When I returned to the training area, I got the feeling that my superiors knew what I had done. Nonetheless, I did not tell a soul; and no one mentioned it to me. I was not back in the test area two minutes before the next one was administered; I felt that I definitely made the correct choice by keeping my mouth shut and not worrying about a way to solve the clogged toilet problem.

The troops were required to provide their daytime contact information. I gave one of my business cards showing, "Deneace Green, B.A., Membership Services Co-ordinator." Almost immediately, my name became a buzz: "Green has a degree; Green is a co-ordinator; Green works for the government; Green. . . ." I felt as though the people around me were suffocating me, as if they were sucking the air out of me; I wanted to be alone, away from people and not just the people in the army.

I overheard WO Ross telling another soldier that "Green passed." He was referring to the battery of unexpected written tests that he and the other superiors had administered to the recruits.

Sunday evening Lloyd came to pick me up. Since he was using my car, he really had no choice; otherwise, he would need to find another way to get himself to work. The recruits were not yet dismissed. He watched a bit of the training. I saw him shaking WO Ross' hand. I noticed that my superiors all became tense and looked apprehensive.

In the car, Lloyd informed me that when he shook the WO's hand, he heard it crack at the shoulder; and the WO looked scared. The Warrant Officer was physically huge compared with him. However, White people's perception of Black people often gets the better of them. My superiors knew that they treated me like shit, and they thought the Black guy was there to "make trouble." Had they known him, even slightly, they would have saved themselves some stress. Nonetheless, their change in behaviour was a lesson for me. It confirmed that they were well aware of what they had been doing to me.

— Chapter 11 —

Weekend 6: January 1998

The Military Having Impact on Human Core

For these two days, we reviewed everything we had learned thus far; then we started training in hand grenades. While doing some outdoor activities, we had to pretend that our partner was seriously wounded. Military rules dictated that we leave behind neither an injured person nor any weapons. Most of the female recruits could not even lift their partners, not to mention carry them a specified distance along with all their gear. When I picked up my partner, her gear, and her weapon—while never putting down any of my own gear—and started running to my destination, everybody started cheering for Green. My physical abilities were not dependent on their discretion; considering the pathetic performance of all the other females, their physical weakness, they could not find a reason not to give me the recognition I deserved. Even Garant, who could not stand me, cheered.

I don't acknowledge people whom I cannot stand. One night, I chose a particular spot to lay my sleeping bag. This meant Garant could not sleep beside her pal DaCosta. When Garant lay down beside me, thinking I would move, she was in for a disappointment. However, DaCosta lay on the other side of me, and I knew what she was thinking; therefore, I asked her if she wanted to trade spaces. I did DaCosta the favour because she was tolerable. In fact, I liked her.

Garant, on the other hand, I hated more with each passing weekend; and a story she would tell in the months to come caused me to increase the depth of my hatred for her. Her story was that she had stopped at a coffee shop to get a coffee and a muffin; the coffee was not hot enough for her, so she shoved it back at the server behind the counter and berated, "This is 'unacceptable!'" She was quoting her superiors, as they berated us about our performance and dress being "unacceptable." As her story continued, the server quickly apologized and got her an "acceptable" coffee. Garant was obviously taking the army much too seriously—she believed that her treatment of the server was funny and justifiable. I pictured the server who, according to Garant, was a new refugee woman from war-torn Somalia. The newcomer, apparently, did not realize that military attire does not mean anything in the larger Canadian community: nor in the army for that matter. As Garant stood in the summer-like morning sun, by the main doors of Dennison Armoury, still holding her freshly bought coffee in a paper cup, telling how she belittled the woman, I pictured Garant in a nursing home; I pictured her helplessly lying in a bed, eating shit, in what should be her twilight years. Considering that servile jobs are reserved for minorities, I pictured a Somali nurse's aid watching her as she ate her own shit.

Garant was not the only recruit on whom the military was having an impact. There was absolutely no room for privacy. I was in a toilet stall, trying to be as discreet as possible with my bodily functions. The Asian female recruit and her White "friend" were just outside the door—a small change area—having a conversation; two other females not involved in the conversation were present. Against my wish, my body decided to release gas very loudly. I figured that if I kept quiet, everyone present would pretend they did not hear it; thus, I could continue to show my face in public. The Asian recruit paused, then said, "That's a nice, healthy, fart." Her response gave me the courage to say, "Excuse me." She responded, "Why? It was a nice, healthy, fart." With that I was able to finish what nature had dictated and walk out of the stall without feeling that sense of uneasiness one feels when caught violating a normal code of conduct: I farted in public, and I was not dying of shame.

Sunday afternoon, DeGroot got promoted from Corporal to Master Corporal (M/C). The event was nothing fancy, just the troops called to attention in line formation, in the gym; after which, Warrant Officer Ross presented DeGroot with his stripes. DeGroot beamed, while trying to contain the smile that kept creeping back to his face until I left for home. Ludwig was to be promoted to Master Corporal as well, but the army is never on time with gear. Hence, there was no insignia available for Ludwig and he had to wait until later to be promoted.

— Chapter 12 —

Weekend 7: Early February 1998

Outdoors for Twelve Hours in the Winter

Before we left the garrison to head for Base Borden, we were sent to the supply room in small groups. Master Corporal Gardner was responsible for handing out supplies. In addition to my washbasin, he gave me a small metal ladle. Sometimes White people do things for me without knowing why; perhaps their guilt briefly gets the better of them, as in this case. Gardner reached into the container and came up with a small metal ladle; he looked at it then, switched it to his other hand; he reached in again and came up with a regular size metal basin; and for some reason, he decided to put the small ladle into the washbasin and hand them both to me. This ladle came in very, very, handy out in the fields.

After collecting supplies, the troops lined up in the parking lot with their gear in front of them—duffel bag, sleeping bag, helmet, etc. In keeping with military rules, recruits removed the bolts from their weapons, placed the bolts in the left inside pocket of their jackets, loaded their gear onto one of three rented school buses and then took a seat on the same bus. The ride took about one and a half hours. We went north of Toronto to Base Borden. It was dark when we arrived at the base.

We were required to safety and content check our weapons as soon as we arrived; therefore, in sections, we were lined up for inspection outside the buses. One recruit could not produce the bolt for his *wifle* (rifle). Our superiors searched every crevice of the bus and the surrounding areas for a bolt that did not surface. The next process was to thoroughly search the recruits' belongings. There was talk about calling in the military police. As the guy was escorted off to answer for his lost bolt, I thought, "Thank God, he is not Black." I think this unfortunate, or careless, recruit was returned to his unit. The rest of us were told that if the bolt had been a magazine, we could not have proceeded until it was found; and charges would definitely have been laid.

When we got to our barracks, the search for the bolt continued. Corporal Heather was required to search each female recruit's belongings. When she got to my stuff, she said, "Now, here is a girl who knows how to pack." I always pack more than I need, and I had my toiletries nicely laid out in a sack for such purposes—even though my sack was floral, i.e., pink, beige and yellow, not fit for the military. She felt something hard in my belongings, and said, "Oh! My! God!" The male military personnel, including WO Ross, quickly found themselves at my door, but they did not enter the room. What she felt was my toothbrush case. I know WO Ross was relieved it wasn't the bolt; I felt his relief as he exhaled without even realizing what he had done. Corporal Heather just said, "Oh," again and continued to search while repeating, "Here is a girl who knows how to pack." When she left, I heard her telling the males waiting outside my room, "It was just a toothbrush case." It was after 11:00 p.m., and the next day was going to be a long one, so we were told to wash and go to sleep. I did not do picketing (keeping watch for an hour) that night, but I am sure some of the recruits had that *pleasure*.

The troops were awakened at the crack of dawn. In fact, dawn had not yet cracked because it was still pitch-black outside. Boy, was I in for a surprise! I believe this was the first day of my life when I actually spent more than 12 hours outside in the winter. After our superiors conducted the morning inspection, we were taken out into the fields by military trucks. We received a lecture on what we should expect—we would be there all day; what we could and could not do—put nothing except water in our water bottle; and how we should get our meals—we were to walk through the portable canteen (a truck), collect our food without delay, and keep going; find a spot in the camp area to eat.

I knew that my water bottle acted as a thermal flask as well as a cooler. I considered the temperature and decided to put hot water in my water bottle. This was a good decision because, when I started to *feel* the cold, my warm water was my saviour. My superiors must have thought I was hard of hearing because on three separate occasions throughout the day, shortly after I had taken sips, Master Corporal DeGroot, Corporal Ludwig and WO Ross, respectively, inquired as to the contents of my water bottle. They could not complain when I told them it was hot water, which soon became warm water. This is so typical of how White people watch Black people and allow their suspicions to get the better of them. I wonder if they were thinking that I sneaked brandy into the field. I would not put it past them. This is my life. Of the more than thirty recruits in the field, why were they asking me what was in my water bottle—especially after they saw me fill it with hot water? Could this have been their way of trying to engage me in conversation? I doubt it, although it was a very slight possibility.

We did three hours of outdoor survival training. First there were lectures, then pitching tents, spotting camouflaged enemy, and measuring distance by counting steps. During the camouflage exercise, as we walked towards the *enemy*, I thought I saw Master Corporal Gardner hiding among some twigs and snow. I called out, "I see him. I'm going to shoot him!" Of course there were no bullets in our guns, but we pretended. Other troops thought they saw another "enemy" and pretended to fire. When we got too near to the "enemy," DeGroot ordered us to halt. Gardner then showed himself. He said none of the recruits shot in the correct spot. Gardner had to make the point that, "Green was not even close." Mind you, he kept on moving from one area to another. Furthermore, this person's character is such that even if there were real bullets in the guns and he surfaced with blood all over him, he would have said he was not shot by anyone in the group.

Lunch time rolled around rather quickly. We followed the same procedure as for breakfast. The group, including Master Corporal DeGroot, joked about my willingness to shoot Gardner. In the afternoon, using a portable gas burner, we were trained on how to keep a fire going. The warmth from the fire did not make any difference to me; the heat was too minimal to make a difference.

Jealousy of other people is a feeling I very rarely feel; but when I saw Corporal Heather snugly lying in a tent, I felt jealous. The jealousy did not last long, as I thought, *"Once I get through basic training, I, too, will start enjoying the good life."*

Corporal Heather's work for that day was simply to remove herself from her tent for about four minutes, to tell the recruits that it is important to keep their clothing dry when going to sleep. She said that during her basic training, she thought that if she wore a lot of clothing she would be warm in her sleeping bag. Therefore, she went to sleep in clothing that soon become wet from her sweating. She did not sleep, but instead shivered all night. The next night she followed her training and slept in a dry thermal shirt, and she was able to sleep quite comfortably. It was too damn cold for me to be doing any sweating during the day; months later, however, when I thought the weather was warm enough for me to go to sleep in damp, sweaty clothing, I experienced what Heather was talking about; and I thought, *"She actually knew something other than how to provide sex for the men in the military."*

In the afternoon, we made "hot" chocolate on our group's portable burners. Although our water did not come to a boil, recruits were taking a sip in turn and passing the tin can around. What should have been hot chocolate looked more like muddy warm water. DaCosta and Bezchilbuyk offered the can to me. I do not share drinks from one container, so I politely declined both offers. DeGroot asked me why I did not drink some, and I told him that the hot water from my water bottle was enough. He knew my real reason for not drinking the so-called hot chocolate, and I knew what he was thinking: "Green! You are not an individual!" Every time I did not conform to the group, he reminded me, "Green! You are not an individual!" My response still rings in my brain today, *"Oh, yes I am."*

While the troops were sitting around, listening to M/C DeGroot give a lecture on how to build and maintain a fire, some of them took the opportunity to have a smoke. DeGroot ridiculed the smokers for what they were doing to their bodies. Then he ridiculed his mother for smoking when she was pregnant with him. He claimed that his mother damaged some of his brain cells. Personally, I thought he was quite intelligent; and if I were going to be stuck out in the wilderness, I would want to be stuck with the soldier who displayed the best survival skills; and that was DeGroot. As he berated the smokers, I watched his small head bob up and down on his excessively long neck, and his body squiggling, and I thought, "*Rather than blame his mother for damaging his intellect, he should blame her for damaging his physical appearance.*"

That night Bezchilbuyk and I shared a tent. I slept quite well, considering it was my first night sleeping out in the wilderness in the middle of winter. In the morning, as we were packing up our gear, I noticed something: There were electrical wires buried under the leaves on the forest floor. I thought, "*How the hell did they get electrical wires all the way out here? What the hell kind of* wilderness *is this?*"

It was Sunday, and since we had to clean the barracks before we went home, we left the wilderness mid-morning. We had to get down on our hands and knees to get rid of the scuffmarks on the floor.

The troops were moving from one location to another. I was directly behind Garant when she opened a door and as she passed through ordered, "Green! Hold the door!" I shook my head, trying to grasp the order, before realizing that I was holding the door and everyone was passing through as though it was my job. Without regard for whoever was the next to pass through, I released the door. That feeling of wanting to be away from people deepened within me.

Corporal Ludwig's insignia had arrived and he was promoted to Master Corporal Ludwig.

— Chapter 13 —

Weekend 8: February 1998

Learning to Crawl

We were taught the Leopard Crawl and the Monkey Run. The Leopard Crawl entails lying on your stomach and resting your rifle across both arms, bent at the elbows; then, crawling along while staying as flat on the ground as possible. The Monkey Run allows you to ease your body off the ground; however, you are still on all fours while running from one location to another with your rifle slung over your shoulder. You would think these recruits who were in their early twenties (except for Garant and Kerr who were in their mid-thirties) were actually in their late fifties or early sixties. At one point during the Leopard Crawl, Private Goudett (another recruit) and I were so far ahead that he said to me, "Hey, Green. We don't have to hurry, eh. Look how far behind us they are." He was obviously tired. I was tired too, but stopping was not on my mind. He just didn't want me to pass him and allow everyone to see a "girl" ahead of him. I answered, "Yeah. Okay," and slowed to a more comfortable pace. I was actually crawling in the snow, and I was not feeling the cold. All the recruits had started in a straight line, but some reached the finish line three to five minutes after Goudett and I got there. In all fairness, some went around trees, and others tried to avoid slushy puddles; however, most just did not have the physical ability to effectively carry out the exercise—scary, considering we were crawling fewer than three hundred metres.

Goudet was another person trying to get onto a police force, but he was too blatant in his criminal activities. He had been found guilty of robbing some sort of business; and according to him, police recruiting will never get past "a stupid thing I did when I was younger." He had not changed a bit. He was not shy about telling a group of recruits that he and his buddies went to a bar the previous summer, a bar into which the owner had refused him and his buddies admission. He had produced a police baseball cap and a police T-shirt and had told the "owner" (a man) that if he did not let him and his buddies into the bar and give them free drinks, he would go get more of his police buddies and "tear the place apart." The owner complied.

Before I joined the military, I would have thought the tale was a good "story." Now, I was exposed to people who freely acted out the baseness of their thoughts. A fine police officer Goudet would make! At the time, his civilian job was some form of lab technician. He told us of autopsy slides that he observed and wondered about how people who conducted autopsies continued to smoke after removing black mushy lungs from the dead bodies of people who smoked. I realized just how useful he might have been to society as a police detective, when he told us of an incident where a bunch of specialists were looking at a slide but could not see a bullet. Goudet and an old specialist were still examining the slide when Goudet spotted the bullet at the very top; the bullet almost did not make it onto the slide. Too bad he allowed his criminality to get the better of him, a trait that was so entrenched in him that he could not be anything other than a criminal of some sort. I do not for one moment think that Goudet's career aspirations combined with his mentality are a rarity. Keep in mind that most people in the army aspire to be police officers, including Gardner and Ludwig. I have some stories I could tell you about police interaction with Black people, but they are not my stories. Perhaps, one day, two of my brothers will put their stories in writing.

The next day, we had more of the Leopard Crawl. We, in One Section, were to compete against Three Section. DaCosta certainly had it rough during this exercise. She and Bezchilbuyk had to carry the only two C9 weapons while the rest of the section carried their C7s. I noticed DaCosta struggling with the weapon during the practise, crawling through the snow-covered terrain; however, her spirit was unbroken. She encouraged our section—after DeGroot briefed us on our strategy—by giving us a pep talk regarding Three Section: "Their morale is going to be low when they get here; they are wet and cold; and they are angry at Sergeant Mahood." I thought, *"We are cold, too."* Apparently, Mahood had been herding his section like animals; and the troops were not amused. Mahood liked to think of himself as a god: This was evident from the first time I observed him marching through the gymnasium in his police uniform. Whenever he lost at anything, he swelled as if he was about to explode. Despite struggling with a much heavier weapon than the rest of the troops—except for Bezchilbuyk, who had the other C9—DaCosta had the strength to assess the other section, motivate her own section and strategize. She was only twenty years old, but a true leader. I was glad I "failed" the C9 test; otherwise, I am sure I would have been stuck with carrying one of them. No, thanks!

DeGroot was a pain in the ass, but we could not help liking him. He was serious about leading his troops, and we could tell that he cared about us. He cared that we were cold and wet climbing through the snow. Each time he turned around, his eyes scanned his troops to make sure we were all present and breathing; and although DaCosta was struggling with the C9, he must have thought she would be stronger as a result of her struggles because he did not instruct her to switch rifles with a male counter-part. As a result, followed by willing troops, he marched on up the snow-covered hill. The difference between One Section and Three Section was that One Section wanted DeGroot to win. We were bonded to him because he cared about us. Whereas, Mahood alienated his troops; and they were angry at him.

We spotted Three Section coming up the hill: dragging their tired, wet, asses. We waited for DeGroot to give the word of command before we pretended to fire shots. They got close, charging at us like they knew no fear. Degroot gave the command to "char-r-r-rge!" into them with our bayonets, the tips of our rifles. I got carried away and jabbed at a Chinese male who came at me—his face looked too scary; his growling sounded fierce. I was surprised to see him go down, holding his upper arm. I probably would have jabbed him again if he had not said, "Green! You jabbed me really hard you know!" As he didn't want to look like a weakling, he quickly composed himself and re-entered the battle; and I did, too. We fought on until my side won.

Who really wins in a fake battle, or even a real one, for that matter? My section felt victorious, but my personal victory was short-lived because the sights fell off my weapon. DeGroot laid into me. He yelled, "Green! You saw me tighten my sights before we went into battle! You should have tightened your sights too! Whatever I do, you do!" Of course, a chit followed this berating. This was a time when I felt that the victories in my life are most often short lived.

— Chapter 14 —

Weekend 9: March 1998

Lessons in Loving Myself

Like all the other weekends, we met at the garrison Friday at 1900 hours in the gigantic training arena: the gym. Along the training arena were many offices and storage rooms. Chang, the private I had jabbed, was there. I had just arrived and was looking for a spot for my gear. He was exiting one of the offices. When we intersected, he said to me, "Green! My arm is still hurting me, you know! I still have the bruise!" I told him that I was very sorry and I really did not intend to hurt him. I didn't jab him with much force, but the tip of a C7 rifle can do a lot of damage when it is placed against flesh—even with minimal force.

Chang was a Chinese from India. He was probably forty-five years old. He had immigrated to Canada about five years previously and was desperately trying to get back into the dentistry profession. During basic training, his civilian work was as a dental technician. Essentially, he was making dentures for a living. He often talked to me about the expenses he incurred for each test he wrote in seeking his licence to become a dentist in Canada.

After assembly and inspection, we travelled to Base Borden. When we got off the bus and lined up outside the barracks, Sergeant Cherniawsk said he was surprised to see that only three women remained in One Section: Green, Garant and DaCosta. I had noticed that three weekends earlier. For whatever reason, I guess the full day ahead of us, our superiors sent us to bed within an hour of our arrival.

Early next morning, we ate breakfast in the canteen. It was big, clean and well stocked. We lined up for our meals based on rank, with privates being first in line. Recruits could ask for what they wanted, but they could not point. I was enjoying the chicken fingers until I bit into something that tasted like shit smells, like rotted potatoes. DaCosta noticed my face and asked, "Green, what's the matter?" I shook my head, signaling that nothing was the matter. Her attention forced me to keep the shit in my mouth longer than anyone should have to endure. I looked around and saw my superiors looking at the people seated at my table. I then snatched some serviettes and as discretely as possible emptied the contents of my mouth into the serviettes. I did not want to drink anything to swallow the remnant, so I generated as much saliva as possible and spat it into more serviettes. For the rest of my breakfast, I sniffed the chicken fingers before putting them in my mouth. Long after breakfast, I could still taste shit in my mouth. The repulsive and abiding taste caused me to wonder *why*: *"Why, in all my years on Earth, I had never had such an experience? Why did it happen in the army? Why did it happen only to me?"*

The superiors gave the usual safety lectures. After that, they taught us how to use a hand grenade. We practised removing the pin and putting it back. We learned that the grenade would not go off unless the pin was removed and the clip came off; therefore, if we replaced the pin, the grenade was still perfectly good. We practised removing the pin, throwing the grenade and taking cover. On my first practise throw of an empty grenade, DeGroot squeezed his lips together, shot his head from side to side and from deep down in his gut, through his clenched teeth, demanded, "G r-r-reen! Why did you throw it so far?" Then he ordered, "Go pick it up and do it again!" I did as I was ordered and thought, *"I thought the whole point of throwing a grenade was to get it as far from you as possible."*

Lunchtime came quickly, the meal brought to us by a military truck. WO Ross took this opportunity to let us know that the following weekend we would be spending the entire time outside. There would be no barracks on Friday night and Sunday afternoon.

While we sat around having lunch on the grass, a major from another unit tried to entice us into joining the Canadian Air Force. He said to me, "If you were younger." Afterwards, he said, "If your eyes were better." There is always an excuse. Since I could not do anything about my age, thirty-three, I thought, "*Why the hell is he even mentioning it to me?"* It is a game they like to play: "Look what you could have . . . but oh, so sorry." A red-haired sergeant tried the same shit on a different day. "You could go to Bosnia," he said, "but oh, you are not in the Regular Force." I thought, *"Why the hell would I want to go to Bosnia? Do I look like I care to find out how many bullets it would take to kill me?"*

It was during this meal I noticed that Private Kerr was not able to control her farts. We ate, and she farted. She said, "Pardon me. I've got gas," and kept on eating like her farting was no big deal. People looked at each other and kept on eating. Kerr kept on farting every two minutes, and I stayed away from her backside—literally. She was probably in her late thirties, White, with short orange-red hair and pleasantly plump. A Black woman would have been ostracized for farting uncontrollably, even once. Just because the Asian female recruit had put me at ease when I farted in the toilet did not mean all the other people around would have been as tolerant.

Kerr inadvertently helped me to find comfort with my race and my hair. Two days in a row, she borrowed my metal washbasin so that she could wash her hair in the field. Although her hair was as short as a man's, it needed washing daily because the grease it naturally exuded made her look like a wet, shiny, rat. She would use as few as five cups of water to shampoo and rinse her hair. She appreciated the metal ladle Master Corporal Gardner had given me, at least as much as I did. I fully realized its value the first day I had to wash my face in the field; having the ladle enabled me to utilize the water in my basin to first brush my teeth and then wash my face without having the soap on my hands transferred to the water in the basin. Had it not been for the ladle, which she used to scoop the water from my washbasin, Kerr would have needed to borrow someone else's basin. You see, a condition of my letting her use my basin was that clean water only was to be in that basin; and that included no one else's cup, her hands or anything else small enough to use as a scoop. *I am always cautious about germs being transferred to me.* Her most sacred parts did not get washed as often as her hair; during the early months when we trained at the garrison, instead of showering she would change her panty liner. According to her, "As long as it's changed, I am okay."

When the time came for recruits to throw live grenades, they were taken four at a time to the training structure. At first, the explosions were so loud that recruits jumped with fright each time a grenade went off. Sergeant Cherniawski reassured the recruits that they were not in any danger. I noticed how people were not as rattled by the explosions once they had thrown a grenade and returned to the building.

Master Corporals Ludwig and DeGroot watched me like hawks. When it was my turn to throw a grenade, Ludwig came into my concrete cubicle with me. It was standard practise to have a superior with a recruit; however, he looked like he was waiting for the grenade to fall out of my hand so that he could pick it up in time to throw it out into the exploding zone and save the both of us. I kind of enjoyed the tension he was feeling, knowing that I had his life in my hands. I guess he was disappointed that my throw was well past the average female distance. Despite the noise from other people's grenades exploding, when I returned to the holding structure, I fell asleep in a sitting position. Some other recruits had also fallen asleep. Cherniawski looked around the room at the recruits sleeping in the sitting position, others just resting, and commented on how people became relaxed as they grew accustomed to the noise and the vibration of the building.

The Sunday field exercises included training to hit an aerial target from the ground with a hand-held rocket launcher. When Sergeant Cherniawski finished introducing us to the various parts of the launcher, the captain fired a rocket into in the sky. Points were usually awarded for being the first recruit to try a newly learned skill. When DeGroot asked who was ready to try it, of about thirty recruits, I was one of five who slightly raised their hands. DaCosta's and Garant's hands went up a little slower and a little lower than mine, so DeGroot picked me to go first. After the rocket left my hand, I felt that my thumb had gone with it. I looked at my hand; my eyes were seeing my thumb attached to it but my senses were telling me otherwise. I did not let anyone see what I was feeling. I dropped the shell of the hand-held launcher into the basket provided for collecting them and stepped aside to make room for other recruits.

After two other male recruits let off their rockets, the captain let off his second one. He and everyone, except me, watched it rise as high as it would go in the sky and then make its way to Earth. I watched his hand. He did not make it obvious if the launcher had the same effect on his hand as it had on mine; however, he then said to our immediate supervisors, "They don't have to fire one unless they want to." Although I could see immediate relief on their faces, I was rather surprised when both DaCosta and Garant quickly refused DeGroot's invitation to try a rocket launch. Almost every recruit declined the opportunity to try a launch, and I was happy not to try a second one.

When Sergeant Cherniawski introduced the troops to the C-10 rocket launcher, I literally prayed to God that I would not be required to fire it. I thought that if the little hand-held launcher nearly took my thumb off, this one, which was almost as tall as I would be sure to kill me. I felt that my prayer was answered, when the only requirement was for the troops to pretend to fire it. The launcher was designed to be fired by two people: The person doing the actual firing would put the launcher on his shoulder; a partner would hug the person firing around the waist and anchor himself as firmly as possible, as the shooter fired; at the same time, the partner would pull on the shooter to keep the shooter from flying forward. If a partner were not available, the shooter would need to find a strong enough tree and firmly secure his/her body behind the tree when firing.

If there were not a strong enough partner, nor a secure enough support, the shooter was advised never to fire the launcher.

On the way home, I told Lloyd of my experience with the chicken finger. True to his character, instead of even trying to support my thought that the incident might have been deliberate, he quickly defended people he had never even met: "No one would deliberately do something like that; you just had a bad piece." His response reminded me of why I had not told him about my other experiences in the army or any other aspect of my life. The conversation lasted less than three minutes; yet, it was one of the longest we had engaged in since our first three weeks of living under the same roof.

— Chapter 15 —

Weekend 10: April 1998

I Observed, I Spoke, I Cried

We arrived at Base Borden by chartered buses, as usual, and lined up in our respective sections. There was no Private Garant. Sergeant Cherniawski approached me and asked whether I had seen or spoken with Garant. He obviously left Toronto thinking that Garant would be at Base Borden when the rest of us got there, since she had the privilege of driving herself. Garant was above the team. While the rest of us who had cars were required to meet at the base in North York/Toronto and take the bus to Base Borden, on more than one occasion, Garant was allowed to drive her car to Base Borden and park there for the weekend. Apparently, Garant did not bother to inform her superiors that she didn't feel like "playing" with us until late the next morning. How do I know this? Cherniawski approached me not once, but twice, asking for Garant's whereabouts—even though he knew we were not friends. In fact, even Garant's friend, DaCosta, did not have any information regarding her whereabouts.

Cherniawski was making the most pathetic excuses for Garant, "It's not like Garant not to show up like this. Maybe she is sick. Maybe she forgot we are training this weekend." Inside, my head was just shaking at the injustices of this world. I thought of the Friday night, during the first few months of training, when I decided to stay home because my body was just too exhausted to do any drills. Lloyd had called-in to report that I was sick; Cherniawski had called my home and had ordered me to show up next morning; yet, they had logged it in my file as "Failed to report."

I believe Garant's refusal to show up Friday evening was our reason for not going out in the field that night. After all, WO Ross had made it clear that we would be spending the entire weekend out in the field; but how would Garant find us?

The next morning, as we were getting ready to go out to the field, guess who stepped out of her car? You got it. She walked over to One Section. Lieutenant Nguyen called her a short distance away from the group and asked, "Where were you?" You see, she was not to be embarrassed before the rest of the group. With her head bowed, she replied, "I was sick, Sir." The Lieutenant replied, "You should have called." Her response was, "Yes, Sir." The Lieutenant then walked away. No big deal; nothing on her file for neglect of duties; no chits; no picketing; no yelling; nothing. Garant and I were in the same army, same section, same superiors; different race, different rules, and no different from the larger society. Sometimes I scream with my mouth shut.

I have always hated having my period, but this weekend my period turned out to be a blessing that was not in disguise. It was tear gas weekend. I did not want the tear gas powder in my hair. The superiors spray the recruits with real tear gas as the recruits run through a tunnel-like structure. I knew it would make me cough, probably until I peed myself. For extra support, and since mine were not readily available, I borrowed a sanitary pad from a corporal. She told Warrant Ross that I was on my period. This was one of the few times I was glad the people in charge totally lacked the ability to be discrete. I thought asking a female for a sanitary pad would be a woman-to-woman issue; instead, the WO announced that women on their period should not go though the gas chamber because the chemical causes women to menstruate heavier than normal and can cause irritation. Not going through the gas chamber did not mean relaxation for me though; I was required to carry water for the troops to wash their hands and faces once they had gone through the chamber. Did the WO not know that lifting thirty-pound containers of water would also make my period flow heavier than normal? Nonetheless, I was quite happy to make the trips with a corporal from another unit. He was White, approximately twenty years old. As he backed the truck into the water storage area, I was to use hand signals to tell him when to halt. I signaled just after the truck backed into a small stack of empty plastic containers. It was our little secret, to save his ass as well as mine. He said, "Don't say anything to anyone." I thought, *"I guess my parents do not know how the real world functions, because they would have instructed me to tell my superiors and accept the consequences."* Here I had someone younger than myself, albeit a corporal, teaching me how the real world operates. The scratches in the paint job of the truck and the dents in the plastic bins were not going to make a difference in their ability to function.

Dalel suffered as a result of the gas chamber. The poor girl coughed and coughed and coughed. On the truck going back to the barracks she was hyperventilating and coughing; therefore, Cherniawski told her to sit at the back of the truck—he knew what was coming. About thirty seconds after she moved to the back of the truck, she leaned over the back door and vomited. Then she kept right on coughing. The tear gas was still burning her lungs and hindering her breathing. As she slumped on the bench and rested against the inner side of the truck, her small body looked almost lifeless.

Cherniawski commented that the army was not going to take the dangerous side-effects of the gas chamber seriously until someone died and the family sued. Dalel's reaction to the gas chamber could very well have made Cherniawski's comment a prophecy; she had a serious heart defect. Had her team members and I known how serious Dalel's situation was, I believe they would not have openly rejoiced at her suffering; yes, some of the guys actually hounded her when she started vomiting. Cherniawski watched Dalel closely, but that was all he could do. He spoke openly against the gas chamber aspect of the training. In my thoughts, I agreed that it was unnecessary suffering for the troops: eyes burn, skin burns, throat burns, lungs burn, breathing hindered, and the repulsive taste of sulfur.

We had lunch out in the field. I observed Corporal Dennis, one of the two Black female corporals assigned to help among the three sections. She was sitting alone, facing the trees that grew just below the area where she sat. Even after finishing her lunch, she remained seated. Not only was she physically alone, she appeared lonely. DaCosta's observation was different: "I don't know how she tolerates the guys in the army; she is so much more mature than they are." I thought, "*We (black) learn to tolerate a lot of things so that we can eat and keep a roof over our heads.*"

I noticed Major Jensen with a small group of officers. They were clearly not present as a part of our group because while we (25 Medical Company) and two other companies (the Infantry and the Engineers) were having lunch, the major and his team, including our captain, were on the firing range practicing.

After lunch, I noticed that there was no bleach in the water for rinsing our dishes. I thought it best for me to not wash my plate. I could not believe the number of people who were washing their dishes in the dirty, soapy, water and then dipping them in the murky, rinsing water. DaGroot and Ludwig stood watching the recruits wash their plates and utensils in filth. They knew that they had messed up, but said nothing. The WO and the lieutenant came, saw the situation, but said nothing. Almost teasingly, Corporal Dennis said to me, "Green, aren't you going to wash your stuff?" I replied, "No, Corporal." She looked contented. We knew why I was not washing my "stuff," and I knew why she was not pressing the issue. The other superiors knew that I did not wash my plate and utensils, but no one insisted on my doing so. I bet I knew what they were thinking though: "*Green! You are not an individual*"; therefore, the words echoed in my mind, *"Oh, yes, I am."*

Corporal Dennis asked to borrow my lip balm. I was curious to see if she would actually use someone else's lip balm. I handed it to her. She turned the rotating bottom of the plastic tube that caused the balm to protrude from its cylindrical case. Then, she gently rubbed one index finger along the newly exposed part of the balm and handed the tube back to me. She rubbed her finger on her lips—another lesson for me. I felt satisfied that she was comfortable enough to approach me for something she needed. It seemed the other Black female assigned to help the three groups, Corporal Miller, was not available for training on this particular weekend. This left Corporal Dennis all alone to deal with people who would like to erase her and her kind from the planet Earth.

We spent a large part of this weekend on the firing range. We practised shooting at a target from a standing position, a kneeling position, and from the prone position (lying on our stomachs). Then we were tested on all the positions we had practised. At one point, my section was up for the prone position. My spot was in a puddle of muddy water. I intended to lie in it, but I was mustering the courage. As I stood there looking at the puddle, DeGroot ordered, "Green! Adopt the prone position!" In my mind, I had already adopted the prone position; then I heard for the second time, "Green! Adopt the prone position!" Some things are not as bad as they look; even in the mud, I could be comfortable because the water did not penetrate my outer clothing.

I aimed for my target's chest, but somehow I ended up blowing out its crotch. My officers instructed me to readjust my sights, which made no difference. Members of One Section alternated between firing at the target and putting-up the target. Each time I did a round of fire, the person responsible for my target would check with me, "Green! Were you on number twelve, or eight, or three, or . . . ?" No one ever asked me about a target that was not mine; in other words, my colleagues and superiors always knew my target and asked me about mine only. Since my bullets always landed in the same area of the target, I was billed as "the person who blows guys' balls out."

My shooting group switched with the group that was monitoring the targets. We were given a few minutes' break. I headed for the portable toilet. A private—the showoff named Stone who kept targetting Dalel and whose neglect in favour of self-exaltation had caused his partner to fail the C-7 test—saw me heading for the toilet and decided to make a dash for it. I just shook my head. Master Corporal Gardner saw what happened, but he did not insist that the private get out of there; instead, he merely said, "Nice way to treat your team member."

Master Corporal Gardner and Sergeant Cherniawski were responsible for the target area while Master Corporals DeGroot and Ludwig, WO Ross and Lieutenant Nguyen were responsible for the personnel.

Throughout the day, Gardner whined and complained about the officers: He made fun of them; shaking his head, he kept on saying, "Stupid officers, don't have a clue." I really don't think he meant *all* the officers. I think his remarks were really directed at Lieutenant Nguyen, but he used "officers" to cover his racism. It clearly annoyed him that Nguyen, an Asian, was telling him, a Caucasian, what to do.

The group responsible for monitoring the targets was marching back to our resting area, when I smelled shit. I didn't say anything. However, it didn't take long for another private to announce, "Someone's got shit in their pants." For those who looked at me, I just looked at them as if to ask, *"Don't I know how to wipe my anus?"* I bet I knew who had the shit in his pants, because he was in the toilet too long to have been taking a leak; and when I went into the toilet after him, there was no toilet paper therein. Could it be that even though he dashed past me, he still did not make it to the toilet in time? I felt no pity for him because he could have said, "Sorry, Green," as he ran past me on the way in or walked past me on the way out.

The incident prompted WO Ross to give us a lesson on what to do when there is no toilet paper. According to the WO, "Rip the sleeve off your T-shirt, and use it. This is often why you will see soldiers in the field with no sleeves on their shirts." I would never have a need to use my shirtsleeve because I would not be caught out in the fields without my feminine wipes—if for nothing else, to ensure my private parts and my hands are kept clean. I cannot say the same for Kerr. Earlier that morning, when she saw me cleaning my hands with a wet wipe as I exited an outdoor toilet, she said, "Green. Can I have one of those? I won't tell anyone else you've got them." Not long after, DaCosta also asked me for one; and after that, Corporal Dennis asked for one.

I was up for another round of shooting when DeGroot noticed my gloves and asked, "Green! Where did you get the gloves?" I responded, "I bought them on Queen Street, Master Corporal." He responded, "Were there any more?" I responded, "No, Master Corporal." I felt his disappointment because I knew that he was asking out of more than mere curiosity. He was not the only person who noticed my gloves; but the others put up with the government-issued gloves that had no padding, caused hands to become dry and blistered, and did not fit unless worn with government-issued mittens. I was thankful that he did not order me to use the government-issued pair; in that case, I would have gotten more that a chit for "insubordination." A few other people had gloves they bought themselves, though they were not nearly as soft and padded as mine.

DeGroot could not see my elbowpads and kneepads under my clothing, so I did not have to answer for wearing them. I was thanking God for my good fortune and His foresight because there was no way I could jab my elbow into the ground and comfortably aim my rifle without having a reasonable amount of padding, which the army did not supply. I also gave God thanks every time I was required to kneel and then stand or kneel and then lie flat, when target practicing. Even though the kneepads did not totally eliminate the pain I felt each time my knees hit the ground, I would have been rather ungrateful to not acknowledge God each time He buffered the pain. I thought about Kerr; in the first few weeks, I had seen her nursing her knees when she got up from sitting on a bench at the armoury. She had asked me not to say anything or else, she thought, she would have been kicked out of the army. She was slow in the physical exercises, but she was coping. Perhaps she too knew the benefits of kneepads.

On my final round of shooting in the prone position, which was a test, I fired a round after the order to "cease fire." I heard "fire," but I didn't hear "cease" and fired another shot into my target. DeGroot sent me to the WO. He asked me what had happened, and I told him. He told me to join Three Section in the camp area, and that I was not allowed to continue my firing test.

I was sitting in the camp area observing the squad firing on the range when an incident happened that caused me to really question whether I belonged in the army. Two Black girls—about twenty years old, from the Engineers unit—started calling me "Princess," and the taller and better looking of the two made a general statement which was obviously directed at me, "If you can't stand the heat, get out of the kitchen." Instead of getting annoyed, I addressed them as "my loyal subjects." This made them laugh and made me realize that people I don't even give a second glance have a tendency to watch me intently. The instigator had come from Jamaica within the last six months. She was fairly tall (perhaps 5'7"), dark, short-haired and somewhat good looking. Her mannerisms showed that she came from an undesirable background, perhaps the ghetto-area in

Kingston or Spanish Town ghetto: the worst places to live in Jamaica. The other was just a follower, trying to fit-in. She had a light-brown weave in her hair, combed into a ponytail. Just below the base of the ponytail, at the top of her neck, I saw the biggest *whole black pepper grains* I had ever seen in anyone's hair. *Black pepper grains* are knotted hair, that rolls into clumps, at the nape of Black people's neck. Apparently, she never used a mirror to look at the back of her head; and somehow, it never occurred to her to randomly comb back there. I guess she figured that since she could not see them, neither could anyone else. If I, a Black woman, felt creepy-crawlers each time I looked at her *black pepper grains*, I could imagine how repulsed her White counterparts felt; for to them, the *black pepper grains* must have appeared to be stationary black bugs.

At just about dinnertime, 25 Medical Company as well as the Engineers and the Infantry had gathered in the camp area. The officers were finished practise shooting for the day, and the major, accompanied by the captain, approached the camp area prior to their departure. They spoke briefly with WO Ross and Lieutenant Nguyen; after which, the Major asked the entire group, "Does anyone need anything?" Even though he appeared gentle and sincere, I felt sudden tension in all my superiors—even more so with Ross and Nguyen. I was the only one, of about fifty troops, to respond by saying, "Yes, may we please have some bleach for the dishwater?" The major's head moved in the direction of the WO and the lieutenant. The major did not need to ask them anything before the WO spoke up to say he would ensure that disinfectant would be made available. I was too dumb to realize that I really was not supposed to speak up. Most of the troops were grateful, I am sure; nonetheless, a few individuals made quick eye contact with each other as if to say, *"Does she realize what she just did?"* Truthfully, I did not. It was not my intention to embarrass my superiors. If I had that portion of my life to live over, I would simply ask one of my superiors to provide disinfectant.

By the time the troops finished dinner, bleach had miraculously appeared in the rinse water. As I dipped my plate in to rinse it, I looked up and saw DeGroot smiling at me as if to say, *"Happy now, Green?"*

At the end of the night, when the names of those who had passed the range section of training were called, mine was included. The WO commented, "She didn't even finish the test." Some of the other recruits, including some from Two and Three Sections, approached me and said, "Way to go, Green." I felt proud of myself, and I felt even better when Ludwig's girlfriend—a corporal of East Indian descent—could not account for a "lost" ammunition magazine. Her losing a magazine was evidence that I was not the only "incompetent" around. I expected it to be a long night in the field, searching for the magazine in the dark, while waiting for the military police. She was antagonizing all the recruits who helped her with the distribution prior to entering the field, as well as the other recruits in her unit. I loved the way she ignored me. I overheard one private from her unit, a Black man named Adofo, remark to another, "Imagine that, she can't even count," alluding to the fact that she had miscounted from the start. It was at this time I noticed that Adofo liked to stay in close proximity to me. He was about my age and very handsome. He had a sly look, which made me want to keep my distance from him even before I knew that he was a Muslim; the two and three wives relationship just would not work for me.

Lieutenant Nguyen and Warrant Ross must have been satisfied with the "miscount" assumption because they gave the order to get ready to return to the base. I had let my body wind down to relax for the truck ride back to the base, when Nguyen and the WO informed us that we would be jogging the seven miles back to the barracks; not only would we be jogging the seven miles back, but we would be jogging with our rifles on our shoulders, our equipment belts around our waists—including water bottles—and knapsacks on our backs.

I was at the head of about fifty troops, along with Lieutenant Nguyen, Master Corporal Gardner and about six male recruits, including Bezchilbuyk, Goudet and Adofo. As I ran, my gear pulled me sideways which at times caused me to bump Nguyen. This caused him to run slightly ahead or behind me in order to get back on the outside of the troops. I was wondering why Nguyen was not just staying out of the way, until a male private said to me, "Green, Sir has to run on the outside." I decided to reduce my pace so that the lieutenant could run without my interference; but apparently wanting me to stay at the front, he said, "Come on, Green." He was polite, and I would have picked up my pace again had it not been for Gardner who had to insert his White trash character and yelled: "Green! You're gonna have to do better than that if you wanna join the RCMP!" I could not believe the guy was sharing my business with everyone. Do you see why I correctly labeled him White trash?

We were ordered to stop. I decided to take the opportunity to adjust the strap on my rifle so I would not be drifting off to one side so much. Gardner started in again, "Green! Don't put it down!" Since I wasn't putting the weapon down, I ignored him and continued. He continued to bark, "I said . . . " while stomping towards me in his unavoidable jig. When he got intimidatingly close, he finished his bark, "Don't put it down!" He got angrier than his usual self, as if he wanted to hit me. I prepared my body and fist to gladly return the favour.

I spoke, "First you talked out my business [his bitter comment about my wanting to join the RCMP] in front of everyone, and that is not enough?" The lieutenant realized that telling me to stop would be useless; therefore, he motioned at Gardner to leave me alone. Poor Gardner: He had a Black subordinate ready to fight him and verbally expressing herself without restraint; and he had an Asian lieutenant telling him he could not express himself. How that must have stung.

At the end of the run, two other recruits and I were ordered to remain at the location while Gardner took the rest of the troops for their warm-down exercises. Master Corporal Seiki, an Asian, took the three of us for our warm-down. This was probably the only time throughout my basic training that any of my superiors exercised any precautions regarding racism. They kept me away from Gardner. They did this knowing that if he got in my face while conducting the warm-down exercises, I would not hesitate to retaliate. In addition, they knew I would not follow his power-hungry commands. It was a good call on their part.

Sunday afternoon, at the barracks, I noticed the female corporal who had lent me the sanitary pad. I approached her and said, "The pad you loaned me, do you want it back?" The woman looked at me with scorn and said, "No," while apparently still wondering, *"What the hell . . . ?"* She actually thought I was offering to return the *used* pad. I know I should have asked, "Do you want *one* back?" However, since she thought so little of my intellect, I decided to let the situation rest. Shaking my head, I walked away to direct my energy at anything or anyone other than her.

As the bus started back to Denison Armoury, a sense of sadness engulfed me. Incidents that occurred throughout basic training were flowing through my mind. I thought about the way my superiors dealt with Garant's not showing up for training until late Saturday morning, without calling. I thought about the way Ludwig failed me on my C9 Performance Check, just to win a bet, and got away with it. I thought about how Cherniawski gave me chits just for the hell of it and then jeered me about being *green*. I thought of DeGroot's never missing an opportunity to single me out. I thought about how deep Gardner's hatred went for me because of the colour of my skin.

I heard, "Green! Green! What's the matter?" The voice was DaCosta's. She continued, "Green is crying." I felt the tears on my cheeks, but made no effort to wipe them. I continued to look straight ahead when I heard myself say, "Do you care?" Everyone went quiet, watching and waiting to see how the "show" would progress. By the time my eyes met DaCosta's, I heard myself again, "Do you really care?" DaGroot got up from his seat, stepped out into the aisle, looked at me, but said nothing. He knows something about people; thus, he knew when to keep his mouth shut. It did not matter to me how people interpreted my tears. Although tears are usually seen as a sign of weakness, my tears give me strength; it is as though they say, *"Here is a reason to go on; here is your source of determination; here is your will to fight; here is the peace you need to make it through this."*

After we had returned to Denison Armoury in North York, Gardner, with the usual jigging of his body, walked over to me, shoved a piece of paper at me and stated, "Green! Sign this! You are out of here!" I was sharp in telling him, "I am not signing anything." What I really wanted to tell him was to go shove it up his ass. WO Ross, who had accompanied Gardner said, "Green, this is the army." What he meant was that I was supposed to obey my superiors. Realizing I was not going to sign the paper, Gardner headed back to the office from which he came. The WO followed him.

DeGroot came by to inspect my utility belt. He did not find anything that warranted a chit. As a result, he could not find an explanation as to why it kept bumping the lieutenant as we jogged the previous night. Obviously, Bezchilbuyk had done an outstanding job assembling it. For me, the reason for drifting to the right was obvious: There was too much weight on that side of my body; the knapsack leaned to the right, and my water bottle was to my right; the rifle on my left was not enough weight to balance the gear on my right.

Shortly thereafter, I was called to the office. Nguyen and the captain were there. As soon as I sat down, Warrant Officer Ross entered the room. He stood the whole time and watched intently. Nguyen was the only superior who did any talking. He wanted to know what had gone on between M/C Gardner and me on the march, as if he was not present when the incident occurred. He gave me the opportunity to express myself. I told him that Gardner had no right to expose my business, and that his remarks about officers during target practise were unacceptable. The lieutenant indicated that there would be further dealings with the matter.

At the end of the meeting, the lieutenant looked at me in a peculiar way and said, "Green, I've never met anyone like you: Some things you just excel at, and some things you just don't get." He looked puzzled. I think he was referring to my written work compared with my practical abilities, especially my marching—my marching was pathetic. A few weekends before, we had done an unexpected test that eliminated more than half the remaining recruits. I heard it said, "Green passed," as if they were expecting Green to fail. That was the weekend when I clogged up the toilet and did not report it. I had figured out how they amplified everything I did;

therefore, I was not about to bring more attention to myself. I was learning how the real world works. It's too bad I am such a slow learner.

As instructed by Lieutenant Nguyen, who informed me that I should respond in writing, I wrote a letter about the incident with Gardner and handed it to Master Corporal DeGroot. I was ready to do battle the next weekend.

Master Corporal Seiki was assigned to Two Section, but he invited all the troops to his house to see his military memorabilia and go to a range to do some target practise. I had no interest in going, until DaCosta approached me with a personal invitation, "Green, a few of us are planning on going up to Master Corporal Seiki's on Saturday. I am driving. Do you want to come with us?" I accepted only because she was sincere in asking. In all honesty, after the way I treated her on the bus, she would have been well within her right never to speak to me again.

At 10:00 a.m. on Saturday, we met at Denison Armoury. I was rather surprised to see that the group consisted of Garant, DaCosta, one other White female from Two Section, and me—surprised because I had expected to see people only from One Section. While we waited for Master Corporal Seiki, Garant took the opportunity to bask in how she had just berated a server in a coffee shop about her coffee being "unacceptable!"

We followed Master Corporal Seiki to his home in Newmarket, which is about forty-five minutes' drive north of Toronto. I thought of Seiki's selflessness: coming to Toronto on a Saturday just to escort us to the firing range. Bezchilbuyk and two other male recruits made it to Seiki's house on their own. I believe Seiki's mom let them in, because they were at the home when we arrived.

Seiki's collection of military memorabilia was indeed quite impressive. He showed us antique military clothing, bullets, and weapons that were catalogued in military magazines. I looked at Seiki's dad and saw that he admired the interest his son took in educating us about his collection.

Seiki provided the bullets and the guns we used at the range. We each had two rounds of shooting, using handguns. His demeanour made us comfortable; on the firing range he was calm and respectful, unlike DeGroot and Ludwig.

Seiki decided to stay at the range and continue his target practise. Bezchilbuyk and the two other males went their way, while DaCosta, the girls and I went to a nearby McDonald's restaurant. Bezchilbuyk's name came up in a conversation about desirable men. I made it clear that if I were younger, Bezchilbuyk would be mine—highly unlikely, but it made a nice dream.

Later, I was telling a friend of mine, named Carlene Harris, about the incident with Gardner. She was a lawyer I met while working at Coca Cola Bottling Ltd. Like me, she was Black and able to get employment only as a customer service representative. Carlene left Coca Cola and managed to get a job in another call centre, I believe working for a telephone company. Carlene interrupted me mid-sentence, "Wait a minute, Deneace; is this guy a smoker who walks with a jiggle because one leg is shorter than the other?" I exclaimed, "Oh, my gosh! Do you know him?" She responded, "He is a loud mouth, White trash who works in the collections department, and he is always talking about his importance in the army." Now I knew why the poor guy was so miserable and hateful: If you worked in the collections department, trying to reach deadbeats who do not want to talk to a money collections agent, you, too, would be hateful. Sorry, I could not feel the pity I just expressed. The guy was just too full of hatred and anger.

— Chapter 16 —

Weekend 11: May 1998

A Hearing Permeated With Racism

Would you believe Gardner did not show up for the hearing regarding our confrontation in the field? This is the typical behaviour of cowards. They attack whom they view as the weak; and when they realize that the "weak" is not so weak, they decide to run and hide. I felt greatly disappointed and deprived of my opportunity to let Gardner know that I was fully aware of his blatant display and verbalization of his racism, particularly when he tried to code racism as ". . . those Jamaicans in the Caribbean." He denied me this opportunity to tell him that his code was transparent, and that even in the army I was still entitled to a certain level of privacy.

The matter was taken before the major. Major Jensen asked me whether I wanted an apology from Gardner. I replied, "As far as I am concerned the matter is closed." I don't believe in accepting or listening to an apology which comes only from the mouth, and not from the heart. I apply the same principle when I extend an apology.

Corporal Dennis (a Black woman) was assigned as my assisting officer. Before we went into the hearing, we were instructed to wait outside the major's office. During our wait, Corporal Dennis informed me that she was very proud of my standing up for myself. I felt supported, a support I needed but did not expect. I did not choose her to assist me; a superior had ordered her to take the job, and her silence had made me wonder about the resentment I thought she must have felt at being thrown into Green's battles. Her remark to me was another example of people noticing me when I am not aware that they even see me.

My self-esteem was so low, long before this point in my life, I thought people had stopped seeing me. I felt very insignificant, almost invisible: since graduating from university and not being gainfully employed, a failure as a mother, and rejected by a man who himself was a reject. I thought, *"If* he *can reject* me, *why would anyone else notice me?"* Thankfully, my lack of self-esteem had not diminished my will to fight—at that time.

Now that I knew Corporal Dennis was aware of my struggle against racism in the army, I wondered why she had so quietly tolerated such blatant racism and how she coped when *she* was targeted. Considering Master Corporal Gardner's remarks about Jamaicans, I was surprised to find out she also was Jamaican and that the other Black corporal had Jamaican parents. Within the hour, I would get a chance to see how she coped.

Since the rest of the troops had already left for Base Borden, the captain drove Dennis and me in a military truck. He proceeded to tell me that harassment and racism are not at all tolerated in the army. He tried to get confirmation from Dennis, but all he got was, "Sir?" As in, *"Sir, come again?"* Then she remained silent. Her reaction taught me something about not succumbing to the pressures of a superior, while not going against him; she coped. The captain continued, "The army is not your bread-and-butter, so your full-time job should take precedence over the army." This was the only time Corporal Dennis verbally agreed and nodded her head to any of the captain's statement about the army. The captain's statement was in reference to the Friday night I chose to stay home because I was too exhausted to tackle basic training, and the first two weekends when I was a few minutes late getting to the garrison after working downtown and dealing with downtown Toronto traffic on a Friday afternoon.

Months later, Corporal Dennis would reveal to me, "Green, some of the stuff that is written in their [our superiors'] personnel files would blow your mind; you would not believe some of the stuff they do and get away with." Administrative clerks get to see a lot of *private* information. She continued, "My superiors know about the stuff that still happens to me, and they say nothing." It was as though she became more ashamed than afraid to talk about the racism she was still experiencing. I thought, *"They have succeeded in putting you where they want you—in your place."* Despite not having the fire to fight for herself, and knowing the army's ironclad resistance to change, she did not discourage my will to fight. For that, I am grateful.

— Chapter 17 —

A Trial Permeated with Racism

Both my children had abandoned me; but since it was Mother's Day, I still felt very much like a mother—a grieving one, but a mother nonetheless.

We assembled into our sections as usual before we were dismissed for meals. WO Ross reminded the troops that the ground was dusty and he did not want sand in his food; therefore, we needed to pick our feet up when we went to collect our food. To my surprise, WO Ross called me and three other women out of the line, acknowledged that we were mothers, and gave us the privilege of obtaining our meals first. Not long after, I heard the WO sternly reminding some guys to pick up their feet because he did not want sand in his food.

Private Stone felt the need once more to display himself. Apparently, after the day's training, when we sat down to clean our weapons, Dalel was walking through the woods. Stone, sitting in his little group, called out,

"Hey, I see a monkey walking through the woods." Dalel confronted him, and he brushed her off. Dalel complained to one of our immediate superiors, who sent the complaint up the chain of command. It went all the way to Major Jensen. What I found interesting was that the military put Dalel on trial, as if she was the one who made the derogatory remark. It was not surprising that Stone denied he was referring to Dalel. However, it was surprising how his "team members" covered for him. According to Stone, he asked his team members if anyone *saw* a monkey in the bush. What difference does it make? The fact is, this guy called a Black person a monkey, and he did so knowing what this connotes for Black people; and to add insult to injury, our superiors treated Dalel as if she was paranoid. Their attitude was, "How dare you accuse someone of displaying racist behaviours?"

Although Dalel was not present for training the following training weekend, the major conducted interviews regarding the racist remark. During my interview, he asked me if Stone treated me the way he was accused of treating Dalel. I replied, "He's never bothered me." He then asked why I thought he wasn't treating me the same as Dalel. I answered, "For one thing, I am bigger." He and the other officers present looked at me as if I was not *with it*. They, like most people, underestimated me because of my height and size (5' 4"; 120 pounds). I added, "Stone and some other unit members get frustrated with Dalel, because sometimes she does not do well in certain physical activities." The major explained that Dalel has a heart condition that affects her physical abilities. There, again, was a total lack of discretion; I did not need to know that, but it caused me to remember the day she nearly died after she was ordered through the gas chamber. To make light of Dalel's complaint, the major said, "You should hear what my wife calls me sometimes; she even calls me a big ape." White people just do not get it: They do not realize that a White person being compared to a monkey is vastly different from a Black person being called a monkey by our former "masters," who saw us as simply *black* and not people—hence, the African slave trade and the rape of Africa.

While Stone never used a derogatory remark to me, were I asked if he treated me the way he treated DaCosta and Garant, the answer would have been a resounding "no." At the time, I did not interpret his behaviour as racist; I thought he just did not like me. However, I am now more attuned to subtle racist practises and behaviours.

Two training weekends after Stone made the derogatory remark, all the witnesses were called. We were seated on the bleachers in the gym, while immediate supervisors took turns giving us feedback on what had been taught since the training began and what we were to expect in the next few weekends: amongst other things, nighttime exercises, overall examinations and, ultimately, graduation. Periodically, Stone and Dalel returned to the group and, between witnesses, were called away individually and together. Dalel was notably drained from having to defend herself, "for accusing someone of being racist." The outcome was that Stone and Dalel gave each other a lame apology in the presence of the unit. What did Dalel do to warrant an apology to Stone? This was my first lesson in how people get away with racist practises in Canada these days, but it was only a taste of what was to come in my own life.

Master Corporal Seiki invited the troops—One, Two and Three Sections—to go to the range again. I wondered whether his extra effort at cohesiveness within the unit was to soothe out the tension therein. It certainly felt that way, even if his true motive was to bring our awareness to his collection of military memorabilia.

—Chapter 18 —

Saturday, May 16, 1998

I invited my dad and Lloyd to target practise at the range with Master Corporal Seiki. Carlene—my friend who had enlightened me that Gardner was a miserable collections agent working in a call centre—invited herself along. Seiki gave us a quick lesson in firearms safety and proceeded to guide us in shooting. I wanted my dad to hit the target, so I let him have my turns. Lloyd was not so generous; he was not going to give up what may be his only opportunity to fire a gun. Carlene was too happy to start shooting. She looked like she could easily become a master at hitting the target. I started calling her "Miss Aggressive with the Weapon." She called my dad "trigger happy" because his finger was always touching the trigger, though it should not be touched unless you are ready to fire the weapon. Seiki invited us back for more practise on our next weekend off. We accepted.

On the way home, Lloyd said he needed to stop in Newmarket to look at a second-hand van that was on sale. I knew our budget; I knew the cost of insurance; I knew the cost of repairs, even though he was a "mechanic"; I knew what his classes at the DeVry Institute had cost me, for which he did not produce a certificate. I told him that we could not afford another set of expenses. He argued that he just wanted to stop to have a look at it. Had I known how devious he really was, I would have guessed that he had already purchased it.

My dad, being the peacemaker that he is, suggested that since the mechanic shop was on the way home, it would not hurt to stop for a few minutes so that Lloyd could have a look at the vehicle.

Carlene, my dad and I stayed in the car while Lloyd went into the mechanic shop to have a "look" at the van. Once back in the car, he tried to get my dad to side with him by telling my dad about the "great deal" he was getting on the van. My dad did not take the bait. That, I am sure, did not surprise Lloyd; it had always burned him to the core that there is not a soul on Earth who can put a wedge between my dad and me.

We dropped Carlene off and then my dad. I was not surprised that my refusal to waste my money on a second vehicle would cause Lloyd to engage in his usual passive-aggressive behavior. He stopped talking to me. His refusal to speak to me did not bother me in the least. We would usually go for days without seeing each other; and when we did see each other on good days, conversations lasted only seconds.

— Chapter 19 —

Weekend #12: May 1998

Weekend Basic Training Extended

None of our superiors had the decency to tell us that it would require more than twelve weeks to complete our basic training, due to the Quebec ice storm having delayed our starting. Instead, they simply kept our training weekends going as if we would not notice. I noticed, even though I did not confront any of my superiors, and I am sure others noticed but were too afraid to question the extended training.

The troops were on the bus at Denison Armoury, waiting for our superiors to give the orders to leave for Base Borden, when I was called to the office. The issue was my hair. They had concerns about my helmet not fitting properly, due to my braids. I had no intention of taking out my braids. When I returned to the bus, Goudett asked me, "Green, what's their problem?" When I told him, he responded, "Well, they didn't have a problem with it all this time."

About two minutes later, Dalel was called off the bus. A sergeant motioned to the driver to pull out. The troops burst into cheers. If the superiors responsible for our training decided that they did not want you to continue training, they would call you into the office and give you your documents for returning to your unit—the part of the army that accepts a particular applicant as a recruit and is responsible for deciding whether to keep that particular recruit and send the recruit on a future basic training course, or whether to release the recruit from the army; the part of the army that the individual joins. Our superiors administered surprise tests to the new recruits in order to fail as many as possible and send them back to their units, in the hope that they would leave the army. I was the only Black recruit in a unit of thirty remaining recruits, the remnants of the three original sections. Thank God for the two Black female corporals who came along as "helpers."

As the bus drove away from Denison Armoury to go to Base Borden, Goudett commented that Dalel attacked him for saying Black people in Africa are stupid. What he had actually said was, "They cannot see that the United States gives them just enough food to keep them alive and more than enough guns to kill each other, while America laughs at their stupidity." Goudett is Caucasian, but I do not interpret this as a racist statement; it is a fact. I believe Goudett was illustrating a parallel between the way the Canadian Army treats its recruits and the way America treats Africa.

Not five minutes after the bus pulled out of the garrison, a few recruits lit cigarettes and started smoking. The smokers held their cigarettes out the window of the bus. The wind blew a chunk of lit tobacco right into my bosom. DeGroot saw, looked at me to ensure that I was okay, then stomped his way from the front of the bus to uncomfortably close proximity of the recruit and barked: "Watch your cigarette! You just burned Green in the c-h-h-h hest!" The anger I saw coming out of DeGroot far exceeded the constant anger I carry around with me. We all have issues that touch certain nerves and send us off into extreme emotions: For me, it is the constant pain of how racism affects my life; for DeGroot, it was the constant effects of his mother's smoking on his life. Although I saw him as very intelligent, his view of himself was quite telling in his own statement: "She [his mother] damaged some of my brain cells because she smoked so much when she was pregnant with me!" Despite grinding his teeth constantly, the only other time I had seen DeGroot display such levels of hatred and anger was that day in the field when I first heard him make that remark about his mother.

DeGroot's anger at the incident was such that I felt sorry and scared for the recruit; I would have been gentler with the guy, but DeGroot did not give me the opportunity. Furthermore, since I was so tired from a week of work, I would have just let it go—especially since I was unharmed. White people amaze me: DeGroot did everything in his power to keep me in "my place," but he was genuinely concerned for my physical well-being. Where racism was concerned, he could not feel for me; in fact, he perpetuated it. However, where a threat from cigarette was concerned, he looked like he could have killed for me—using his bare hands. I guess it was okay for him to keep me from progressing, as long as I was not killed by cigarettes in the process.

Upon arrival at Base Borden, our superiors immediately ordered us to bed. Just as my sleep was getting good, I was awakened to do a turn at picketing. The hardest part of picketing is getting dressed for it, which led me to conclude that soldiers who are required to picket during the night should simply stay dressed. My partner was a male private I did not recognize, as I was too occupied with accommodating the sleep in my body; from the way he stood in slumber, he obviously felt the same as I. The designated picketing spot might as well have been the front door of the barracks; our distance from the barracks provided no lead time for us to warn the company of impending danger. We got up and got dressed to picket only a few feet from the entrance to the building. We were too close to the barracks to provide any real safety for the people inside. Moreover, we were under lighting. Had enemies been in the dark, they could have shot us like sitting ducks. Leave it to DeGroot to figure this out. He came out of wherever, and in his cover of night voice told us, "Move further into the dark. Take ten steps forward. Do that now!" He took those ten steps right behind us and then disappeared into further darkness. The private and I stood shoulder to shoulder, our rifles slung over our shoulders. About two minutes passed before he spoke, "Green. Is that you?" I answered, "Yes." Only then did I realize he was a recruit who had emigrated from South America. He wondered aloud, "I wonder how long they are going to keep us out here." I answered, "It can't be more than another hour," even though I was preparing my mind for an all night stay. We both knew we should not have been talking: nearby enemy.

Looking back, I now wonder what part his heritage played in his fear of the dark and the army environment. You see, being of South American descent, he most likely had first-hand knowledge of the atrocities of their past and present civil wars; he probably entered Canada as a refugee from those very atrocities. Although we did not have watches, I think we picketed for no more than fifteen minutes. Each shift is supposed to last for an hour. I like those types of surprises; however, I could not help thinking, *"Why did they bother waking me from my short sleep?"* I fell back to sleep almost as soon as my body hit the bed, but it seemed I had slept for about a half an hour before it was time to start the day's training.

Warrant Officer Ross started the day's training by instructing us on how to measure distance by walking. Ludwig was supposed to demonstrate. Do you remember my telling you that he was as dumb as an ox? Here is some proof. WO Ross instructed the guy to walk towards the fence and tell us the number of metres between the fence and the troops. Instead, he started walking in the other direction, towards no-man's-land. To make matters worse, he had walked about ten metres before the WO called, "Ludwig, the fence." This was another time his looks saved him from ultimate embarrassment. He smiled and shook his head, which caused the troops to see it as a silly mistake instead of a dumb blunder.

At another field location, we were given a map and told to find various points using this rule: "In the door and up the stairs." In other words, move your finger from left to right on the map; then, move your finger towards the top of the map until it touches the targeted location. I noticed that everyone in my group was hitting the wrong point. The younger of the two East Indian brothers used his finger while repeating the rule, and he was the first to get it correct. I was the third person after him. DeGroot came over to our group, "Green! Find. . . ." I used the ruler and my finger, and BINGO; I found it. He looked disappointed—there was nothing about which to ridicule me.

When it got dark, we had to measure distance by first finding a spot on the map and then walking while counting each step. Each step is considered one metre. This skill is still valuable to this day; I know exactly how long it will take me to get somewhere by driving, simply by measuring the distance on a map using a ruler and then dividing the number of kilometers by one hundred to get my travel time. For example, if from point A to point B measures fifteen millimetres, and we consider each millimetre to be an hour's drive, assuming we are traveling at a hundred kilometers per hour, we should be at point B within fifteen hours. I was taught this in high school and perhaps elementary school, but it did not register until I learned it again in the army.

We were about to do a tour in what appeared to be an unexplored part of Base Borden's bush. Corporal Dennis was dishing out chores. She assigned me a thirty-pound radio battery. The moment two recruits saddled it onto my back, my back pains were unbearable—thanks to the Coca Cola Bottling Ltd. I thought, *"Does Corporal Dennis not know the weight of this thing? Did we not bond after she used my lip balm? Could she not pick one of the able male recruits?"* I concluded that, psychologically, she had to pick me. It was reverse racism; had she not picked me, people—both recruits and superiors—would most certainly have concluded that she spared me because I was Black. That kind of judgment would have been a small price to pay to remove the pain from my back.

I carried that thing for about one and a half hours and never said a word. Master Corporal Seiki led his troops carrying the receiver as though there was no heavy battery included in anyone's load. He is the type of guy who does not harass anyone; and since I did not complain, he must have thought the battery felt like a one-pound weight to me.

When DeGroot came to check on the troops, he asked, "Green! How long have you been carrying that?" I replied, "Since we started, Master Corporal." He gave the other recruits shit for not looking out for their team members. He immediately assigned the battery to another recruit and told him to trade off in fifteen minutes. Corporal Dennis should have stipulated this in the beginning.

DaCosta and Garant were winning in the trench-digging exercise. Each team was given two shovels, a mini one and an almost average size one, and each team was comprised of two or three recruits. I don't know what technique DaCosta and Garant figured out, but they sure put everyone else's team to shame. My team had two males and myself; yet, DaCosta and Garant were emptying their trench three times faster than my team. Mind you, one of the guys on my team was not worth a damn. I cannot stand lazy men. DeGroot and Cherniawski were too happy to flaunt Dacosta and Garant's progress in the faces of the other teams, particularly the teams with three men. Let me point out that these trenches are dug in sand, and they are emptied and refilled by every recruiting class. Knowing how Garant was favoured, to ensure the winning outcome, I would find it easy to believe that she was assigned to a very recently re-filled area.

At one point in the digging, in order to gain ground, I took off my outer shirt—leaving my T-shirt. This of course exposed my elbow pads. DeGroot commented, "Green, you're wearing elbow pads?" I answered, "Yes, Master Corporal," while thinking, *"What the hell do you expect? Don't you know my elbows hurt when I fire the C7 from the prone position?"*

When the trench was deep enough for us to stand inside, I noticed a small worm going about its business of pushing and wiggling through the soil. Normally I would have been scared of it; now, after being out in the fields so long, I just figured, *"This is life in the army."*

When it got dark, I thought about the worm maybe crawling into my clothing; however, exhaustion would not allow me to worry much about a worm that was primarily concerned with finding a new home.

Sleeping in a trench wasn't so bad. Two people stood watch while one slept, on a rotating basis. The lazy recruit on my team was perfectly contented to sleep all night. I sensed that he was afraid of the dark, as every two minutes he tried to make conversation with his male partner; this, I concluded, was not to see if the person was awake but because he was scared. What really ticked me off, however, was the frequency with which he wanted to know the number of minutes left before his picketing duties would be over. I thought, *"This is exactly how you behaved the other night when we picketed together."*

It became apparent that we were not picketing in vain when, at about 1:00 a.m., a fire fight started. It seemed that a team of soldiers was approaching the trenches in which we were sleeping. The sound of plenty of gunfire was getting closer by the second. DeGroot gave the order for the team to the right of DaCosta and Garant to fire. Next, he ordered DaCosta and Garant to fire their weapons. The flashes of light appeared to be coming from high-powered weapons. When the flashes were within a few feet of my trench, DeGroot gave the order for all three of us in my trench to "fire at will." Frankly, I could not see what I was shooting at; nonetheless, I let it rip. I still do not know how they got the place to light up as if real bullets were coming from our guns. It was beautiful, better than firecrackers in July.

At about 2:00 a.m., the WO ordered the troops to bed. I was so exhausted that I did not remove my outer clothing—combat pants and jacket—or inflate my air mattress. Instead, I just climbed into my sleeping bag and went off to sleep. Not even ten minutes later, the lazy recruit was waking me up because he and our other team member were sharing the tent. As he called in a hushed voice, "Green! Green!" I ignored him. When the other team member called my name, I moaned an answer; but I just could not move. I decided that they would need to make themselves as comfortable as possible in the available space, because I was not getting up until morning. The obvious thought for the reader is, *where is your team spirit?* My answer: "It disappeared on Weekend #10 when my superiors ignored Garant's AWOL."

I heard the WO over me saying, "Just sleep in that end." Did this young man really need someone else to tell him that? Even if I were "awake," did he think I was going to give up my spot so that he could take it while I slept at the inner end with less air? He reminded me of that Middle Eastern glutton, who kept on praying every half hour or so in those first few weeks—before he failed and was sent back to his unit. For the record, if the glutton were a Jamaican, I would label him *Jamaican glutton*. Likewise, if he were Canadian White or Aboriginal or whatever, I would still label him accordingly as a *glutton*.

I paid for my selfishness, big time. It was May, but the hard ground gets very cold at night. At first, I did not feel the cold because I was hot in my sweaty clothing; but as my body temperature dropped, I felt the cold. I thought one side of my body would warm up the ground and the sleeping bag would keep the other side warm. I thought wrong. There was a whole lot more ground to warm up than I had body with which to do it. I started to shiver. It was then I remembered what Heather said about her experience of going to sleep in too much clothing during the winter, and I regretted not taking it seriously. There was no way I was going to get up to go looking through my backpack for a dry T-shirt. I suffered until the sun came up, and even then I was still shivering.

The main thing I have to say about the ready-to-eat packages of food is, "They should be called *sugar packets*." The content looked like beef stew, but it tasted like sugar; in fact, it was much sweeter than sugar. I might as well have been drinking a bowl of syrup. Also, I do not think anyone ever got those packets warm on those things the army likes to call portable stoves.

Sergeants Cherniawski and Mahood decided to have a tour-of-duty the night following the unforgettable flashes of light. DeGroot assigned the "little troops" their spots and took Garant and Bezchilbuyk (the *elite* recruits) on the ambush against Mahood. Even though Garant was telling some people in our section how easily DeGroot defeated Mahood, there would have been no difficulty in determining who won: Mahood was still angry the next day, relentlessly barking at his troops. I can still hear DaCosta saying, "He hates losing." My guess is, Mahood was so busy looking for Cherniawski that he totally overlooked the DeGroot factor. I imagined DeGroot took him out in such a way that his incompetence became obvious to his subordinates. I had never seen a grown man who was such a sore loser, nor who was so delighted to take out his shortcomings on his troops. First of all, the night was so black that you could not see even the person next to you. A private would be solely dependent on his/her superior for complete guidance. Yet, this sergeant treated his troops like trash because "they" lost.

— Chapter 20 —

Saturday, May 30, 1998

A Turning Point

My dad and Carlene were waiting for Lloyd and me to pick them up, to go target practicing with Master Corporal Seiki. Lloyd casually informed me, "I am not going, because I have to do some work on the van." I paused to let the information register, while he just walked past me to use the phone. I said to myself, "*I pay your rent. I pay your phone bill. I pay your cable bill. I even pay for your classes at the DeVry Institute of Technology because you don't have any money, even though you go to work every day. So, how the hell can you afford to buy a van?*"

Instead of verbalizing my thoughts, I ordered him to hang up my phone. He was sitting on my bed, ignoring me, so I attempted to take my phone from him. His response was to kick me. I reached for the base of the phone and, before I knew what happened, blood was oozing from his forehead. The blow caused him to pause and obviously wonder what the hell had just happened. He dropped my phone on the bed, touched his forehead, got up and went to the bathroom saying, "I am going to call the police." I stayed put. My thought was, *"Deneace, call the police."* He stood at the top of the stairs verbalizing his thoughts, "You are lucky I don't beat women." No answer was going to come from me because if he had known me, he would have known that I do not speak when I am ready to kill. He then walked down the stairs saying, "I am going to call the police."

I called my dad, who said, "You go ahead and call the police too." I hung up the phone and followed my dad's advice. Within minutes, a male and a female officer were at my door. After the officers took my statement, one commented, "We just saw him at the Seven Eleven [store]. He said 'Hi' to us." The officers left my apartment to pick him up. While they were gone, I gave myself some therapy: Lloyd would drive around the city and collect every piece of electrical garbage he could find, then bring it to my home. I smashed every piece of his junk, and got some relief from doing it. Anger management classes required? No, that was enough therapy to last me for a while.

The police officers escorted him back to the apartment, to get some of his clothing. He started to complain to the officers about my smashing his stuff. I think the officers were sympathetic to me because they discretely told me that he could take me to court to pay for the damages. I nodded, indicating that I would not cause any more damage.

While Lloyd was upstairs packing his clothing, the officers examined my wall hangings: my University of Toronto Bachelor of Arts degree, and my Seneca College Honours Law Enforcement diploma. They also examined my graduation and class graduation pictures on the walls. They wanted to know who else lived in the house. I am not diplomatic, so I gave them the answer they were seeking, saying, "They are all mine." Then they wanted to know what I did for a living and where I worked. The title Membership Services Coordinator sounded impressive to them. The Ontario Network of Employment Skills Training Projects (ONESTEP), to them sounded like a place of great importance. The female complained to the male, "It makes you wonder what we are doing, eh?" If they only knew; the job was nothing more than that of a telephone solicitor, a telemarketer.

The officers felt that I was educated enough to write my own police statement. The female handed me her notebook, and I wrote.

The officers left my home, taking Lloyd with them. A condition of his release was that he would have no contact with me until after court, that the situation was being treated as a domestic assault.

Carlene was more concerned about me than her missed opportunity for target practise. Master Corporal Seiki, like Carlene, took the broken appointment very well. I gave him no details, but he was happy to reschedule. I told him I would let him know when I was ready.

Lloyd phoned my parents to complain. My mother offered him shelter in her and my dad's small, one-bedroom apartment. He found refuge elsewhere, through church members.

— Chapter 21 —

Weekend 13: June 1998

I Shared a Victory; The Last Weekend in the Field

I was glad to see Dalel had returned. I was ecstatic to learn the reason for her being pulled off the bus the previous training weekend. She had been accepted into medical school, and her dad wanted her home immediately to take care of more-important business. Here was a fighter: Her mom and dad never wanted her in the army; the people in the army did not want her in the army, but she stayed. Her dad cried when she was accepted into medical school and was very happy to take out a $70,000 second mortgage on the family home. She did so well on her MCAT that Columbia University gave her a $10,000 scholarship. She attained something that Garant, DaCosta, Nguyen and Chernaiwaski could not; she got into medical school; she was living her dream; she was going to be a doctor.

I shared Dalel's victory: An underdog in the army had just moved to the top of the social hierarchy, and her acceptance into medical school was a reminder to me that "what is for you is for you." You see, she wrote the MCAT just to see how well she would do; then, she applied to medical schools just to see if she would get accepted. In her first attempt, she excelled in both. In fact, earlier that same week, she went to the University of Toronto to complete some paperwork. There she saw Cherniawski sitting on a bench. He sat there staring into space for about an hour; then, he just got up and left. She had witnessed Nguyen on a number of occasions at the University of Toronto, trying to get his medical training going; and the irony is, she was not even trying—she just wrote the test to see if she would do well. From here on in, I addressed Dalel as Doctor Dalel. Every time I said, "Doctor Dalel," I felt the venom spew from just about everyone around; and I loved stinging them.

We didn't even bother to stop at the barracks in Base Borden; we went straight out into the middle of nowhere. I don't know what the recruits were supposed to learn from this exercise, because we were simply divided into groups of two or three and placed in particular locations until a superior found us in the dark. Looking back, this exercise was obviously for the corporals and master corporals rather than for the recruits.

When they had found us, our superiors marched us to our camping site. We could not see each other; however, DaCosta's teeth glowed in the dark—too much professional cleaning, perhaps by Garant who was a dental hygienist. Had those been my teeth, Cherniawski would surely have given me a chit. He was still using the word "discombobulated" at every turn. The WO told DaCosta to "stop smiling; otherwise, the enemy will see us." We knew the Warrant was joking because we were already found, and not by "enemies."

This weekend we were to be tested on all the skills we had learned in the field: tying knots; finding our way in the dark by measuring distance on a map and walking the required number of steps to find objects placed by our officers; disassembling and reassembling our weapons; digging trenches and re-filling them; and properly camouflaging ourselves in order to avoid enemy detection.

Along with our regular superiors, trainers from other units were there to have their units tested and to help with the testing of our unit. Stations were set up for the recruits to demonstrate their skills.

I had just finished digging my trench when DeGroot ordered me to go with him to get water. Each full bottle weighed thirty-two pounds, and I was ordered to carry two while he carried his stick. He walked slightly ahead of me, his small head bobbing up and down as if repeatedly trying to bump the sky. At first I was not giving my all to carrying the bottles, as I thought he would turn around any second and say, "Green! I will take those." No such luck. I realized that I needed to dig deeper for more strength to make it back to the trenches. When we were about a hundred feet from the WO, DeGroot said, "Green! Do you want me to take those?" This was my answer: "No, Master Corporal." I was thinking, *"Why the hell should I let you have any of them now? Look how far I came."* I saw the smile on his face, even though his back was to me. Approximately ten steps later, he said, "Green! Do you want to join the infantry?" (his unit). This was my opportunity to do what I joined the army to do, train to fight. However, the racism had gotten to me; and I no longer felt the desire to give my all to the army. My answer was, "No, Master Corporal." I realized he was proud of my tenacity, my determination to get the two thirty-two-pound jugs of water to our destination without his help; and from the feeling of satisfaction I felt emanating from him, it is safe to say, he thought he had finally "moulded" me. It was wishful thinking on his part. I am still an individual, and my stubbornness is an innate gift from my maternal grandmother.

I was about three steps from my destination when one of the bottles just about slipped out of my hand. DeGroot could not resist, "Those last few steps are always the hardest, eh Green?" I overheard him telling the WO that I refused his help. The troops were so eager to get the water, I felt like a saviour watching them gulp it down as though their lives depended on that one drink.

The feeling I was experiencing from my heroic act of supplying drinking water had not worn off before DeGroot gave me a chit, for allowing the grass on my helmet to get too dry. The grass on the helmet was a part of my camouflage outfit. The logic is to blend in with the field. Thus, while doing the Leopard Crawl test, I was required to put grass in the netting on my helmet to blend with the grass around me. Apparently, the grass on the helmet was to be changed often enough that it blended with the undisturbed grass; but I was no longer crawling through the grass; I was on my feet. Consequently, if he felt the need to give me a chit, it should have been for not putting a branch in my helmet—as he had done to fit the trees. He was wearing a seven-inch tall branch with grass around it. I thought about the speech he had made after the sights fell off my weapon, saying, "Green! Whatever I do, you do." Oh please. Was I to mimic him down to the branch? Furthermore, I could not see the grass in my helmet, but I guessed I should have looked at the other recruits around me. As soon as I got my chit, the others scrambled to put fresh grass in their helmets. It required "Green" as the sacrificial lamb for the other recruits to put green grass in their helmets; "Green" was grass.

It pays to be in the right place at the right time: Starting with Garant, a trainer from a different unit was about to give us three females an individual test on firing the weapon. Garant's face looked like she had already failed the test; so, Cherniawski quickly stepped in, took the test sheet from the other sergeant and dismissed him by simply saying, "Here, I'll do it." The relief on Garant's face was undeniable. Cherniawski saw me watching him intently and ordered, "DaCosta, Green, get over there." We took up our positions beside Garant in grass and bush about a foot high. The test was virtually non-existent; Cherniawski gave us the most basic drills imaginable. This was the only time I ever had such an easy break in my military career, despite the fact it was a parasitic break. I got a break because of Garant getting her usual breaks.

I observed Master Corporal Gardner exercising his White supremacy on an East-Indian sergeant from the engineering unit, who was working with him on the *counting distance by steps* part of the testing. The sergeant was eating sunflower seeds. Gardner was taking the sergeant's sunflower seeds in a way that must have been exasperating to the sergeant. Obviously, the sergeant did not want to deny Gardner the seeds for fear of reprisal. If you do not appease your White colleagues, you will be ostracized; if you are ostracized, you may find your career grind to an abrupt halt; or worse yet, you may find you have no career. It boiled my blood to see how this White master corporal was treating this older sergeant. After repeatedly helping himself to the sergeant's sunflower seeds, Gardner said, "Gimmie some more of those!" while reaching into the bag of seeds that the sergeant was still holding. Gardner saw me watching him and knew what I was thinking: *"Write a letter."* Whereupon, he turned the scene into a joking matter: shaking his whole body from side-to-side while repeating, *"Gimme some-a-dat."* I did not buy it; and neither did the sergeant; nevertheless, he had to grin and bear it. I can still see the other recruits' faces as they observed the situation, feeling sympathy for the sergeant; he was playing a role to which he had become so accustomed in this society, that he bravely endured his degradation as a natural part of life.

It was dark; even so, we kept right on training. After all, we still needed to be trained in how to use night vision and how to distinguish which shovel was being used in the dark. At a distance from us, DeGroot had another trainer dig with a small shovel and a regular-sized shovel. In the dark, he said, "Green! Which shovel is that?" I guessed the large one, when deep down I knew it was the small one. He took one of his usual fits: "You have been using the 'portable' all day; you should know the sound of it by now!"

Garant got to spend both nights in the military vehicle because she was *sick.* Only Garant and perhaps DaCosta could get away with spending the night in a nice, warm, comfortable truck while the rest of us froze our asses off in our sleeping bags. It was June, but the weather can get quite cold at night when you are in no-man's land.

I guess Cherniawski knew how I was feeling about Garant being exempted from certain tests and sleeping in a heated, comfortable, accommodation, i.e., in the military truck with padded bunks and all. That Sunday afternoon, a few hours before we started preparing to head home, he said to me, "Green, you did better than Garant this weekend." The man actually allowed himself to believe, and expected me to believe, that Garant did better than I throughout basic training. The human mind is an amazing thing; it can bring itself to believe anything is true.

— Chapter 22 —
Weekend 14: June 1998

Graduation Weekend

The Queen's Regulations and Orders clearly states that it is illegal for a superior to fraternize with recruits; yet, a corporal from another unit was openly dating one of his recruits; and no one bothered to address it. There they were in the gymnasium, the night before graduation. She was perched on his lap, as though sitting upright on a chair, facing forward, in her tight white half-T-shirt which barely covered her upper ribs and her low-waisted blue jeans fastened not more than an inch above her pubic area, her navel on display with a ring therein, for all to see, as he made circles around her ringed-navel with his index finger. Guess who graduated at the top of her unit?

Despite Garant's minimal participation during the last field weekend and her not showing up one Friday night, she graduated as Number One Candidate. DaCosta knew she or Bezchilbuyk was the true Number One

Candidate. Nonetheless, she grinned and bore the injustice. Through her smiles, I could see the hurt. She was in an awkward situation: She and Garant had bonded and become best army buddies; how could she make a case against her "friend?" Moreover, how could she justify herself getting the award over Bezchilbuyk? She did the smart thing by keeping her mouth because it all worked out well for her. That is, in the next course, the Qualification Level 3 (QL3), she would claim the Number One Candidate award and the course sergeant as her husband. That, too, was a whole other case of fraternizing.

On this graduation day, Dalel and I became very *important* to the unit. It was so ironic that the two people the immediate supervisors fought so hard to have dismissed from the army now became very important to them. Graduation is a good time for the army to sell itself to the public. Strategically placing two Black females in the graduation march and ceremony would yield the highest prospects for more Black recruits. Their purpose was quite obvious in the way the superiors, from corporals to lieutenants, kept pulling Dalel and me to the front of about sixty recruits, using phrases such as, "All the ugly and tall people in the back; and, Green, Dalel, to the front." Again, the superiors were making me sick with their saying, "Watch myself," when teaching the recruits the graduation march.

My mom, dad, and my brother Worrel came to my graduation. Worrel was their chauffeur, as usual. My dad confirmed what I have always known about my luck. He was able to capture on video every recruit accepting his/her graduation certificate—except me! As soon as my name was called, the camera stopped recording. That could also have been because my dad wanted to get such a good picture that he ended up getting nothing. He said, "Deneace, you really are bad lucked."

It was no surprise that only one-third of the original class graduated. Observers at the graduation would never know they were observing a skeletal class, because the superiors combined Sections One, Two and Three to make it look like a reasonably sized class of approximately thirty. Additionally, to make the proceedings appear even more impressive, the ceremonies for the Engineers and the Infantry were held along with mine (25 Medical Company).

The graduates who wanted to pursue medical training went off to do their QL3 course. Since I was to do administrative work, my further training was to start in the fall. I was looking forward to what I felt would be a well-deserved break.

– Chapter 23 –

Life After Basic Training

Shortly after basic training was completed, I was riding the subway train when I bumped into Dalel. We chatted about various things that were going on with us and acknowledged one thing we clearly had in common: We would not forget the racism we constantly encountered in the Canadian Armed Forces. I phrased it, "A lot of it had to do with our colour." She chose to put it into clearer perspective, by retorting, "It had *everything* to do with our colour!" It mattered to neither of us that most of the people present and listening intently were White and middle class. Dalel informed me that I was a source of strength for her. She said, "Green, I always watched what you were doing, and it helped me to get through a lot of difficult times." I had no idea I played such a role in her army life—another classic case of how people who I do not really notice tend to zero in on me. I am not sure if Dalel went on the Qualification Level 3 (QL3) course over the summer months, before she left for Colombia University medical school in the fall.

When I reviewed my Qualification Level 2 (QL2) course report (the overall basic training report) and saw the petty issues that were documented to make me appear totally incompetent, and therefore deserving of my placement at or near the bottom of the class, I felt the need to respond in writing. I sent a four-page letter to Lieutenant Colonel von Bulow, addressing all my experiences and concerns, including the following:

1. Green displayed poor attitude and tardiness;
2. Green left her weapon unsecured;
3. Green dressed improperly;
4. Green failed her C7 Performance Check;
5. Green failed her C9 Performance Check.

Lieutenant Colonel von Bulow obviously forwarded the letter to Major Sutherland, who, instead of addressing any of the issues, simply wrote his own letter dismissing me, noting, "Green is incompetent, and she is complaining to cover her shortcomings." This was no different from how Major Jensen had turned Dalel's complaint about Stone's racist remark into an attack on Dalel—for her daring to call Stone on his racism.

If I had failed my final C7 or C9 check, I would have been sent back to my unit. I wonder how these two checks showed on Garant's report, since Bezchilbuyk and DaCosta were the only ones who *passed* the primary C7 Performance Check; the other ten recruits failed, including Garant, and any candidate who fails any part of the course cannot be Number One Candidate.

To make matters worse, I had admitted to failing a test that I passed (the C9 Performance Check). The racist major backed his racist counter-parts, and repeated their assessment of me in more simplified terms. Where was I to turn when the major, who had never observed me in field training, chose to label me *incompetent* without questioning me himself? Now, in addition to the garbage written about me by my immediate supervisors, there was also a letter in my file, written by the major, labeling me as *incompetent with shortcomings*. Besides, my racist immediate superiors kept on telling me, "Green, you passed the course; what's written in your course report means nothing." I thought, *"If . . . it means nothing, why write it?"*

What they could not grasp, or better yet, what they did not want me to grasp, was that anyone reading the report would not know the circumstances surrounding the incidents and would, therefore, see the incidents as major issues. They knew exactly what they were doing; they knew they were deliberately sabotaging my future.

I want to tell you how Private Stone finally let his impulses get him into deep trouble during a party given by someone in the QL3 course.

I was talking to a corporal, one of the Black females on my course. She asked if I had heard about the situation with Stone. I answered with sarcasm, "Is there a *new* situation with Stone?" She proceeded to tell me. There was much drinking, and smoking, and "carrying on" at the party. Stone was openly approaching people for sex. No one was obliging him. He somehow managed to lock a Black male private in a bathroom and told him, "I have done women; I have done men, but I have never done a Black guy." The captive insisted on being let out of the bathroom. Stone kept him confined and attempted to "do" him. I do not know how much "doing" was done, but it was serious enough for formal charges to be laid against him—I confirmed this incident with two other sources in the unit. Perhaps that was what it took for Stone to get the psychological treatment that he so desperately needed.

Was the army partially responsible for what happened to Stone's victim? Based on the following facts, you can decide. Fact one: Stone was not generally held accountable for his actions. Example, even though the WO told him that he was directly responsible for his partner's passing the C7 Performance Check, he caused his partner to fail by ignoring him and telling a bunch of fabricated stories to everyone present. Fact two: He openly targeted Dalel during line-ups in basic training, and was never called on it by his superiors. Fact three: He called Dalel a monkey, in the presence of his peers, and his superiors defended him while making Dalel out to be paranoid and petty. I think all the passes Stone got in the army combined to get him to the place in his head where he felt that he could get away with rape.

— Chapter 24 —

The Incident: A Day I Should Have Skipped

Fall came. Military duties resumed; in that, I was supposed to start my administrative training. I was talked into going on a field-training course. I did not want to go; I went just to make-up the numbers—to make the weekend more worthwhile for the organizers. This favour indelibly altered the course of my life and put me through a living hell. I thought I had seen racism at its finest during basic training; but it was on this weekend that my education began, in how and why racism is practised so blatantly in Canada. This was when my consciousness of my true hatred for most of humankind really started to take shape.

It was October 1998, and I was on the firing range shooting at my target. I was obviously doing well, as usual, because all my bullets were hitting the target—albeit in the groin area. Sergeant Michaud (I am told Michaud means *wicked* in French, and he was French) approached me after a round of firing. According to him, I was not holding the C7 rifle correctly. I explained that I needed to hold the rifle the way I did because I could close my right eye while looking through my sights with the left, but I could not do the opposite. His doubtful response was, "You can't open the right one, eh?" I answered, "That is correct." I was wishing he would just leave me alone, since my strategy had gotten me through basic training without complaint from people who pecked at me just for the sake of it. Instead of wishing for him to leave, perhaps I should have prayed.

As soon as Cherniawaski started giving the next round of commands—which were already difficult to hear, due to the ear plugs everyone on the firing range was required to wear—Sergeant Michaud asked me, "Where are you shooting on the target?" This forced me to engage in conversation with him, causing me to miss the commands Cherniawaski had just given. However, I did hear the part about firing five rounds into the target. When I fired my first shot, I realized no one else had fired. Michaud immediately booted me off the firing range and told me to go see my Warrant Officer.

Warrant Officer Ross informed me that I most likely would have to pay a $50 fine for firing the bullet before time, and that I was done shooting for the day. That seemed like a reasonable punishment to me, even though Michaud caused the misfire.

Since I was done shooting for the day and there was plenty of daylight left, I had lots of time to ponder my future in the army. I sat in the approximate spot where I had seen Corporal Dennis eating alone, some months prior. I thought about how Garant had become the Number One Candidate before she even started basic training, and about how Ludwig failed me on the C9 Performance Check even though we both knew that I passed. I thought about how Cherniawski threw chits at me left, right and centre while adding, "It ain't easy being *green*," knowing full well what he meant by *green*. I thought about how Gardner wanted to fight me because he felt that I was taking something from him, since the RCMP was showing an interest in hiring a *black*. I thought about how DeGroot ignored Garant when she did not bother to show up for training without calling, but documented me, who had called, as "Failed to report for duty." I thought about how DeGroot documented me as "Left weapon unsecured," when he knew very well the weapon was in no danger; and how the major labelled me, "Incompetent with shortcomings." I recalled how Lieutenant Nguyen pulled Garant aside to find out why she did not show up for training, because she was too good to be disciplined like the rest of us, and how Garant never even received a chit for not showing up—but my not showing up was recorded for all time. I thought about my field training always being a part of my life; and why I had joined the army in the first place. I considered how the army had affected my life by being a hindrance rather than help, and I asked myself whether I would risk my life for the people in the army and for the White people who really *own* Canada in the larger society. The answer was a resounding, "No!" It was time for me to leave the army.

As it turned out, Michaud was not only racist, he was also on a power trip. Later that night, he informed me that I would be formally charged for the misfire. Additionally, I was to do picketing duties (guard the weapons) while he and his peers went out drinking. Also assigned to do picketing duties was Corporal Pierrie [sic]. Why? She too had misfired. This could have seemed like a coincidence—two Black females doing picketing duties for misfiring. However, four people had misfired:

Private Green, Corporal Pierrie, Lieutenant Koth, and Private Lo. Corporal Miller witnessed Lo being taken off the range for his misfire. She also witnessed Lieutenant Koth being allowed to continue firing after he misfired. To add insult to injury, both Koth and Lo were allowed to go out drinking; in short, they were not penalized for their misfire. Michaud was able to administer as many punishments as his cold, hateful, rotted heart desired.

Other immediate superiors saw the injustice and decided to shorten our picketing duties, considering the weapons we were guarding to be safe in a locked closet within a locked room. Corporal Crumb (a female) released Pierrie and me from picketing duties.

When Michaud, or "God," returned to the barracks and found that Pierrie and I were not in the spot he had planted us, he took a fit. I thought he had gone mad. Luckily, hitting was no longer allowed in the army; otherwise, he would have been too happy to bring out his stick or fist, or whatever else he could get his claws on.

I was talking on a wall-mounted telephone, about ten feet from the door of the room that held the weapons. The demon started shouting as he walked towards me. When he got to about twenty centimetres from me, he stopped and continued to yell—stifling me with his alcohol breath. Any reasonable person would know this was punishment enough; but let us not forget, he was not a person and he was not reasonable.

The demon thought his actions were something of which to be proud: Private Adofo saw him early the next morning, bragging about how he "bawled out Green last night." I had met him only the previous day, but he *knew* me: You know one *black*, you know all. If there is a place in Heaven for this guy, then, Lord, send me straight to Hell.

Evidence of Michaud's drinking the previous night showed up in a private's behaviour the next morning;

in that, as opposed to having a hangover, he was still drunk—a testament to just how much alcohol they were gulping. Being a private, his superiors would not have allowed him to drink more than they, themselves, had drunk. The private was of South American descent, Spanish speaking. I heard him before I smelled the alcohol on him. I lined up behind him for breakfast in the cafeteria. He passed me a tray and said, "Green, go ahead cause you're a lady." He growled loudly and looked behind himself, then turned around to move forward in the line. I wanted to tell him to be quiet before his superiors heard him, but he looked behind himself again, saw all males lining up behind him and said, "These mother fuckers are not getting ahead of me. Go ahead, Green." I was sure he was going to be severely disciplined, a thought to which he appeared to be oblivious. I thought, *"In his state of mind, this guy is still able to extend courtesies to a female, but he is not able to keep his mouth shut."* Furthermore, he was falling down. I saw WO Ross and two corporals observing him. The WO told him to get some black coffee with his breakfast. He slurred something to the effect of, "Don't . . . tell me what to do." There would be no discipline for him, because his superiors had taken him out drinking.

Corporals Dennis and Miller were being given more active roles in our training. The privates were lined up in the hall of the barracks, listening to instructions from Corporal Miller. I was admiring her very slight British accent and the clarity of each word. That accent coming out of a White woman would have been envied. I was annoyed that some of the privates were listening as though they were having trouble understanding what she was saying. The corporal stopped her instructions and asked the most overtly gawking private, "What's the matter?" The private responded, "I can't understand what you are saying." The corporal straightened her back and paused briefly before asking, "Which one of the words do you not understand?" The private could not pick a word; so, the corporal continued her instructions. I noticed how everyone, including the most overt private, was suddenly able to easily comprehend the same accent coming out of the same person. I thought, *"Good for you. They thought they were going to make you keep on repeating yourself."* Corporal Miller had been around long enough to know the "games" White people play to keep Black people feeling inadequate. At the time, I did not know that her abrupt response somewhat reflected the anger she was feeling about the way Michaud was treating Pierrie and me—compared with the way he treated Private Lo and Lieutenant Koth.

The reader may be asking, "How could a sergeant discipline a lieutenant?" The answer is quite simple: Michaud was in charge of the firing range; although Lieutenant Nguyen was overseeing the activities, it was Michaud who was directly responsible for the operation.

Pierrie suggested we each write a letter to our senior superiors regarding Michaud. I did; she did not. My letter brought more charges against me, which further propelled me down the path started by my biography in basic training.

The Pierrie Factor

I should have known that Pierrie had not written a letter. We were in the change room the following Thursday night, when she asked to see my letter but made no mention of hers. I could make a dozen excuses for her as to why she did not write the letter *she* suggested. Instead, I would much rather look at the facts: This woman set me up to fight her battle for her. When people encourage you to do anything, think about their motive;

assess the situation from all angles, and act only if the action is one you would take without input from anyone.

Within minutes of my handing-in my letter, Lieutenant Koth and his cohort—a superior I had never before noticed—pulled me aside and demanded that I released the source who told me that he had misfired. He could not even muster the anger he wanted me to think he felt when he made his demand, and he was rather amused when I told him that I would not reveal my source. My source, Corporal Miller, had told me that if I revealed her as the source, she would deny that she had told me anything. She was assisting Cherniawski on the firing range when she observed Pierrie, Koth, and Lo misfire.

Although Miller gave Pierrie *shit* for setting me up, Miller was not the type of person one would want as a friend. She was willing to testify, but only if it was done in court. Corporal Dennis approached me and said if the matter went to trial, she would be willing to reveal what she knew, though she quickly added, "What do I know?" I believe Miller's input caused Master Corporal Scarrett—a Black man to whom the other Blacks in the army referred to as Uncle Tom—to approach me. He offered me a White woman as an assisting officer. I told him that unless I had a Black woman to represent me, I did not need any help. Where race was concerned, I no longer felt the need to protect anyone's feelings. Adofo—the seasoned, Black private—approached me with his support and his willingness to testify. I had to ask, "Why is everyone coming to me about going to court?" Adofo responded, "Green, they all look to you because you are not afraid to stand-up for yourself." Wow! They had found a scapegoat.

— Chapter 25 —

My Day Job

The army, my day job, and my anger at Lloyd were taking a toll on me to the point where insomnia and fatigue set in. The racism at work was no different from the racism I was experiencing in the army. I introduce this part of my life at this point to tell you how Lisa, the Conference Co-ordinator who participated in the job interview, became a source of support to me. Lisa had left ONSTEP about four months after I started working there because of the internal politics and the death of a building maintenance man who had a heart attack and died in her arms, despite her best efforts to administer cardiopulmonary resuscitation (CPR) to him. He died in the lobby of the building, as a result of clearing snow. Lisa felt his death would have been avoided if it had not been for the demanding executive director, Sandra, insisting on comfortably parking her sports car in the heart of winter.

Lisa and I remained friends. She would call me at work sometimes to get the scoop. Why? Only she really knew. When I leave a place of employment, I could not care less what goes on there. Nonetheless, the new executive director, like the former one, wanted her four employees to stop everything when she entered the office and worship her as she engaged in one of her 'look at me' routines. I refused to worship her; saying "Good morning, Bernadette" was acknowledgment enough for me to get back to my work.

One day I was to organize a conference in a church, for about fifty people. As well, I was to get donations for the conference. I was doing okay making my requests by telephone, when Bernadette arrived in the office with her "look at me" self. She butted into the conversation, saying, "Tell him you want the location for . . . [date]." I repeated her request. She continued, "You want it for . . . [time]." I repeated her request. Her pal, Karen, joined in the dictation, "You need . . . [chairs]." I repeated it to the man on the phone. Bernadette and Karen continued their dictation until they were satisfied.

I thought nothing more of the conversation until a few days later when Bernadette approached me with a verbal reprimand about my "tone and demands" to the man at the church. My first thought was, *"A Christian called to complain?"* My next thought was, "*Why did he not tell me 'no,' if he felt that I was rude and forceful?"* I wracked my mind, trying to remember when I had been rude to a potential donor. Bernadette wanted me to call him and apologize for speaking to him "that way." She reported that the man went as far as to say, "She was talking to people in the background, who were egging her on." I suppose Bernadette did not clue-in that she was one of these people in the background ; or perhaps she, like Sergeant Michaud, simply wanted to distance herself from any negativity coming her way because of Green. Bernadette had approached me shortly before the lunch hour. I called the man and apologized. It burned me to the core.

I had to talk with someone; and since Lisa was aware of how executive directors and other ONESTEP employees could be, I called her at home. By the time I got the first sentence out, the tears were rolling down my cheeks. I will never forget Lisa for her next statement, "Deneace, I am coming down." I told her no; I would be okay. She responded, "Do you have your purse with you?" I said, "Yes." She responded, "Deneace, just go home. Don't even bother going back for the rest of the day." I was shocked, because the thought never even occurred to me. Lisa picked up on the sense of confusion I was feeling about going home then and there. She continued, "Just call Bernadette and tell her that you are going home because you are not feeling well." I did just that.

I should have stayed home another day. When the other three employees had left the next day, Bernadette called me into her office. She wanted to discuss my leaving at mid-day. I told her that I was upset and rather than taking out my frustration on anyone, I went home. She responded, "Nice spin." Everything I said, she twisted. Finally, I just flipped. I sat up in my chair, leaned forward to her, looked her in the eye and said, "Bernadette! Stop twisting my words." I very slowly repeated myself, "Stop. Twisting. My. Words." She rightly got scared because if I had attacked her, I do not believe I would have remembered to stop. Her defusing skills paid off for the both of us, when she said, "Okay Deneace; I just wanted to make sure that everything was okay." It scared me how quickly the power in the room switched from her to me, though I took her statement as the cue that I should leave. As I left, I felt her relief and the grinding feeling that my time at ONESTEP was near the end. I trembled at the thought of how close I had come to going to jail for assault.

I relayed the incident to Carlene, telling her that I wished I knew how to relate to White people who constantly try to treat me like a child. She said, "Deneace, you dealt with Bernadette the right way; you got her off your case." I did, although not without planting a seed for her to get rid of me.

— Chapter 26 —

Lloyd Was Back

Many of the things I did for Lloyd, I did because of his mother. She, too, was a single mother left to raise her children on her own. She had her first child out of wedlock. The father of the child went off to England (as did many Jamaicans in the 1960s) to "make a better life" for the child and mother. Not long after he reached England, he "forgot" that he had left a woman, Lucille, and a child behind. *Fortunately* for the woman, she was yellow-skinned—an asset desired by Blacks who cannot get past their Colonial mentality. Not many years had passed before Lucille got married to Lloyd's father, who treated her like royalty—the skin. Unfortunately, the marriage lasted only twelve years; the man took ill and died. She was now left to raise the five children she had borne him, plus the one from the "forgetful" man. Lloyd was the husband's second child and he was only eleven years old when he lost his father; the elder brother was twelve.

For whatever reason, the "forgetful" man visited Jamaica and decided to take his daughter to England with him. The child was then in her early teens. Lucille still had to contend with her other five children.

When all her children were grown, the "forgetful" man visited Jamaica once more and remembered that he "loved" Lucille. He invited her to England and married her there. Three years later, he died of cancer. With his pension and estate, Lucille was able to return to Jamaica before she reached the official retirement age. She did well in the end, but the bulk of her life was no picnic. You name it, she suffered it; including unimaginable physical abuse from men who came along after the death of Lloyd's dad and before her marriage to the "forgetful" man.

Lucille appeared to be a tender-hearted person who cried easily, but she could be just as cunning as Lloyd: The leaf never falls too far from the tree. Nonetheless, when I consider her life and her struggles, her life was not very different from mine (this book is not about that part of my life); thus, I would do more than what was reasonable to ensure that I did not add to her pain. I did not want her to deal with the pain of her son ending up with a criminal record for domestic assault.

Moreover, I knew the pain of racism Lloyd was facing at work; I knew how he felt as he observed White people, who had been on the security guard job for only a few weeks, become his supervisors—including some whom he had trained. I wanted to help him in the assault case pending against him for kicking me. So, I wrote a letter to the judge.

On the day of court, while I was standing in the witness box, the judge asked me to read the letter. My voice broke as I started; but the presence of my dad in the courtroom helped me to compose myself quickly and read from the heart. I read that a criminal record would further debilitate his chances of gaining meaningful employment, and that the underemployment situation created a great deal of stress in our marriage. I read that his law-abiding nature could be seen in the way he obeyed the police release condition of not contacting me until after court. This may have been something he was glad to get from the police, which saved him from the social implications of not wanting to reconcile. I further read, "I am a strong, independent, woman who is able to take care of myself." This was in response to a call I had received from the Victim Assistance Unit, offering me counseling and court protection from Lloyd, when a meaningful job was what I needed.

Lloyd tried to make a case for himself by stating, "I lived in the home; so, it was my phone too." The judge corrected him, "It is Ms. Green's apartment and *her* phone." Since Lloyd had wisely pleaded "not guilty" and since I spoke on his behalf, admitting that he kicked me and I hit him, the judge found him *not guilty*.

The judge taught me something about body language: He observed me while I gave my testimony; analyzed the way I leaned back and lifted one foot—indicating that as Lloyd kicked me and I moved backwards, I grabbed the base of the telephone and slugged him. My belief is that the judge chose to indicate to the Crown and the police officers that he believed that I did act to protect myself.

Lloyd came back to my home that same day, immediately after court. Why? I have yet to figure out the reason. However, I believe it was for social implications; he wanted people—my parents, his mother, church members and his friends—to believe he wanted the marriage. Nothing changed. We were still not talking nor having sex. I was not about to sneak around; therefore, after about a month of passing each other like shadows in the house, I told him that since we did not have a sexual relationship, I would be getting my sex elsewhere. He had no answer, neither did I expect one.

— Chapter 27 —

Stuck In the Army

Ironically, now that I had finally made the decision to leave the army, I was stuck; I could not leave with charges pending against me.

Captain Chamberlain brought me a Black, female assisting officer, Captain Pamela Evelyn of the Canadian Air Cadets. She had been walking through the massive parade area, on her way to her office, when Captain Chamberlain approached her. He spoke with her briefly, and then brought her to me. Captain Chamberlain was not on my QL2 course, but he was a captain in 25 Medical Company—a typical middle-aged, fit, White man.

It was not long before Captain Evelyn would admit to me that, at first, she felt that I could have been overreacting regarding my statements about the racism I was experiencing. However, after she interacted with Michaud a few times, she said, "Deneace, I don't think you have a problem; your complaints are legitimate. You would never guess what that guy did. He came into my office, saw me sitting there, did not acknowledge me, and instead started making his case to one of my lieutenants." She went on, "My lieutenant said to him, 'Why don't you speak to Ma'am directly; she is sitting right there.'" She continued, "Deneace, the look on his face said, *'I cannot believe* 'she' *is my superior.'"* After he gathered his composure, his attitude towards her was not very different from his attitude towards me. In fact, as stated by Pam, "He treated me the same way he treated you." He disregarded her each time he passed her in the common areas.

It was almost a year before my case went to trial. The delays came from Lieutenant Colonel von Bulow; he was always away on the scheduled nights, on one pretext or another.

One old fossil who was about to retire—I was told he was Major Sutherland—was on his way out of the office one Thursday night. He spoke to me, saying, "You should be commended for pursuing this. A lot of people would just drop-off their gear and walk out; but you are seeing this through, and for that you should be commended." I stood there and thought for a moment, because if that was indeed Major Sutherland, he was the same officer who had labeled me "incompetent with shortcomings" when I first complained. My mind went back to the recruit who, in the first few weeks, had dropped his gear and told the WO to go fuck himself. I was not about to give them the satisfaction of giving me a Dishonourable Discharge by dropping my gear and running away; I wanted my day in court.

On one of the nights when I showed up for trial and the lieutenant colonel did not, a corporal informed me that my *dog tags* had arrived. I found it odd that the tags arrived during my process of trying to leave the army. I would have taken them as a keepsake. Considering that my name was engraved on them, they were useless to anyone else. A sergeant—the same red-headed man who falsely tried to entice me into going to Bosnia—overheard the conversation and said, "Don't give them." I might as well have been a tree, where the sergeant was concerned, by the way he gave the order without regard for my service and my feelings.

Since Captain Chamberlain was much more accessible than Lieutenant Colonel von Bulow, Captain Evelyn spoke with him a few times. During one of those meetings, Captain Chamberlain made a statement that Captain Evelyn interpreted as a "backhanded compliment." He stated, "She [Private Green] is the type of person we want in the army." I guess I had the right characteristics but not the right skin colour.

My witnesses and adversaries gradually disappeared. Pierrie quietly transferred to Ottawa, but not before apologizing to me for burying me in *shit* and informing me, "Traditionally, my people [Guyanese—self-identified as Black with Aboriginal blood] run rather than fight." Adofo resigned from the army. Lieutenant Koth resigned and moved to the United States. Corporal Miller and Corporal Dennis were promoted to Master Corporals. Master Coporal Skerrett soon became Sergeant Skerrett. I thought, *"Is this not my life? I am carrying the shit, but everyone is moving ahead as a result of my stirring the shit."* I waited patiently for the trial.

— Chapter 28 —

May 1999: A Glimpse of Used

In March, Bernadette had given me a month's notice that she would not be renewing my contract. She gave me a glowing reference letter. This helped me to immediately obtain another contract position, this time at the Jewish Vocational Services of Toronto. I started working in early April.

Lloyd was doing "volunteer" jobs when he was not fixing his van. He offered me a ride to work a few times, and I accepted. Therefore, when he borrowed $800 from me for repairs on his van, I loaned it to him. Oddly enough, my car had reached its end, and I did not want to spend any more money to keep it going. Lloyd no longer needed to fix it because he now had his van. Let me point out that prior to Lloyd's "fixing" my car, there was nothing wrong with it.

He looked very uncomfortable having me in his van. I noticed there was no glove compartment; so, I asked,

"Where is the glove compartment?" He responded, "There isn't one." I asked, "So where do you keep your stuff?" He responded, "I don't need to keep anything in here." I rested the conversation.

It was Mother's Day, and he was driving us to church. He started the van; and for no apparent reason, it lunged forward and immediately stopped. The storage compartment, containing his passport and other important documents, slid out from under my seat and stopped when it made contact with my calves. I looked at him; I looked at the storage compartment, and then I looked forward. That was the moment when I knew I was done with the relationship.

I went for altar call at church. I cried. The men are supposed to get dinner for the ladies on Mother's Day. Lloyd went and got my dinner as though we were a couple in love. I thought, *"You really are an anus; you are such a good actor; you do know how to treat a woman, but only as a show."*

I knew that I wanted him out of my home, but for his mother's sake I did not want to put him out on the street. As he drove me to work that Monday morning, I lectured him about giving up the "volunteer" job at the mechanic shop and looking for paid employment. My mouth popped open when the guy responded, "So, where do you think I got money from to put new wheels on the van?" I closed my mouth because I knew what I needed to do; it was time for him to go.

That evening, I took the mattress off my bed and placed it on the carpeted floor in my daughter's (Deneka) abandoned bedroom. I kept the box spring. After the first night's sleep on the box spring, I realized that I should have kept the mattress and given him the box spring. Deneka and Allin (my son) had moved their furniture out of the apartment, enabling Lloyd to take over both of their rooms: He filled Allin's with electrical junk he found in dumpsters belonging to second-hand shops, and Deneka's with his clothing—clean and dirty, as he could no longer access the closet in Allin's room.

I had told my parents of the situation; therefore, when Lloyd called my mother to complain that I had put him on the floor to sleep, she quickly blasted him.

A few weeks later, he packed and left. I bought boxes and packed the remainder of his belongings, which he collected a few weeks after he left. Within a few months, he visited my brother, Lennox, and then my parents to inform them that he had bought a four-bedroom house.

Upon hearing this news, during our telephone conversation, Lisa asked me, "Do you think he was hoarding all along?" I responded, "Apparently."

My sister Arlene had a totally different response from Lisa's, saying, "You see? If you had been patient, you would be living in it!" I thought, *"I would rather live in a trench than live in the same mansion as him."* She obviously did not know him; she knew only of his pitiful, "poor me" stories. I cannot blame her, since it was those same "poor me" stories that got me to marry him.

Details about how Lloyd fully fits into my life is found in my second book, entitled, My Thoughts, My Life: The Life of a Black Woman Living in a White World, "Used."

— Chapter 28 —

The Trial That Never Took Place

Finally, after almost a full year of waiting, the trial for the misfire occurred in September 1999; eleven months had passed before Lieutenant Colonel von Bulow finally realized that I was not leaving the Canadian Armed Forces before I got a trial.

It was probably the only trial where no one spoke except the judge, the lieutenant colonel. As soon as Captain Evelyn and I entered Lieutenant Colonel von Bulow's office, he said, "The charges are dismissed. You are free to pursue your military career." He informed Captain Evelyn that she could assist me in removing *anything* from my file that was contentious. The captain and I, upon leaving the lieutenant colonel's office, immediately walked into the administrative office and requested my file from Master Corporal Dennis. I chose to leave my letter to him in the file, which meant the lies my immediate superiors wrote also stayed in the file.

My goal was to leave a paper trail that might be useful to others enduring the racism that I endured.

This perceived generosity on the part of the lieutenant colonel was not for my benefit; it was for the benefit of 25 Medical Company—there was talk that the situation could have had the company disbanded. Those in command, including Major Sutherland, would have needed to look for a placement elsewhere; but not before answering as to why they allowed such racist practises to permeate the company. Sutherland had attacked me to protect himself.

Ironically, by the time I left the army, I was back to doing customer service work; I was back exactly where I started. I guess this is the difference between real life and Hollywood. If it were Hollywood, everything would work out well in the end.

Have you wondered why, two years after I started the process for the RCMP, I was still waiting? Well, let me tell you. . . .

Part 2

My Thoughts, My Life: Institutionalized Racism in the RCMP

— Chapter 1 —

My Experience with Racism While Trying to Join The Force

I wanted to be a police officer because I cared and I believed that by "serving and protecting" I could make a positive difference in people's lives. I applied to join the Royal Canadian Mounted Police (RCMP) because I had an education that more than qualified me for a position, and because I honestly believed I had an equal chance of employment as the other people applying.

Canadian society overtly expects its citizens to shun *systematic racism*. However, through life experiences, I have learned that, often, those who should be most passionate about not practicing racism are in fact some of its worst perpetrators. It is through experience that I have arrived at this conclusion: The Royal Canadian Mounted Police, as an organization and as individuals, definitely practise a very finely honed racism. They have public policies against racism and discrimination; and yet, in their selection process, they are masters at rejecting candidates that they deem *racially unsuitable*. This is my story of how I was sidelined and victimized by their racist policies, and of the effects of the experience on my life.

July 1997

My experience with the RCMP started in July 1997, when I attended a recruiting seminar in Newmarket, Ontario. The presenters encouraged the eligible attendees to apply for employment as *regular member constables* and handed out information packages to most of the approximately fifty people who attended. As I browsed through the seventeen pages of recruitment information, I felt elated and very hopeful; I felt that once I passed the entrance exam, I would be sure to land a position. After all, my lifestyle and education reflected the type of people the RCMP was seeking to hire. That is, I fit within mainstream society; I graduated high school; I was over eighteen years old; and I was mentally and physically fit.

Although none of the attendees verbalized a question, which I am sure most of us were thinking, the recruiting officer who did most of the talking, Wanda Jackson, answered it when she said, "A score of 100 out of 145 on the RCMP Recruiting Selection Test (RRST) is a really, really good score." That information prompted a White man, an obvious member of the military, to ask if there would be special consideration given for military service. Wanda replied, "No."

August 1997

I wrote the RRST with approximately fifteen other people. There were three White women in the group, and I was the only Black person.

September 1997

I received a letter from the RCMP informing me that I was successful in completing the Recruit Selection Test with a score of 89/145. The pass mark was 84/145. The letter further stated that my name would be placed in their Initial Ranked List (IRL) in an order based on my test result. This process was contrary to the recruitment information package and statements made at the recruitment session, where females and minorities were strongly encouraged to apply, because the RCMP was trying to bridge the gap between the number of White male members of the force and other groups within the community.

I was not happy with my score, but I was comfortable with it because—if, according to Wanda Jackson, "100 is a really, really good score"—I knew from my experience in classrooms that it would be difficult for most people writing the test to attain a score of 100.

The letter further outlined the selection process, noting that a selection of candidates was made every six months and that the next selection would be in October 1997. Those selected would be sent an application based on priority, and they would be invited to an interview. Those not selected would receive formal notification in the form of a letter. Additionally, if after being considered for two consecutive selections from the Initial Rank List an applicant is not selected, that applicant's file is closed. If the file was closed and the now non-applicant was still interested in a position with the

RCMP, as a regular member constable, the former applicant must wait for one year from the date he or she first wrote the entrance exam and then write it again.

Finally, the letter reminded the reader that candidates selected from the Initial Rank List are required to obtain a physical abilities certificate known as the Physical Abilities Requirement Evaluation (PARE).

October 1997

I received an employment application package from the RCMP, indicating that they were satisfied with the results of my test and were interested in continuing the selection process.

The information in the package required me to provide a daily account of my whereabouts and activities for the last ten years. I found the process time consuming but not difficult, because I had lived in only two places in the last ten years; and when I was not working and taking care of my children, I was going to school and taking care of my children. They wanted birth dates and contact information for my seven siblings and my parents. They wanted information on my friends, my bank accounts, and social organizations. . . . I felt as though I was being stripped naked, as though I was selling my soul. I looked past the invasion, towards a worthwhile job.

November 1997

I took the Physical Abilities Requirement Evaluation (PARE) and failed the pushing component, which was included in the timed portion of the test. The pushing component entailed pushing metal weights against springs, to measure physical strength resistance.

According to the RCMP's recruiting literature, *Staffing and Personnel Branch, revised by "O" Division Recruiting (96-03), Physical Abilities Requirement Evaluation (PARE),* "The applicant is allowed a maximum of 4 minutes and 45 seconds to complete this phase of the PARE." *See Appendix 1, the PARE.*

I spoke to the proctor, Claire Shaw, about what to do regarding a PARE re-test. He answered, "The RCMP will have to set up another one for you." Additionally, Claire informed me that he would be sending a copy of my results to RCMP Recruiting.

I kept my copy of the PARE form, and waited for the RCMP to contact me for the interview portion of the application process and a new PARE date.

— Chapter 2 —

Changing the Rules to Keep Me Out

January 1998

I received a letter from the RCMP informing me that since I had not submitted my PARE Certificate, my application was being "carried over to the next cycle," which would be April 1998. I called RCMP Recruiting to get clarification on the letter, because it appeared that while I was waiting for information from the RCMP for a PARE re-test, they were waiting for a certificate they should have known was not coming. They should have known because Claire Shaw faxed them the list of candidates he tested and the result of each candidate.

Karen Cleary answered my phone call and informed me that she was quite sure that I would be included in the April selection, and that I would be sent for another PARE after the selection.

"Included in the next selection" meant not that I would be considered for an interview and PARE; rather, it meant that my name would be placed back on the Initial Rank List—back to the step in the process where I had started, the test-scoring hierarchy.

May 1998

A letter from the RCMP arrived, informing me that my file was closed. It said in part, "The number of positions available and your test score determine your standing. In excess of 630 applicants competed in the last selection and only those candidates with the top scores were selected. The cut-off score was 100/145." The letter further stated, " . . . only those candidates with the top scores were selected."

The letter they sent me in September 1997 said that a score of 89/145 was acceptable for further consideration in the application process. Arbitrarily raising the score eliminated me from the application process. My file was closed without an opportunity for me to raise my score or to become more competitive with a largely new pool of applicants. Assuming that the RCMP was telling the truth regarding their selection process and my test score, I fail to understand why they even bothered putting my name back on the Initial Rank List. How many of the few members of minorities who apply are eliminated this way?

I might have ignored this example of systematic racism, if the RCMP had not been advertising itself as an organization seeking to reflect society by leveling the playing field for females and minorities by streamlining the hiring process—meaning, focusing on a particular group that suffers social, economic, or gender disadvantages within a larger group. My thoughts were, *"How many of the candidates with whom I had tested were female and of a minority group?"* Considering that standardized tests are skewed in favour of urban, middle-class White males, is it not systematic racism to encourage minorities to apply and then evaluate them with the same criteria as middle-class White males? What happened to the RCMP's "targets set for employment of women, visible minorities and Aboriginal peoples?" Apparently, the targets are real only in their propaganda but not in their hiring process.

According to the RCMP recruiting literature, *Staffing and Personnel Branch, revised by "O" Division Recruiting (96-03),* "Long range targets have been set for employment of women (20%), visible minorities (6.3%), and Aboriginal peoples (5%)." See *Appendix 1, General Recruitment and Special Programs, page 3*. I thought, *"Considering that I was the only Black person (and female Black at that) of fifteen people who wrote the exam, how would the RCMP's target be reached if the stated groups are targeted in theory and promotional materials but eliminated in practise?"* If after passing the entrance test, females and minorities are treated no differently from middle-class White males (who make-up the bulk of all police forces in Canada), how will the RCMP ever reach its long-range target? The bottom line is this: I am arguing about the way the RCMP contradicts *its own* hiring policies, not what might be viewed by some as preferential treatment based on my being Black and female. Although, considering the dominant versus subordinate statuses within any society, one can hardly make a persuasive argument that *altering* the rules for non-Whites would be preferential treatment. How else would the playing field be levelled in the Canadian society as it is, with all its racial and social inequalities? Do Whites not get preferential treatment by virtue of being White? Do White males not get the greatest preferential treatment by virtue of being *White* and *male*? I feel angry that I need to argue this point so fervently in attempts to persuade anyone of the blatant, systematic, racist formula the RCMP uses to select candidates from its pool.

Analysis

I thought of the venom spewed at me by just about all of my classmates, during my law enforcement studies at Seneca College, because they believed I could get onto any police force based on my race alone. In their thoughts and snide remarks, repeatedly they said, "She has an unfair advantage; she'll get on [a police force]." In their opinion, the fact that I was an honour student, studying policing, had no relevance to my chances of being hired as a police officer.

I suppose if I approached the situation from my classmates' perspective—looking at police recruitment posters and information packages that seemed to say that minorities would be welcome almost without regard to qualification—I too would feel that there was indeed an advantage for minorities.

The hostility I felt from my classmates was not limited to the classroom or to people applying for jobs in policing. The Canadian government's job-postings always encourage minorities to apply. What do you think is the reasoning behind this overt call for minorities to apply? I will tell you.

In general, Asians (including East Indians) are apparently able to hold their own in medicine, business and law—the core elements of our society; they are able to maintain a strong degree of autonomy in the areas that matter most. Their history is also very different from that of Africans and Aboriginal peoples, in that the Asians were not dispersed; their customs, traditions and ideologies were not obliterated by the Western European influence; they managed to maintain their culture and cohesiveness. In contrast, Aboriginal and African people were de-humanized and displaced from their societies. Africans, especially, were dragged away from everything they knew, physically beaten, burned with sizzling hot iron to be identified as disposable property, and indoctrinated into believing that they are inferior to White people—a legacy Black people are still struggling to overcome. The Africans who remained in the *Motherland* experienced no fewer atrocities—*a detailed account can be found in the book entitled "King Leopold's Ghost," by Adam Hochschild*—than the ones who were dragged away into a life of perpetual torture. This torture exists today in the form of poverty.

If people believe there is a chance for them to break out of poverty, get a better job, they have an incentive to remain within the confines of the law and endure whatever hardship until better comes along. In my case, I will remain a law-abiding citizen, living in poverty, because I need a clean police record to get a job of substance; I care about my reputation. The hope of a chance works for me: I just need to get a good education and remain within the confines of the law, legally and morally. The hope of a chance keeps me in my place within society.

On the other hand, White people remain hostile to minorities they perceive as having an advantage. What would you do if you were a White person feeling that rules exist to displace you from your position of power? If you have blood in your body, you would do whatever you needed to do to keep your power. I cannot blame you: The feeling is innate, the will to survive. Who controls this society? Who controls government organizations? Who are the gatekeepers for jobs? To whom are you going to give a job, if you identify with him/her racially and feel that the individual is at a disadvantage, at risk, while someone with whom you have no connection has an advantage? I did not need a degree in sociology to teach me this; but it helped.

In summary, the government overtly encourages minorities to apply for jobs, to give them hope for something they most likely will not get; but, for the most part, the hope keeps society stable. Furthermore, the perception that there is a chance that White people are in danger of losing their place in society gives them strong incentive to maintain the *status quo*. The whole construction of institutional or systematic racism may be unintentional. I, however, strongly doubt it. That is, individuals make up the government, and individuals have an innate desire to seek and maintain their personal interest.

What about those members of minorities who "get in"? I would answer: "That is exactly my point; there is a chance for me, too." The worst part of "getting in," is when the hostility grows because of the perception that *she* "got in" only because of the colour of her skin; that *she* had to be better than *all* the rest is of no consequence.

August 1998

I re-wrote the RRST. That is, for the second time, I started the process from the beginning. I noted that the pass mark was still listed as 84/145. This time, of the fourteen people taking the test, there were two minorities present: myself, and an East Indian fellow who appeared to have been giving more of himself to the process than (in my opinion) the job was worth. I came to this conclusion because I had decided to use the bathroom before sitting a test for two and a half hours. As I stood outside the door, I heard him gagging, then spitting, then running the tap water. The sound of the running water was different from that of a person washing his hands;

it sounded more as if he was using his hand to channel water to rinse the sink. I had no choice but to wait until he was finished. He walked out of the bathroom looking physically weak, as though he should have been going to bed instead of to a test. I had seen that look before, during first-year exams at the University of Toronto. I walked into the one-stalled bathroom and saw remnants of vomit in the sink. I thought, "*Why didn't he gag into the toilet, or at least use toilet paper to remove the chunks of regurgitated food from the sink?*" Looking at the remnants caused me to ponder about the toll this process was taking on the applicants; yet, the RCMP was treating me as though my participation in the process required no effort—not even the fact that I started my day at 5:00 a.m., to ensure that I was present for the 8:00 a.m. exam.

October 1998

I received a letter from RCMP Recruiting informing me that my test score was 99/145. However, I was not to be included in the October selection, even though my test was written in August. My getting the letter in October was a clear indication that I was not considered for the October selection.

I had written their test twice. I had observed the small number of minorities present for the test, and the RCMP was still distributing material encouraging minorities to apply; yet, they by-passed me twice. First, they told me that my score was not high enough, not above 100/145; and the second time no reason was given, even though I received a letter stating that I passed the test.

— Chapter 3 —

Processed Like Gold Through Fire

July 1999

I received my second employment application package from the RCMP. The enclosed information confirmed that 84/145 was still their pass mark; consequently, the rejection based on my not scoring at least 100/145 was a lie in the most blatant form—unambiguously written on paper.

September 18, 1999

I took the Physical Abilities Requirement Evaluation (PARE) for the second time, the only Black person of eighteen to take the test. This time I passed with 37 seconds to spare, in the total time of 4 minutes and 8 seconds (see *Appendix 1, PARE*)—the only successful female of six. The next step was for me to call RCMP Recruiting to make an appointment for an interview. Clarie Shaw, the proctor, would be faxing my PARE results to RCMP Recruiting (and then he would courier the original document); but just to be on the safe side, I also faxed my copy to RCMP Recruiting.

September 20, 1999

I called the RCMP to set-up an interview, and I was told that I could not set an interview date until the RCMP's medical expert had examined my medical records, which they had requested from my family physician. This was a side effect of my being hurt while working for Coca Cola Bottling Ltd.

October 15, 1999

I received a phone call from the RCMP to schedule my interview.

November 14, 1999

I attended a six-hour interview in London, Ontario. Although I was not barraged with questions for the entire six hours, by the time the fingerprinting, questioning, waiting, breaking for lunch, and enduring more questioning and processing had ended, six hours were gone. If a candidate does not pass this interview, his/her file is closed. During the interview, Sergeant Crowder confirmed a statement made by Karen Cleary, of the RCMP support staff: "If you leave the country, your file will be closed." Karen had made this statement to me because of my discussing my job offers in Korea with her.

Sergeant Crowder and I also reviewed my bankruptcy issue. During this review, he left the interview room to discuss it with his supervisor. When he returned, he informed me that, "If there was a problem with your bankruptcy, the interview would have been terminated at this point; and your file would be closed." He continued to interview me. I thought, "*Wow! I am being tested like gold through fire.*" I started to understand what Christians of old meant when they quoted that scripture from the Bible, although they were referring to their earthly passage into Heaven.

Early December 1999

I received a letter from the RCMP informing me of the date scheduled for my psychological testing by an RCMP psychologist. The letter also included information regarding a physical test with an RCMP physician and a dentist of their choosing.

Mid-December 1999

I received a letter with a conditional offer of employment from the RCMP. The conditional offer stated, in part, " . . . be expected to enroll within the next two to twelve months."

— Chapter 4 —

More Processing: The RCMP *Lost* My File

January 05, 2000

I completed the psychological test (administered by a psychiatrist), which consisted of approximately 560 written questions designed to analyze whether a person would be "psychologically [and ethically] fit" to become a police officer. The questions were repetitive but worded differently to test truthfulness.

After the written test, the psychiatrist asked about my sleeping habits. Based on the way he yelled and just about jumped out of his skin when I walked into his office and greeted him, I thought he needed more than good sleep—he needed medication to calm his nerves. Granted, he had his back to the door, sorting papers; but it was broad daylight and office hours, the time of day when people are expected to walk in.

Before I left his office, I could see why the poor man was so jumpy. He regularly dealt with RCMP officers, who were either over-the-edge psychologically or just at the edge.

One example arrived in the doctor's office about two and a half hours after my arrival. He was the average-looking White male—the type I often look at and think, *"The world is his."* I cannot figure out how he found his way to the office, because he entered in a zombie-like manner. He stood looking into space and did not sit when the doctor offered him a seat, but continued staring blankly. The doctor gently, physically, guided him in sitting down, saying, "Please sit down and tell me how things are going." Evidently, the doctor knew it was safe to make such a statement in my presence; he probably knew that the patient would not talk. The police officer's head trembled slightly from side to side as though he were trying not to deal with a very tragic issue. I assumed that the doctor must have been preparing himself mentally for this patient, when I walked in and caused a fright.

I am telling you this story about racism, but I am convinced that God saved me from the RCMP for a good reason. He did not want me to end up in the psychological state of the officer I just described.

In this same month, the RCMP started interviewing my references.

Mid-February 2000

The RCMP instructed me to attend a medical clinic of their choosing, where a specialist employed by them gave me a complete physical examination that included eye and ear examinations. Also, an RCMP-approved dentist examined my teeth and took about 16 x-rays.

I noticed two other RCMP applicants, male and female Caucasians. The male was somewhat amicable towards me: He greeted me and introduced himself as Mark; conversely, the female behaved coldly towards me, as though she would rather I did not acknowledge her existence. Yet, she latched on to Mark so tightly that I thought they were a couple; I thought she was a jealous girlfriend who was ensuring there was no room for anyone else in Mark's life, not even room enough for him to be amicable to a stranger. I guess the psychological testing does have some value, because it eliminated her from the RCMP's application process.

February 26, 2000

I showed up for the Final PARE at Pickering High School just east of Toronto. Terry Alexander, whom I met in college in 1989—I will tell you all about Terry in my second book, in a chapter of my life entitled, *When Terry Called*—and Pamela Evelyn, my assisting officer from the Canadian Armed Forces, accompanied me. Every since I can remember, Terry has made notes about everything; therefore, I was not surprised when he took out his pocket-sized note pad and started documenting events as they occurred. In fact, because he recorded names as they were called for testing, he was able to tell me the number of people ahead of me to do the test.

Unlike Terry, who is a White guy, wherever I am, I look around the room to determine its social composition: First, I look to see if there are any Black people; second, I look for the total number of people; and third, I look for the number of females. This is a common trait for Black people; any Black person who tells you otherwise is likely lying. Thus, even without Terry's documentation, I would have known that there were about eighteen people taking the PARE that evening; and that I was the only Black person included.

Mark from the medical centre was present. I asked him about his 'other half.' He replied, "She and I spoke a few times. The last time [we spoke], she told me that she did not make it past the psyche," meaning that she failed the psychological test. I thought, *"Umm, if she shunned me, someone who is applying for the same job as she, someone who would be her peer and perhaps even her co-worker, how would she deal with illiterate or poor or retarded . . . or Black people?"* I further thought, *"Umm, I wonder if the test determined that she was too 'elite' to become a police officer."*

This time around, I completed the PARE with 16 seconds to spare, as against 37 seconds previously. After comparing my score with the score of other applicants, it became clear that just about everyone's score had declined. Mark concluded that the decline in test scores had something to do with the Christmas Holidays.

Late February 2000

I faxed my PARE results to RCMP Recruiting and followed-up with a phone call to confirm receipt of the fax. This confirmation gave me the opportunity to ask Karen Cleary, one of the administrative contact personnel, about my file. Karen informed me as follows: "Your medical is back and everything is fine." She further told me, "Your background investigation is due back by March 20, 2000. You most likely will be enrolled by April."

March 16, 2000

I faxed updated information regarding my employment to RCMP Recruiting, London, Ontario. I had obtained employment as a customer service representative for Georgeson Shareholders Communication.

March 31, 2000

I called RCMP Recruiting, London, regarding the status of my application. Karen told me that my file was due back in London by the end of April 2000. Notice that this new date is well over a month past the date she gave me in late February.

Week of April 26, 2000

I called Recruiting in London to inform them I was moving and to provide them with my new address and phone number. I asked about my file. Karen answered, "It is still not back yet."

May 05, 2000

I called RCMP Recruiting to confirm that they had my new address. Karen confirmed that they had my new address. I took the opportunity to ask about my file. The answer, "Your file is still in Toronto."

May 30, 2000

A member of RCMP Recruiting, Rick Morris, called one of my references, Annette Grandison, at work because (according to him) he did not have a phone number for me since I had moved. Rick left his phone number with Annette, telling her to tell me to give him a call. Remember, I had given my new address and phone number to RCMP Recruiting in April; and on May 5th, I had called and confirmed that they received the information.

May 31, 2000

I returned Rick's phone call to Annette Grandison. Rick wanted to know the names and dates of birth of my children—information I had provided in both applications. He also wanted more information regarding my employment history—information that had to be included in my application.

During our conversation, I asked Rick if there was a problem with my file. He answered, "No. It is a human resources issue." Rick's answer echoed what I had been hearing from RCMP Recruiting since March 2000.

June 05, 2000

Rick called my place of employment. He interviewed my supervisor, Wade MacKenzie, for about 30 minutes. He asked Wade about my sexuality. To be exact, he asked, "Has Deneace engaged in any inappropriate sexual behaviour at work?" My supervisor gave me a very good reference. I heard from Wade later, that when Rick was told how I ended up on my supervisor's team, he responded, "Wow!" In order to be on this team, the elite team, an employee must be exceptional in the performance of his/her duties.

Saturday, June 10, 2000

Rick called another of my references, Carlene Harris, for a second interview. This interview was conducted over the phone. He did not ask any questions to which he did not already have the answer. He asked about my sexuality, drug and alcohol abuse, my children, my family, and whether I was a loner. Carlene was interviewed previously, in January 2000.

Tuesday, July 04, 2000

PARE test results are good for only six months. I was getting worried about my PARE expiring on August 26th. I called RCMP Recruiting, London, to determine the status of my file. Karen answered, "Your background investigation is not complete." I voiced my concern about my PARE to her. She responded, "You will need to do another one. The RCMP will pay for it." How many applicants are required to do the final PARE twice? I immediately called Rick in Toronto. I reached his voice mail and left a message. He returned my call, informing me that, "I am not going to explain it! Your file is back in London!" My first thought was to call London again, but I did not want to upset them.

Please note that the candidates with whom I did the final PARE, on February 26, 2000, went off to basic training in April 2000; meanwhile, I was passing up jobs elsewhere and still waiting around for someone to tell me where my file could be found.

In their recruitment information, *Revised: "O" Division Recruiting (96-11), Appendix 1, Application Process for Regular Member Constable,* RCMP recruiters write the following: "All applicants are afforded the same priority and method of processing and once an applicant is selected to proceed to the interview stage, the average processing time is about 4 months." See *Appendix 1, Application Process For Regular Member Constable, page 3.* If every candidate were given the same priority as I, there is no way the RCMP Recruiting would be able to start training a new class every month—frequency of classes confirmed by a constable in the recruiting department, during one of my phone calls.

Tuesday, July 18, 2000

I called Sergeant Crowder, the person who interviewed me in November 1999. I reached his voice mail and left a message asking him to give me a call. He did not return my call.

Wednesday, July 19, 2000

I left another voice message asking Sergeant Crowder to give me a call. Again, he did not return my call.

Friday, July 21, 2000

Vicki, from RCMP Recruiting, returned my call. She had the usual response, "Your file is still not back yet; and when it comes back, it takes time to be reviewed." I expressed my concern about my Conditional Offer, which stated that I may expect to be enrolled before the end of September 2000. Vicki's response, "September is a rough date; it may be later." This was vastly different from the letter I received in December 1999, which stated that I could expect to enroll within two to twelve months. I was interviewed on November 04, 1999. Eight months later, no one in RCMP Recruiting knew where to find my file; this was twice the average processing time. I thought, *"I have lived in Toronto since I was eight years old; other than the United States and Jamaica, I had never travelled anywhere; I have neither money nor assets for which I cannot account; so, what the hell could they be investigating all this time?"* It grieved me to the core that the other candidates who took the final PARE with me were in their fourth month of training, looking forward to graduating from the RCMP academy; yet, my file was nowhere to be found. How is that for "streamlining minority and female applications"?

Mid-August 2000

My friend Annette Grandison saw an article in the Toronto Metro newspaper regarding racism and Black police officers in Canada. It read, "Of the 25,000 police officers in Canada, only 350 are black; and of those 350, only six are at the senior command level." Annette encouraged me to get help from the Black Business and Professional Association. I protested, not wanting to upset the RCMP. She pushed, saying, "Deneace, you need to be proactive rather than reactive." I thought about the conflicting information both Rick Morris, the investigating officer, and Karen Cleary at RCMP Recruiting had given me on July 04, 2000: Rick's saying, "I am not going to explain it! Your file is back in London"; and Karen at London RCMP Recruiting saying, "Your background investigation is not complete."

I thought about Master Corporal Sophia Miller telling me about her dealings with the RCMP. It took them so long to complete her employment application that she got frustrated and did not bother to respond to the RCMP's request for a typing test; and that was where her employment aspirations for employment with the RCMP ended.

— Chapter 5 —

I Refused to Quietly Go Away

Rather than going away quietly, I decided to force some form of action from the RCMP; I decided to take Annette's advice and call the Black Business and Professionals Association.

On my behalf, the Association made contact with the RCMP Board—a body of volunteers who monitor complaints against the RCMP. Mr. Michael Lecky, from the RCMP Board, made contact with an RCMP officer who previously worked in RCMP Recruiting. After doing some checking with some of his former co-workers at recruiting, the officer called me. According to the officer, Karen told him, "I don't blame Deneace for being upset; this has being going on too long. Her file has been sitting in the office for two months, and no one will touch it." He further told me, "If you release this information, I will deny it!"

The officer had a note of irritation in his voice, stating that when he did recruiting, if he had a file on which he could not make a decision, he would bring it to his supervisor and tell the supervisor to make a decision on it. Unfortunately, the people who sympathized with me had no power.

Monday, September 11, 2000

Mr. Lecky, the representative from the RCMP Board, called and left me a voice mail informing me that he would be calling RCMP Recruiting regarding my file. An hour later, Karen Cleary, from RCMP Recruiting, called to inform me that my file was back; however, she needed some additional information—two additional references; my children's date of birth; and my updated employment information. It was a miracle! For months, no one in RCMP Recruiting could provide me with any information regarding my file; however, with the intervention of the Board, it took the RCMP less than one hour not only to find my file but also to respond to me. Now, instead of ignoring me, and hoping I would go away, they were going to have to deal with me; and they were going to have to find some solid reasons to reject me. This is where the Canadian Armed Forces came to be very convenient for them; though the army made their task easy, in the end, the outcome would have been the same. *In the event you have not noticed, they were ready to start digging afresh for reasons to reject my application—starting with more references and my children.*

Their reason for the two additional references: "References need to be people whom you have known for at least five years," according to Karen. Nowhere on the reference form or anywhere else does it state that I needed to know the references for a minimum number of years. In fact, the *RCMP's Friend and Associates Security/Suitability Screening* form states the following:

> *In addition to the character references listed on the form TBS/SCT 330-60 OR 2281, we require that you submit the names of five of your closest associates (friends with whom you socialize regularly, and are not people who you see only in the workplace). None of your associates or references should be related to each other, nor to you. Please list below, giving complete names, addresses (including name of city), and telephone numbers at home and work.*

Nonetheless, I provided the two additional references the RCMP requested: Dawna Davis, whom I had known for about twenty-three years and who was already listed as a reference; and Ovid Noble, whom I had known for eleven years. Had the RCMP dealt properly with my file, they could have contacted Dawna without asking me to provide more references. They wanted two additional references; I provided only one, Ovid Noble; yet, that was sufficient for them because they totally overlooked some of the ones I had provided. I thought, *"If this is their way of treating all applicants equally, then how do they ever get anyone processed within that four-month period?"* What happened to the statements of all the people they had been interviewing, including two people from my Member of Parliament's Office—where I had volunteered? Were they thinking that if they interviewed enough people they would find that I lived a double life?

In addition to the two additional references, Karen wanted to know the date of birth of my two children and my current employment information—information which they had received multiple times. A copy of each child's birth certificate was included in both of my application packages. Further, on May 31, 2000, I provided the RCMP investigating officer, Rick Morris, with my children's birth and my employment information; and on June 05, 2000, he interviewed Wade MacKenzie, my supervisor. On March 16, 2000, I had faxed my updated employment information to RCMP Recruiting and phoned them on March 31, 2000, to confirm receipt of the information. Additionally, my May 5th and May 31st conversations with RCMP Recruiting involved the information Karen was seeking on this day. Were they trashing my documents, or just testing my patience?

September 14, 2000

I called RCMP Recruiting to have three questions answered. Support staff transferred me to Constable Bob Joseph, since he was now handling my file. Our conversation was as follows:

Question #1: When can I expect to do the next PARE?
Answer: October.
Question #2: How long before the additional two references will be interviewed?
Answer: Two weeks.
Question #3: Approximately, when can I expect to be enrolled?
Answer: Maybe one month; maybe three months; one or two troops will be leaving in December and again in January. We shut down for December, and November is fully booked.

The answer to Question #3 was proof that recruits were being processed on a monthly basis, which would allow for the four-month enrollment period after passing the interview.

Considering that my interview was conducted on November 14, 1999, I should have been enrolled in March 2000. The foregoing conversation took place six months after my file was due to be completed and eight months after the final PARE, one of the last stages in the application process. The applicants who did the final PARE with me were getting ready to graduate from the RCMP police academy; meanwhile, I was still waiting and being properly spun.

Saturday, September 16, 2000

Rick Morris interviewed Ovid Noble, one of my additional references.

Sunday, September 17, 2000

Rick Morris interviewed Annette Grandison and Dawna Davis. Both Dawna and Annette could have been interviewed in January or May; however, they were not. Annette gave me her perception of Rick, "He thinks he is in Hollywood. For the full hour that he interviewed me in the coffee shop, he did not remove his dark eyeglasses; and his voice message sounds like something from a Hollywood script." Annette referred to him simply as "Hollywood Man."

Annette found it offensive that Rick asked this question: "Is Deneace a loner?" Annette continued, "If you are a loner, then what am I? I don't have any friends with whom I socialize; and I don't go out." The loner question was not the worst for Annette; what infuriated her the most was when he asked, "Does Deneace have any weird sexual practises?" I wonder how Lloyd Davis (Anus) answered this question. Yes, the RCMP found him and interviewed him too.

During this series of Rick's interviews, Lisa Meecham was included. She was less tolerant than Wade, Carlene, and Annette in answering questions she found inappropriate. I must tell you that Lisa is one of the most levelheaded and diplomatic people I have ever known; but she was not diplomatic in her answer when Rick asked, "Does Deneace have psychological problems?" It was a jolt to her system, and his sheer gall caused her to respond, "First of all, I am not a psychologist, and even if I felt that way about an enemy, I would not have the nerve to put that label on anyone."

Weeks after he had interviewed her, Lisa and I spoke about Rick. Through our phone conversation, I could feel the discomfort she endured when Rick placed her in that awkward and inappropriate situation by asking for her analysis of my psychological well-being. Obviously, my favourable diagnosis from a Registered Psychiatrist and Psychologist, Doctor of Psychiatry and Psychology, employed by the RCMP, was not enough; the RCMP needed further analysis from my friend who had a degree in forestry.

I did not share my frustration with Lisa because she is one of those few human beings who still truly cares about the suffering of other people; she still has the ability to feel other people's pain. She gave mouth-to-mouth resuscitation to an old man—something I would not have done, unless he were my dad—who quickly died in her arms. I did not want her to feel my suffering. Thus, when she asked, "So, how are you doing?" I responded, "Oh, I'm just hanging in there, being patient." Her response reinforced my thoughts of her ability to feel other people's pain. She said, "Deneace. You're brave. If I were in your position, I would be going nuts by now—waiting around for them." I had no idea she knew what I was really experiencing. I thought, *"If Lisa, of all people, feels this way, my situation must really be extreme and evident."*

— Chapter 6 —

Blatant Lies to Keep Me Out

Thursday, October 19, 2000

I left a voice message for Bob Joseph, asking him to call me. Based on the conversation we had on September 14, 2000, my file should have been back. I stayed in contact with Mr. Lecky from the RCMP Board.

Wednesday, October 25, 2000

On the advice of Mr. Lecky, I left another voice message for Bob Joseph, asking him to call me. Also on Mr. Lecky's advice, I left a voice message for Bob's supervisor, C.E. Heikkila, and I left a third message on the receptionist's (Vicki) voice mail. Bob returned my call within one hour. He did not bother to explain why he had not returned my call from six days earlier. Instead, he wanted to discuss the "issues" with my file. The following were his issues and the responses I made to them:

"Some of your close friends do not know that you have brothers. If they are such close friends, why do they not know that you have brothers?"

Response: I did not respond to this *issue* because it came as a shock to me. My only reference who, during the interview, did not remember if I had brothers was Terry Alexander. Terry actually knew that I had brothers; however, since he could not remember certain parts of his own life, due to a car accident, I do not hold this non-issue against him. I bet Bob did not bother to ask Terry if he had any memory issues.

"Dorman and Robin [two of your brothers] are criminals. Would they influence your decisions?"

Response: No, I think with my brain, not my heart. I made it clear to Bob that my brothers have chosen their lives, and I have chosen mine.

Let me briefly tell you how Robin and Dorman became criminals.

Robin lived in a rooming house with his White girlfriend and some White men. The men could not handle the fact the she was giving "it" to a "Black boy." So, they attacked Robin. The girlfriend called the police for help. The police arrived, beat the shit out of Robin, and then charged him with assault. Except for the girlfriend, not one of the witnesses lived to attend trial; they managed to kill themselves in a house fire. God is good. The police officers involved managed to self-destruct in their careers and personal lives. Sounds like a fairy tale, does it not? I lived to see it. Nonetheless, this original charge made Robin a toy for the Metropolitan Toronto Police; they targeted him at every turn. He had his share of fights over the years because he did not "belong" in certain community centres, and his life did not get any better as he and his wife (not the White girlfriend) descended into domestic violence. Had Robin made better choices of friends and relationships, he could have reduced his level of involvement with demons in uniforms.

Dorman became a criminal when, at the age of thirteen, he was in an alley in downtown Toronto taking a piss. A man jumped on top of him and started punching him. He fought back. The man turned out to be an undercover police officer. Dorman was arrested for assaulting a police officer and resisting a police officer. Analyze this: The police officer decided to drop the charges against Dorman, if Dorman dropped the charges against the officer. Dorman dropped the charges. This officer dropped the two charges I just mentioned because he knew there would be lots more from whence the first two came. Dorman has lived a fascinating life at the whim of White people. If he ever decides to reveal his life in a book, I strongly encourage you to read it. Despite the forces against him, he should have and could have made some better choices.

All the other *issues* may very well have been a front to cover the *issue* of Robin and Dorman. Why was I such a risk to the RCMP, other than a real fear of what I would find out about the way they treated Robin and Dorman? I have a sister, Arlene, who had this insight from the time she first learned about my application with the RCMP. She had commented, "Robin and Dorman are going to be a huge problem for you." If this is the RCMP's greatest fear of me, we can see the deep effects of racism on my life. Do not forget that Robin and Dorman became "*criminals*" solely because of their race. If I am being denied a job because of their criminal record, I am still being denied a job based on racism—*systematic racism.*

Furthermore, what about all the White people who got rid of their criminal records via pardons and became police officers? Are criminal relation *issues* limited to Black applicants?

"You had personality conflict with workers at JVS [the Jewish Vocational Services of Toronto]."

Response: I told Bob about the time I had answered Francine Taitt, my supervisor, who was a stuck-up, yellow-skinned Jamaican bitch, by saying, "Yes, Ma'am." I thought nothing of it; however, Francine and two of my co-workers (Louise Salhany and Karen Kerbel, two White bitches) looked at me as though I was from another planet. When Francine finally spoke, she said, "Don't call me Ma'am." I apologized and told her that I did not see anything wrong with calling her Ma'am. With that, Karen and Louise reprimanded me about improper terminology. Luckily, the incident occurred at the end of the day—I went home in tears. When I got home, I checked the term "ma'am" with two people, Carlene Harris and Terry Alexander, and they both agreed that ma'am is a proper term. Bob mentioned that he did not see a problem with the term "ma'am."

I mentioned the time that Francine said to me, "Don't think that Louise treats you that way because you are Black; everyone at JVS has felt the wrath of Louise." Reader, take a minute to assess the inferences in Francine's statement. What would you conclude?

Based on Francine's statement regarding Louise's treatment of me, Bob should have been able to figure out that I was not the aggressor in my conflict relationships with my co-workers at JVS and that my race was a factor. Conversely, he was happy to hear about my *"personality conflict with co-workers"* because he was getting ammunition to reject my application for employment with the RCMP. I could just picture him rubbing his hands together, as if to say, "*Finally, something [ammunition] in addition to the army.*"

Bob was well aware that Annette Grandison was also a co-worker from JVS, but that did not matter because Annette was not serving his purpose; her interview statements were the opposite of what he wanted to record. His statements and his tone reinforced in me that anything that he heard that sounded negative, he would amplify; and anything that sounded positive on my behalf, he would ignore.

Annette had a different explanation of why Louise got away with treating people at JVS like garbage:

> *She was in a car accident while on the job, going to meet with a JVS client. She had hurt her back and was in hospital for a while. Now, she gets away with everything because management feels guilty and they are afraid she will sue. Because of her back problem, she can take time off whenever she wants, and they are afraid to let her go [fire her].*

I mentioned to Bob that I left JVS crying many times, instead of becoming "aggressive" with my co-workers. To Karen, Louise, and Francine, "assertiveness" is interpreted as aggression. I knew that whatever I said to him would not make any difference; I felt that I was being harassed all over again. I thought, *"If I was so aggressive, instead of avoiding me, why did Louise always try to push my buttons?"*

In all fairness to Karen and Francine, they did not push my buttons in the same way as Louise. In fact, one day Karen apologized to me for the way a co-worker had treated me in a general meeting. After the meeting, I sat in one of the interview rooms absorbing why people felt free to target me. Karen walked in and said, "Sorry about that Deneace; you did not deserve that." I told her that she did not need to apologize for another adult's behavior, and I thanked her for her concern. After that incident in the general meeting, I chose not to absorb any more. Between the choice of being a doormat and an aggressive bitch, I chose the latter.

Believe it or not, I actually felt sorry for Francine. She fits into the group to which Americans were referring when they coined the term *house nigger.* In order to be accepted into the larger JVS culture, she had to make her remarks and actions fit with those of the people who mattered in the organization—even when they were contrary to her own. As a general practise, she appeased her White clients and disregarded the concerns of her Black ones. Her Jamaican clients used to complain to me, hoping I could help them.

I understand the need people have to be accepted, to feel wanted, to be a part of a group. While I do not have this desire, I understand why it was important to Francine. She did not understand me, and she knew nothing of my ordeal with people in the Canadian Armed Forces; neither did she know that I could be comfortable sleeping in a trench or lying in mud; she did not know that my interactions with most people drove me deeper into myself. As a result, when she walked into the windowless, six-foot by eight-foot basement office I shared with Annette and a young Italian *stud,* to make her case as to why I should move to the North Office, I kept quiet as I watched her pour out her soul for the pain she thought I was feeling from being isolated. Adding to her pain, or rather my pain, the *stud,* Deno, had pornographic magazine pictures of women taped to his computer. I wanted to laugh; nonetheless, I restrained myself as she made her case, saying, "Deneace, that's wrong. That is so offensive to you. That is so degrading to women." Around her Jewish co-workers, I was the outsider; but on this day her heart was bleeding for me. Physically, she identified with White people more than she identified with me: another legacy of Colonialism.

Annette had her own reason for why Deno was never in the office: "He could not stand being stuck in such close quarters with two Black women." Who could blame Deno, when not many people could stay in a box that size all day even without sharing it?

Deno, Annette, and I were employment consultants/counsellors—of all professions. Do you see the irony? We were *employment counsellors*, but look at our physical and social work situations. Our primary duties involved helping people to find jobs and providing counseling regarding legal and illegal treatment in the workplace.

Deno had a car; Annette and I did not. Deno was able to escape the office by going out to see his clients: Annette and I had no such luxury; we had to see our clients in our box.

When Annette was seconded to a position at another location, I inherited a half of the office as opposed to a half of a desk. The story of how Annette ended up in this box that management called an office is another story of *systematic racism.* The short version is that Annette had an office with a huge window on the main floor. A new employee, a White Jewish woman about her age, loved the view and the space. She joined Annette for lunch in the office each day. Shortly thereafter, about two months after I started working at JVS, management moved Annette to the box in the basement and moved the Jewish woman into Annette's office. I remember how Annette cried as I helped her to move her cardboard boxes from her spacious office into the windowless concrete box to be shared with two other people—Deno and me.

Prior to working at JVS (Jewish Vocational Services of Toronto), the Jewish Holocaust used to grieve me to the core of my being. Not realizing that they, too, had been Black slave owners, I had a soft spot for Jews: feeling that they could sympathize with how Black people were spread throughout the world via slavery, feeling that they understood the effects of racism, feeling that they would not perpetuate it. However, that feeling changed for me after working in a Jewish controlled, government-funded organization. Annette's ordeal with her office, the anger that Louise was able to freely channel my way without fear of discipline, and the constant reminder that "you are different and should be treated *differently* (like a retarded child), and my sentence to a windowless room in a basement moved me into a new psychological space. I no longer felt the Holocaust pain of Jewish people; they had proven to me that I am simply *black.* Many evenings, as I cried while I walked home from work, I wondered how far the people in that organization would go—had it not been for the laws of Canada and government funding for the organization.

People love happy conclusions to stories; so, I will tell you that in addition to the two bachelor's degrees that Annette had earned prior to working at JVS, as she continued to work for JVS, she pursued a teaching degree at the University of Toronto. Some months after graduating, she obtained a teaching job within the Peel Public School Board. Peel, where she lived, is less than an hour away from downtown Toronto. But not quite so fast with the happy ending: Although Annette had been teaching since she was sixteen, and despite the fact that she now had three degrees, her starting salary was substantially lower than that of most of her White classmates who were just starting their teaching careers. Racism, systematic or otherwise, always has *reasons*; and for Annette, it was because she did not have

Canadian teaching experience; teaching in Trinidad was not worthy of consideration.

"You down-played the army incident during the RCMP interview; you said the charges regarding the misfire were unfounded."

Response: I asked Bob to clarify what he meant by "unfounded." According to him, "*Unfounded* means that the incident never occurred." However, according to the Oxford Dictionary, "unfounded means unsubstantiated; without substance." I also made it clear to Bob that *unfounded* was not my terminology. My statement was, "The charges were dismissed." In essence, the charges were indeed dismissed because they were *unfounded.* I further made it clear to Bob that I did not say the incident did not occur, because it did. I failed to see how I down-played the charge, when I made it clear that I was charged; I prepared for trial by reviewing the Queen's Regulations and Orders; I was appointed an assisting officer, Captain Pamela Evelyn; I went to trial; and the charges were dismissed.

I recounted the whole incident of the trial: four people misfiring, yet only two being charged—the two Black females; the other two, who were non-Black and male, were not charged. Bob asked, "Did you tell anyone?" His lack of intelligence started to become clear to me. I answered, "Yes. In fact, I wrote a letter to Captain Chamberlain." I continued, "The letter generated more charges because I refused to reveal my sources to Lieutenant Koth, who tried to intimidate me into revealing my sources prior to going to trial." I told Bob that Corporal Sophia Miller saw Lieutenant Koth misfire; and she saw another private being escorted from the firing range for misfiring.

"You left the army to avoid charges."

Response: I told Bob that Captain Pamela Evelyn, my assisting officer, was present when Lieutenant-Colonel Von Bulow dismissed all the charges and told me that I was free to pursue my military career with a clean slate. Again, his lack of intelligence surfaced in his next question, "Were all the charges dealt with?" I answered, "Yes," and made it clear that whoever told him that I left the army to avoid charges purposely gave him misinformation. In addition, I told Bob that Private DaCosta approached me months prior to going to trial, to inform me that the charges would be dropped because her boyfriend, Sergeant Michaud, "does not even remember what occurred." I offered to fax Bob a copy of the letter that I wrote to Lieutenant-Colonel Von Bulow regarding the incident. Bob said, "Yes." Within three hours of our conversation, I faxed Bob a copy of my letter to the lieutenant colonel, the letter of response from Lieutenant-Colonel Von Bulow and a copy of my release certificate.

Lieutenant-Colonel Von Bulow's acknowledgment of my letter is evidence that I left the army long after the charges were dismissed. The very idea of this being an issue speaks to Bob's intelligence. That is, if an accused leaves the army while dealing with charges, do the charges vanish into thin air? Are the charges no longer an issue? Did I mention that the maximum penalty for misfiring in the army was a fifty-dollar fine? Since Master Corporal Andrea Dennis and Corporal Sophia Miller worked in the administrative department and could verify that the charges were dealt with long before I left the army, I gave Bob their phone numbers.

"You had shortcomings in the army."

Response: Bob refused to explain what he meant by "shortcomings"; therefore, I admitted that I had shortcomings. Bob must be the only person on creation without shortcomings.

Would you believe my admission that I had shortcomings was a big scoring point for the RCMP to reject my application? Can you imagine anyone responding "No" to this statement? Even if I had been Number One Candidate in the army, I would still admit that I had shortcomings.

"You left your weapon unsecured."

Response: I figured Bob was referring to the incident where Michaud tried to kill me with his alcohol breath for not standing at the door, guarding unloaded weapons, located in a locked closet, in a room off limits to anyone. I told Bob that the corporal who was assigned picketing with me had dismissed me from picketing duties; and the corporal, too, was dismissed by a more senior person, Corporal Crumb. Moreover, I did not leave the area; rather, I was using a public phone in the hall where I could see anyone entering or leaving the locked room.

Bob wanted to know whether further charges resulted from my not being at the door of the room where the weapons were kept. I answered, "Yes." He then asked, "What happened to that charge?" I answered, "It was dismissed when the other charges were dismissed." Furthermore, Corporal Sophia Miller informed me that Sergeant Michaud had decided not to charge me for the weapon picket; instead, "god" decided to charge only Corporal Pierrier for not being where he had planted her three hours prior. It mattered not that Corporal Crumb had dismissed Pierrier and me from picketing duties. The rule is that picketing duties last for no more than an hour per shift. Michaud had absolutely no regard for the Queen's Regulations and Orders, because he could get away with it. His behaviour was of no concern whatsoever to Constable Joseph, just as it was of no concern to his superiors in the army.

Considering that we were charged with misfiring and that we were going to court, what made Michaud feel that he could administer punishment before even going to trial? Oh yes, I forgot: He is "god." Corporal Miller had knowledge of the whole incident and a better understanding of how the charges were conducted. Michaud never told me that his superiors did not allow him to charge me for *sloppy weapons picketing*. Instead, I heard it from the following people: First, Corporal Pierrier (who was also charged); then, Private DaCosta (Michaud's girlfriend); followed by, Corporal Sophia Miller (who was assisting on the range when Lieutenant Koth and Private Low misfired); and finally, from Master Corporal Dennis (who was fully aware of the racist practises). Michaud's superiority in rank and *race* would not allow him to condescend low enough to deliver this news to me directly. It pissed-off Miller that a private (DaCosta) was so aware of my business that she (DaCosta) could deliver information to me on behalf of her boyfriend, who later became her husband. Upon delivering this news, I could see that DaCosta was hoping and looking for relief on my face. For all her intelligence, she did not comprehend that the charge in and of itself was of little consequence to me; the racism surrounding the charges was my focus, the reason why I wanted to go to trial.

Later, I realized that Bob may have been referring to the incident where Master Corporal DeGroot gave me a chit for taking about six steps from my unloaded weapon and promptly returning to retrieve it and take it to the bathroom with me. What did it matter? Bob was more concerned about my securing empty weapons—without magazines, in a secured environment—than he was in how racism was breeding hatred within me.

"You were late for training."

Response: I mentioned that I worked downtown, and that I had to go home to collect my gear before going to the army. I was late three times, but not as a result of carelessness. I did my best in balancing my commitments.

"You did not show up for training."

Response: I told Bob about the long hours I had to work preparing for a conference. I was just too exhausted to attend on one particular Friday night; therefore, I left a message, via Lloyd, explaining the situation. I showed up the next morning, and a big issue was made of my not showing up at the appointed time. I thought about Garant, and how she never had to worry about her not showing up and not calling coming back to haunt her.

Corporal Miller told me repeatedly that, "Those things should not even be on your file; they are for course reference only." This applied to Garant but not to me.

I told Bob that, considering that I was leaving the army, I checked with Master Corporal Skerrett (the administrative personnel in charge) as to whether I still needed to show-up for Thursday night drills. The answer was, "No." Nonetheless, there were a number of times when I showed up on a Thursday night to meet with Lieutenant Colonel Von Bulow regarding the charges; and for some reason or other, he did not keep his appointments with me. The Lieutenant Colonel's life was so important that he could just disregard my appointments with no repercussions. It mattered not that I worked all day and had to drag my ass there to find out that "he will not be in." Even so, on these Thursday nights, Master Corporal Skerrett would assign me duties which I never refused.

I told Bob that he was purposely given misinformation by whomever to make the situation appear that I was just careless in not showing up for training.

— Chapter 7 —

Spinning the Web to Keep Me Out

After firing issues at me in the form of accusations, Bob decided to ask me direct questions. His questions and my answers are as follows:

Why did you leave Jewish Vocational Services of Toronto (JVS)?

Response: The position was being moved to a different location that would entail an hour more traveling time for me each day. Also, there was conflict over access to my clients; for example, because of the territorial behaviour of some staff members with regard to various computer databases, I had to travel to another office at the other end of the city in order to copy a simple diskette. This was quite frustrating, considering that the required technology was in the same building in which I worked. When I accepted the job at JVS, in

April 1999, I was told that the Main Information System (MIS) would be up and running within a few weeks. Six months later, because the senior staff could not compromise on which should be their primary database, I was still doing three times the work.

Why did you leave the army?

Response: The misfire incident played a small role; however, I needed to concentrate on my primary job. If I had gotten the army position alone, I would have stayed; but shortly after I obtained regular employment, the army called. I decided to try both jobs. It was too physically demanding to maintain my regular job and the army position. I decided to complete basic training and then take a break. I could not leave my regular job, because it was my primary source of income. The army was part-time—one night per week, and one weekend per month. So, I made the choice to leave the army. Evidence of the physical toll that both jobs had on me could be found in my physician's file. In February 1999, my physician's secretary phoned me at work to inform me that I needed to start taking iron supplements because my iron count was much too low. In addition to dealing with the stresses of both jobs, I was going through a divorce. Ultimately, I wanted to pursue other career options.

Did you have shortcomings in the army?

Response: My answer did not change from the first time Bob phrased this question as a statement. Again, his intelligence showed. I told him about chits I received for not "properly" burning unraveled threads from my military attire, and I also told him about the pants being too short; such that the legs would pull out of my boots each time I sat down or stooped.

Whatever shortcomings I had in the army was of no concern to me, because fewer than one-third of the people who started basic training with me graduated; moreover, most of them had fewer commitments than I. Of the approximately thirty people who graduated with me, only five were still in the army less than two years after graduation.

Bob's final words were, "I will personally investigate this because I am getting two completely different stories. If you are not suited to deal with the army environment, I will not recommend you for training. I will be carefully reviewing your file!"

At the end of the conversation, Bob informed me that he would be contacting Captain Pamela Evelyn, my assisting officer, as well as Master Corporal Dennis and Corporal Miller. I expected him to contact Sergeant Michaud, Captain Chamberlain, and Lieutenant-Colonel Von Bulow.

After my conversation with Bob, I called Captain Pamela Evelyn to inform her of the blatant misinformation that was given to the RCMP investigating officer; that, *"I left the army to avoid charges."* Pamela immediately called Bob to confirm my version (the truth) of the matter. Bob told Pamela that he would be meeting with her for an interview, but he never did; neither did he contact Master Corporal Miller nor Master Corporal Dennis. The misfiring charges were dealt with in September 1999 (almost a year after the incident); my release certificate was dated January 2000, well over a year after the misfire incident; and I was actually released May 2000.

I had pointed out to Bob that I wanted the charges to go to trial so that Lieutenant-Colonel Von Bulow could see the blatant racist attitudes of some of his immediate subordinates—in particular, the way the misfire incidents were handled. Four people made the mistake of misfiring; two went on with their lives as though nothing happened; one had her misfire dealt with *quietly*; and, one (I) has it haunting her eternally. Whatever I did not make clear to Bob verbally, he could have verified through the documentation I ensured had stayed on my file. From this conversation, I knew that it was time for me to start looking for a career elsewhere. I thought, *"What is wrong with this situation? Why is the same incident so trivial for two people and so serious for the other two? I am tired of being treated like shit because I happen to be Black, and that is why I did not go away from the army quietly."*

I remained sitting by the phone where I had spoken to Bob, and I thought some more, *"Is there a place for people like Michaud? Do they get to have it all on this side of the grave as well as the next?"* I pictured Bob gloating at hitting the jackpot with my army situation. I had already known that if the problem were not the army, it would surely have been something else.

Thursday, October 26, 2000

I called Bob Joseph to confirm that he received my eight faxed pages. He confirmed that he received the fax. Also, he stated that he called head office (the Armed Forces) and he still had to look at my file.

As of this date, it had been two years and two months since I wrote the recruiting exam. This delay tactic is not unusual for Black applicants. For example, Master Corporal Sophia Miller wrote the RCMP recruiting exam in 1989. It took one year for the recruiting office to send her a package—this is exactly what they did to me over ten years later, between 1997 and 2000. Sophia wrote the exam with two other Black applicants, and the RCMP hired none of them. Sophia went on to university and joined the army. Since I had already completed my bachelor's degree, I decided to utilize my qualification.

November 07, 2000

I had already passed up three good job opportunities while waiting for the RCMP to make a decision. Deep down, I knew from my conversation with Bob that he was not going to recommend me for a job with the RCMP. Therefore, I decided to accept a job as a counsellor in Blue Ridge, Georgia, USA.

November 24, 2000

I mailed a registered letter to RCMP Recruiting, letting them know how to contact me.

December 11, 2000

I received a letter from RCMP Recruiting rejecting me. I was thankful to God that I was not still in Toronto, waiting around for this new rejection. I was thankful that I had prepared myself, mentally and physically, for this blow in life—my most devastating blow to date.

I had sacrificed two years of my life to waiting. I spent money to attend interviews and fax documents, and made many long-distance calls. I had taken test after test, and passed. I rejected three good job offers. I lost wages due to multiple appointments and time taken off work. I opened myself up to intense scrutiny, violation, and exploitation.

The "reasons" I was given for my rejection are as follows:

> *This decision was made as a result of the findings of our background investigation*

> *into your overall suitability. Currently, there are a limited number of positions available and we have a sufficient number of applicants who are deemed more suitable.*

This was the RCMP that was actively seeking minority and female recruits. *See Appendix 1, General Recruitment and Special Programs, page 3.*

As I stated before, the army was just the RCMP's excuse for rejecting me; if it were not the army, they would have found something else. Except for the phone call Captain Pamela Evelyn made to Bob, there was no conversation with anyone who would tell the truth of the racism that was blatantly practised in the army. Bob never even bothered to interview Master Corporal Miller nor Master Corporal Dennis. Master Corporal Skerrett said he "gave a very glowing" report of me to Rick Morris, but I really do not trust him. He did not earn the name Uncle Tom for having a backbone; he knew how to smile while he was being degraded, pretty much the way I did the first three weekends of basic training—when I had a "good attitude." He even kept his lips glued when his niece was being needled left, right, and centre by military personnel.

The only reason Skerrett gave Rick Morris the interview was because Lieutenant Colonel von Bulow ordered him to do so; the lieutenant colonel wanted no part of Green's problems. Rick approached the lieutenant colonel, and the lieutenant colonel diverted him to Skerrett. Never mind Skerrett. Instead, let us measure the RCMP's *reasons* for rejecting me:

Limited number of positions

On Tuesday, August 15, 2000, the Association of Black Law Enforcers (ABLE) held a conference where the Metro Toronto newspaper published the number of black law enforcers across Canada. According to the Metro newspaper, of the 25,000 police officers across Canada only 350 (not even 2%) are Black. I use the present tense because if you read this documentation of my experiences a hundred years from now and you compare the numbers, you will see that the ratio has not changed—unless a miracle causes systematic racism to dissipate.

Sufficient applicants

How many of those "sufficient applicants" are Black and female? The gimmick about hiring Blacks, particularly Black females, has gone on far too long—over eleven years, if one counts from the time I entered college in 1989 to study law enforcement. If I had known that I was wasting my time, I would not have made such a fool of myself trying again and again: making sure that I did everything possible to meet the RCMP's requirements.

Overall suitability

I am a Canadian. I have lived in Toronto since I was eight years old. I am over nineteen years old (the minimum age requirement for joining the RCMP). I completed grade twelve in a Canadian institution. I am not a criminal. I have a valid Canadian driver's licence. In short, I met all their basic requirements. Moreover, I surpassed their requirements because I possess an Honours Law Enforcement college diploma from a Canadian college, and a double-major Bachelor's degree from the University of Toronto. Black people applying for a position as a police constable believed they truly had a chance. Why play the waiting game with Black applicants to see how long they will wait around? Had I not forced Bob Joseph to act by leaving a message for his supervisor and getting the Black Business and Professional Association involved, how long would they have kept my file in the corner? If the RCMP ever reaches its 20% female quota, I guarantee that Blacks will still not be represented.

Let me make it clear that I did not apply to the RCMP simply because I am Black and female. I applied because I believed that I could make a difference in people's lives, be useful to the community while enjoying a sense of personal pride. I applied because I was more than qualified and because I believed I had an equal chance of employment as other people applying. Two years and four months is a long time to wait to find out that I never really had a chance at all. When I include the first application, the RCMP actually wasted three years and four months of my life.

January 21, 2001

I requested a copy of my file from the RCMP.

May 18, 2001

I received a copy of my file from the RCMP, to find that more than a half of the file had been blotted out; in fact, some of the 11" x 14" pages were blank except for a few lines. Not only were names, addresses and phone numbers blanked out, but also the entire text of what people from the army, and others, had said about me.

The part of the skeletal file that stood out the most was the section by Rick Morris—whom you may remember as Hollywood Man after Annette's interview, where he hid behind his dark sunglasses, pretended he was in Hollywood, and degraded me in a manner greater than I had experienced even in the Canadian Armed Forces.

Hollywood Man's comments played a huge role in my case to the Canadian Human Rights Commission (CHRC). *See Appendix 2 for my responses to Hollywood Man's comments, as I submitted them to the CHRC.* Following my responses to the CHRC, I have included what I really wanted to say to the CHRC but it would have been inappropriate. Let us have a look at Hollywood Man's freedom to express himself while practicing racism.

Excerpts from my file as sent to me by the RCMP

Hand printed notes indicate how I formed my case to the Canadian Human Rights Commission

INVESTIGATION REPORT **RAPPORT D'ENQUÊTE**

OTHER FILE REFERENCES AUTRES CONSULTATIONS DE FICHIERS	DIVISION O	DATE 2000-09-26	SECURITY CLASSIFICATION / DESIGNATION CLASSIFICATION/DÉSIGNATION SÉCURITAIR RCMP FILE REFERENCES CONSULTATION DE FICHIERS DE LA G.R.C. 1999-2678
	SUB-DIVISION - SOUS-DIVISION		
	DETACHMENT - DÉTACHEMENT		

RE - OBJET
GREEN, DENEACE (DOB 66-04-01)
RM APPLICANT
SECURITY/SUITABILITY

1. Form 234 from "O" Division Staffing & Personnel, dated 2000-09-13, refers.

EMPLOYMENT:

2. Source (P) of unknown reliability was interviewed with respect to Green's employment with Coca Cola Canada. This Source says that it is company policy to only say if people have or have not worked with the company. Green worked for Coca Cola Canada.

3. Source (Q) of unknown reliability was interviewed with respect to Green's employment with S & P Data. The Source says that it is company policy to only say if people have or have not worked with the company. Green worked for S & P Data.

REFERENCES:

Green is mature because she brought up her children and they are good children.

Green is responsible as she was on welfare and went back to school. Green has never mentioned any radical political opinions or disenchantment with the Canadian government. Green is not a loner Green does n drink, as she is a Pentecostal. There is no knowledge if Green does drugs. she "can go a little overboard about religion".

↳ For communion, wine is served in church.

Ovid Noble

This is the result of a one hour interview

Green has talked about being a policeman for a long time but never mentioned why she wanted that career ?? that she wanted to get into the military.

Green is considered mature because she had her first child when she was fifteen

Royal Canadian Mounted Police **Gendarmerie royale du Canada**

Why is so much information blotted out?

years old and has taken care of both her children since then.

Green is considered responsible

the only character flaw Green has is that she can get angry, but not explosive. There are no indications of radical political opinions or non-support of our system of government. The only sport she takes part in now is jogging. Green's character strengths are: easy to get along with, people person, manages time well and can reason.

Dawna Davis
one hour interview

The Source says that Green has always been able to take care of her money and always has something in savings.

1

that there has been no trouble with Green

Annette Grandison

Where is the interview from Wade McKenzie?

Green is looking at the RCMP as her second career after her initial career of raising her children.

is impressed with her in how she works toward what she wants in life. Green is spiritual and lives her religion.

⟶ To do otherwise, I would be an hypocrite.

LOCAL POLICE CHECKS:

8. Checks for any involvement with Green identified as a suspect, victim or witness came back with a 'NO RECORD' on September 19, 2000.

0122

Why is so much material blotted out?

Checks done showed no involvement with the Campus Police.

BANKRUPTCY:

Green's bankruptcy. with a total debt of $16,000 on January 17, 1997. The debt was $3,000.00 in credit cards and $13,000.00 in education loans. All of these debts were discharged on October 23rd, 1997. Green's income at the time in the telemarketing jobs could not pay off the bills. If Green had applied for bankruptcy six months later her education loans would not have been forgiven with the change of bankruptcy procedures.

Then, why wait?

Yet, he ridicules me for claiming bankruptcy. I was work[ing] at Coca Cola Bottling Ltd; as a customer service representative.

Then why are they an issue for the RCMP?

Green was unwilling to accept the shortcomings listed at the end of the course. These mean nothing if you pass the course in training situations. They are not recorded anywhere to cause you grief. Any shortcoming Green had she made excuses for and felt she should not get them in the first place. Green took this discipline as a personal attack rather than for what it is meant. Green was described as; "not outstanding, not bad, just a regular individual". Green did not show any leadership as at her rank she would not be given anything to do without supervision just like all the other does not consider Green to be reliable.

Then why have they caused me so much grief!

For what was it meant? Why did everyone not receive the same level of disciplin[e]

Green did not show up as often or as readily as she should have and it was felt that she did not have a loyalty . Green was considered (because missing so many duties) she was just doing this for the money. Any place Green was detailed she would be involved in a clique and it would ultimately show that the clique disliked someone. "Green did not take criticism very well." Green was a personable young lady

Who where the Clique members?

Were they constructive criticisms?

What money? The salary amounted to less than $3.00/hour.

because she is black and made it a racial issue. this was not a racial issue wide variety of racial backgrounds and it is no big deal.

Why were the three black females singled out?

I did not make it a racial issue. The racist people in the army are the ones who made my Colour an issue.

Half page blotted out.

This is as full as the pages in my RCMP file get.

! when put under pressure he noticed that Green became more quiet than normal, withdrew and became defensive.

Michaud

See letter written to Colonel Von Bulow to get a sense of the incidents in the unit.

being picked on because she was black. Th

attitude about discipline in general a

0120

Royal Canadian Mounted Police

Gendarmerie royale du Canada

Why is this material blotted out?

Green was reliable and would suggest better ways to do things

good under pressure

she did not roll over and accept the charges against her. There was no opportunity for Green to show leadership.

If there was something that would get Green in trouble would be her strong will.

INVESTIGATOR'S COMMENTS:

18. Green seems to show some very different work styles between civilian and the military work place. Green has only held short-term employment and this is demonstrated by her work history. The military Reserve job showed that Green could not work in a disciplined controlled work place. Green could not handle criticism and demonstrated that she cannot work in military or paramilitary surroundings. After Green's basic training she only worked at the military about two months then really did not come in again. She was only in the Reserves from September 1997 to January 2000 and rarely showed up. Green's bankruptcy demonstrated she was not responsible with money.

- Most of my bankruptcy was student loans. I could not pay rent, feed and cloth a child, pay for transportation to work, support myself and pay a student loan while earning less than $330/week.

- I had a legal right, in my situation, to declare bankruptcy.

I was not required to be there because I was being released.

Could Rick do what I did on $320/week?

- He did not interview anyone who was not personally involved in the discrimination against me e.g.; Master Corporal Miller, Captain Evelyn, Master Corporal Dennis & Corporal Adofo.

Submitted by:

Rick Morris

Royal Canadian Mounted Police Gendarmerie royale du Canada

- Less than 1/3 of the class graduated from basic training.
- Most of those who graduated left before I did.

Rick later ridicules me for being able to accumulate $10,000 worth of assetts after working for only two years.

My law enforcement studies directly parallel Police college and duties. There is no questi[on] that I did well in a policing environment. The military is not the same as police work.

?

Roval Canadian Mounted Police | Gendarmerie rovale du Canada

Why is this whole Page missing?

This is an example of the blank
pages sent to me by the RCMP.

0117

Roval Canadian Mounted Police **Gendarmerie rovale du Canada**

This is an example of the blank
pages sent to me by the RCMP.

INVESTIGATION REPORT RAPPORT D'ENQUÊTE

SECURITY CLASSIFICATION / DESIGNATION
CLASSIFICATION/DESIGNATION SECURITAIRE

OTHER FILE REFERENCES / AUTRES CONSULTATIONS DE FICHIERS	DIVISION	DATE	RCMP FILE REFERENCES / CONSULTATION DE FICHIERS DE LA G.R.C.
	O	2000-06-13	1999-2678
	SUB-DIVISION - SOUS-DIVISION		
	DETACHMENT - DÉTACHEMENT		

RE - OBJET
GREEN, DENEACE (DOB 66-04-01)
RM APPLICANT
SECURITY/SUITABILITY

1. Form 234 from "O" Division Staffing & Personnel, dated 2000-05-12, refers.

EMPLOYMENT:

3.

Green seems to be doing all right.

0116

Law Enforcement professors

she was a more mature than most of the rest because she was older then most of the others. She worked hard on her assignments and it was felt that she had less opportunity to study because of her family's needs. t she was less worldly than most but was fundamentally honest, determined, cheerful

Green found to be reliable, trustworthy, cheerful, warm and open.

Green was always well mannered, good-natured, spoke well, never a problem

Green is intelligent, intuitive, honest, straight forward, dependable, a hard worker and has a keen sense of responsibility. In discussions she will listen to the other side of an argument but is strong willed as to opinion.

The above are references given by my law enforcement professors. These references are actually police officers or retired police officers.

They are vastly different from the "power hungry" people (immediate superiors) in the army.

Lennox

Green has been talking about working for the RCMP for a number of years. she gets bored easily she is the type that "going to get the position is the challenge and if not challenged during the job gets bored".

Law Enforcement

12. Source (K) of unknown reliability was interviewed reference Green's college education. Source said Green graduated in 1991 in Law and Securities Program with Honours at Seneca College with a GPA of 3.1. Green remembered by Source who taught her two subjects as a responsible student and she got two 'A's' in his class. She was remembered as a student who was irritated by antics of immature students in class. This is all he could remember, as it had been about 7 or 8 years.

Law enforcement professor.

She had no problems in school and her record shows no sanctions.

ADDITIONAL INFORMATION:

14. Green's current residence is Apt. 1202 – 444 Lumsden Ave., East York, ON M4C 2L8 with a telephone number 416-686-[redacted]

I was employed none the less. Otherwise, when I was not in school I chose to spend the summer months with my children.

INVESTIGATOR'S COMMENTS:

Green's file has large gaps in secure long term employment and has references that have not had any dealings with her for years. Green may be happy and confident but she does not seem to be a stable potential candidate.

exaggerated

I graduated in 1996. At that time I was already working. As a new graduate, I had a very difficult time securing meaningful work in the Toronto area. Therefore, I did a lot of volunteer work to gain work experience. Has any employer complained about my work?

Submitted by:

Rick Morris

0114

Refering to my Professor and former church members?

Royal Canadian Mounted Police — Gendarmerie royale du Canada

If yes, my professor was not on my application as a personal reference. My former church members were not on my second application. Why contact them? I was in contact on a weekly basis with everyone listed as a reference on my second application form. Furthermore, the RCMP interviews people who the applicant interacted with in the last ten years.

Started working in 1996. What is considered "long-term employment?" Furthermore, long-term employment was not listed as a criterion for the job.

Earning a lot of money was never my primary objective for working.

Discrimination based on my socio-economic status: subsidized housing and being a mother.

APPENDIX 'A'

Personal comments separate from security file.

INVESTIGATOR'S COMMENTS:

Green has no long-term employment. She demonstrates that she is a project kind of employee who bores easily as suggested by Source (J). Green's education should have enabled her to get better paying employment in the last two years. It should be noted that at the time of the undated security interview Green had assets of $10,000 and liability from eye surgery of $4,400. This amount of savings would have paid over half of the debt that Green had escaped from. I see this bankruptcy as an ethical problem of escaping her educational debts and still ending up with her educational credentials. Now just a short two years later has accumulated personal assets of $10,000. I think this confirms an ethical problem. Green is still living in subsidized housing with her daughter who moved back in. How will she survive without income during the RCMP training period? Will she quit the RCMP after a short period of time as another lark? There is no indication of her ability to sustain employment for longer than 2 years. Green has proved that she can learn but seems to have no ability to apply what she has learned. Leaving her two children off of her 330-60 form leaves much to ponder about. Why were they not mentioned? → How could I hide them? Why would I hide them?

Green's exposure to a military discipline did not seem to be a good situation for her. → Does this mean I am 3/5 human being? This is the premise on which slavery in America was based. she appeared not to be suited to the military and job surroundings that had an expectation of her to perform like everyone else does to make the team work. Not being able to take discipline and blaming discrimination against blacks as the reason she was being disciplined shows that she can not stand up and take responsibility for her own actions. Why were the white people not disciplined?

Green was unsuited to the military. I believe she will ultimately be found equally unsuitable by the Force.

I strongly feel that Green would be an unsuitable candidate for the RCMP.

Rick Morris

I cannot predict what will happen tomorrow, moreover, six months from now. I secured paid employment several months after I declared bankruptcy.

- Two years is a long time to be in a job a person does not enjoy.

- I was working nonetheless.

- Some people get hired on to police forces directly off welfare.

- Some people change jobs twelve times in one year before getting hired as a police officer e.g., the husband of the woman who wrote the book "Cops Don't Cry."

In other words, animals can be trained to do certain tricks; however, animals cannot train anyone.

Their birth certificates were sent in with my application. Therefore, this should not be an issue.

I was offered a teaching position in Seoul, Korea, two years prior; however, I was told by the RCMP (very clearly) that if I left the country my file would be closed. I needed to be accessible.

0081

8

No thought is given to the opinions of my law enforcement professors (police officers); however, the opinions of a few people in the military determines my future.

Am I imagining that Rick has a deep sense of resentment towards me although he never met me?

Part 3

Hollywood Man's Freedom to Practise Racism

The Liberty to Practise Racism in Canada

Sometimes people do things to us that offend us so badly we can never forget. We may forgive them, but we can never forget because the interaction has made an indelible stain on our lives. Some people refer to these stains as "pivotal moments in life"—moments we live over and over, wondering "how?" How can some people be so wicked? How do some people seek to destroy others for the sheer pleasure of inflicting pain? How are some people so masterful at distorting and twisting the truth to suit whatever circumstance they see fit? How are they able to live from day to day, destroying a fellow human being without regard for the long-term effects on the individual and anyone touching the individual's life? I can tell you "why," but I cannot tell you "how." Why? Some people just plain wicked, vile and evil. It is horrible enough that such people exist; the greater misfortune is that, most often, they are in places of power over us. Like great toads, or trolls, or spiders weaving webs of lies and deceit, they sit in judgement over important aspects of our lives. When most people look at the causes of such display of evil, they tend to pity the perpetrators. I, however, feel no such pity. All human beings have free will. With that free will bestowed on us by the Creator, we can choose to hurt and we can choose to heal; we can choose to build and we can choose to destroy. Rick Morris, like every other member of the human race, inherited free will. With his free will, he attempted to destroy me. With my free will, I chose not to be destroyed.

Rick Morris was the RCMP officer who undertook the second background investigation into my case, after my file had been missing for months and I had forced Constable Bob Joseph to respond to me.

When Joseph finally responded, due to pressure from the RCMP Board, it was to inform me that there were "issues" regarding my file.

In the RCMP's file on me, the original investigator, Constable Carey, had noted: "Throughout the course of the investigation, nothing of a derogatory nature was found on the applicant. . . ." Included in the file (now included in this book as the final page of excerpts from my file) was a page titled **Personal Comments Separate from Security File: Investigator's Comments**, written by Rick Morris after he had completed his investigation. Morris took a 180-degree turn from Carey's findings. He twisted every piece of information in such a way that left me to conclude that he used his own mentality and characteristics to judge me.

He never asked me to clarify any of his *concerns*; neither was I ever allowed to address any of the *issues* that he raised. Yet, contrary to the RCMP's denial, it was on the weight of his comments and analysis of my application that the RCMP rejected me as an applicant to join the Force.

I understand better now the concept of 'hired gun.' The RCMP wanted to be rid of me but could not do it without exposing themselves to legal action; consequently, they brought in Morris, who had been trained in human resource management, to find 'reasons' why I would not be a "suitable candidate."

I never met Rick; and each of my two telephone conversations with him lasted less than two minutes—the second conversation lasted only seconds, as he barked, "I am not going to explain it! Your file is back in London."

My friend, Annette, however, had the dubious pleasure of meeting Rick and having her time wasted. She gave me complete details of their meeting during which, according to her, Hollywood Man (HM) never took off his dark glasses and sounded as if he was reading from a script. Annette found even the voice message on Rick's answering machine to sound Hollywood scripted. Thus, she branded him "Hollywood Man," and I found the name to be quite apt.

What follows is a brief sampling of Hollywood Man's comments and my responses, to show you just how deliberately obtuse and malignant Morris was in his treatment of me (extended version to the Canadian Human Rights Commission is in Appendix 2).

HM: Green has no long-term employment.

Response: I graduated from the University of Toronto in 1996, and I started working in 1995—a year before I graduated. Most companies, particularly government agencies, were hiring only on contract. Besides, long-term employment is not a criterion for the position of police constable. It is interesting that when White women are hired by police forces straight off welfare it is neither an issue nor a concern.

HM: She demonstrates that she is a project kind of employee who bores easily.

Response: I admit that if I am not challenged, I get bored easily; police work is very challenging.

HM: Green's education should have enabled her to get a better paying job in the last two years.

Response: Is Mr. Morris admitting that I really became employable only within the last two years? Please note that I applied to the RCMP more than two years before his statement was written. Had the RCMP dealt with my application in a timely manner (approximately eight months), I *would* have been earning more money. As a new graduate without work experience, I found it virtually impossible to get employment in my field of study. Therefore, I had to take customer service jobs until a better job came along. Better offers did come along; however, Karen Cleary of the RCMP told me that if I left the country, "Your file will be closed. We need to be able to reach you." As a result, I rejected multiple teaching opportunities in Japan and South Korea. Some people change jobs twelve times in one year before getting hired as a police officer—example, the husband of the woman who wrote the book, *Cops Don't Cry*. Long-term employment is not a criterion for employment as an RCMP officer.

HM: It should be noted that at the time of the undated security interview, Green had assets of $10,000 and a liability from eye surgery of $4,400. This amount of savings would have paid over half of the debt that Green escaped from. I see this bankruptcy as an ethical problem of es-

caping her educational debts and still ending up with her educational credentials.

Response: I declared bankruptcy in January 1997. I secured paid employment *seven months later*, after doing five volunteer jobs to gain work experience. There was an economic recession in 1997. As for the eye surgery, in order to be considered for employment with the RCMP, it was necessary to meet a specific vision standard. *See Appendix 1, Vision Requirements. For the purposes of my current publication, I would like to add that Rick Morris must be the only human being who can predict his life with certain accuracy: particularly his finances, seven months into the future.*

HM: Now just two short years later, she has accumulated personal assets of $10,000. I think this confirms an ethical problem.

Response: I must have been extremely responsible with money to be able to save $10,000 out of my "low paying jobs." Morris interpreted the situation to suit his purpose. If my intentions were to not repay my student loans, I would have borrowed much more money and then declared bankruptcy. I took minimal amounts of student loans because I intended to pay back every cent.

HM: Green is still living in subsidized housing with her daughter who moved back in. How will she survive without income during the RCMP training period?

Response: I see Mr. Morris' statement as discrimination in the purest sense, discrimination based on my socio-economic status, my living in subsidized housing, and being a single mother.

HM: Will she quit the RCMP after a short period of time as another lark?

Response: I have had an interest in policing since 1988. My studies in *law enforcement, sociology, and political science* are evidence that I have a strong interest in policing. Furthermore, Mr. Morris blames me for leaving what he considers undesirable jobs, "better paying employment." Now, it seems he is saying I should have stayed in those jobs.

HM: Green has proved that she can learn but seems to have no ability to apply what she has learned.

Response: I find this statement personally and racially offensive, considering that the premise of slavery in America [Colonial slavery in general] was that *Black people represented only three-fifth of a human being.* In her book, *How to Be, First Fireside Edition 2000,* (page 158), Harriette Cole reminds us, "People fought against the premise of slavery that eventually stated in the Constitution that our ancestors represent only three-fifth of a man." Animals can be trained to do certain tricks; however, animals cannot train anyone. I find it racially offensive for anyone to say, "She can learn but seems to have no ability to apply what she learned." Even animals can do that. Mr. Morris' statement echoes the treatment I received in the Canadian Armed Forces. Mr. Morris is representative of the type of people who chose not to hire me without work experience. He is perpetuating the statement I often hear, while looking for work: "You have a lot of education, but no work experience." How am I to get work experience if no one hires me? In order to apply what I have learned, I first need to obtain a job in my field of training.

Further response: This from a man who had been with the RCMP eighteen years, at the time, and never made it past the rank of a constable—the lowest rank; at least I have ambition; I do not sit in one spot when there is so much to learn and do.

HM: Leaving her two children off her 330-60 form leaves much to ponder. Why were they not mentioned?

Response: Copies of my children's birth certificates were submitted along with both of my applications; therefore, this should not be an issue. Moreover, both of my children were under eighteen years old when I submitted my applications to the RCMP. *Thus, they were not required as subjects of investigation for the purposes (organized crime, national security threat, espionage etc.) of the 330-60 form.*

HM: Green's exposure to military discipline did not seem to be a good situation for her. She appeared not to be suited to the military and job surroundings that had an expectation to perform like everyone else does to make the team work.

Response: I love it when White people think they know what is best for me. White people also felt Jim Crow's Segregation and South Africa's Apartheid were good for Black people: The Black people who fought against these regimes were also viewed as dissenters who were not good for making the systems work.

HM: Not being able to take discipline and blaming discrimination against Blacks as the reason she was being disciplined shows that she cannot stand up and take responsibility for her own actions.

Response: I do take responsibility for my actions. The letter dated October 25, 1998, after the misfire incident, shows that I do accept responsibility for my actions. I have no problem taking my share of responsibility for the bullet that was accidentally fired. My issue is that four people misfired: two Black women, one White male, and one Asian male. Why were only the two Black people charged?

In the words of Colonel Sutherland, the Commanding Officer replaced by Lieutenant Colonel Von Bulow, "I commend you for seeing this through. Some people would drop their gear and walk away, but you chose to stay through the trial. For that you should be commended." How is that for standing up and taking responsibility for my actions?

Additionally, Captain Chamberlain told Captain Pamela Evelyn that he commended me for addressing the situation. In fact, Captain Chamberlain told Captain Pamela Evelyn, "It is people like her we need in the army."

Of all Hollywood Man's degrading comments about me, this one stings the worst. What he is saying to me is, "How dare you cry racism? People should be able to treat you like shit based on your race, but you should never say it is because of your race; you should say it is because there is something wrong with you." This one stings the most because no one in authority seems to care; it is as though no one in authority is able to understand how racism feels—the anger, the hurt, the frustration, the injustice seems foreign to them. I guess anyone who could enslave another human being really has no ability to feel that sense of "wrong."

HM: Green was unsuited for the military. I believe she will ultimately be found equally unsuitable by the Force. I strongly feel that Green would be an unsuitable candidate to the RCMP.

Response: The officer who conducted the original investigation, M.J. Carey, wrote, "Throughout the course of this investigation, nothing of a derogatory nature surfaced on the applicant. The writer had an opportunity to conduct an employment check on behalf of Milton Detachment." Another RCMP officer who disagreed with Mr. Morris is Sergeant PMP Ohare. He wrote, "It should be noted that all the associates interviewed support the applicant and feel that she will be an asset to the RCMP if hired."

As you can see from these exchanges, Hollywood Man was free to express his thoughts without regard for the truth. He was paid to play a role, and he did it without even remaining consistent in his submission. He did a good job at twisting his script, since accuracy was not a requirement for the role he had to play. He was obviously a man hardened to his job, and one does not need to be a behavioral analyst to conclude that Hollywood Man enjoyed the role he played. Some men like to sit behind dark glasses and torment people to compensate for the deficiencies of their meager manhood. We can safely fit Hollywood Man into this category of men.

Hollywood Man's treatment of me was the catalyst that angered me sufficiently to put my case before the Canadian Human Rights Commission. I intend to hold the RCMP and the Canadian Armed Forces accountable for the *systematic racism* that they will continue to perpetuate until enough people say, "Enough!"

Part 4

I Take My Case to the Canadian Human Rights Commission (CHRC)

June 27, 2001

On Wednesday, June 27, 2001, I contacted Andrew Sunstrum at the Canadian Human Rights Commission (CHRC). At first, I felt awkward telling him about the discrimination I had faced in the Canadian Armed Forces and during my interactions with the Royal Canadian Mounted Police; however, he made the situation easier for me by asking me a few direct questions:

1. Were you discriminated against based on your race?
2. Were you discriminated against based on your gender?
3. Were you denied a job based on discrimination?
4. Has it been over a year since you last had contact with the organization that discriminated against you?

After I had answered Mr. Sunstrum's questions, he suggested that I might have a case and told me to make a written submission to the CHRC.

June 29, 2001

To begin the process of making a submission to the Commission (CHRC), I called Corporal V. Laflamme of the RCMP in Ottawa, on June 29, 2001, to request a complete copy of my file. The copy that the RCMP had mailed to me in May 2001 had more than half of the contents blotted out. Some pages were completely blank, while some had just a few lines left visible. Laflamme informed me that I needed the written permission of the people listed in the file before their statements could be released to me. He and I both knew that the people in the army who had lied about me were not going to give their permission. In essence, I would never get to see the bulk of the information that the RCMP used to make their decision to reject me. Nonetheless, I sought permission from people who would allow me to use their statements. This would provide the Commission with some proof that the RCMP was well aware of the racism I encountered in the Canadian Armed Forces, and that the RCMP perpetuated the discrimination with their own form of systematic racism.

I was living and working in Seoul, Korea by then, and I knew it would take at least a month before I received written consent from the people interviewed by Rick Morris (Hollywood Man); therefore, I decided to go ahead and use the skeletal file to start my case for the CHRC.

October 2001

It was October 2001 before Master Corporal Bernard Skerrett, of the Canadian Armed Forces, finally gave his consent to have his interview with Hollywood Man released; and if it were not for his wife, most likely, I would still be waiting until this day and beyond. Bernard was a sergeant by this time but he used the rank of Master Corporal to ensure that he did not confuse the RCMP: He was a master corporal when Hollywood Man interviewed him.

Bernard had sent me an e-mail of the letter he would be mailing to me. I was relieved to finally receive the letter, even though it was only an unsigned e-mail full of grammatical and punctuational errors. I thought about asking him to send a proper letter; but when I considered the further delay that I would incur in getting my file to the Commission, I decided to proceed with it and let him bear the embarrassment of his poor writing skills. The four months of waiting and reminding (begging) him was enough effort spent.

With the letter (e-mail) finally in hand, I was able to send my submission off to the CHRC. I chose to proceed instead of waiting for copies of the authorized statements I was going to request from the RCMP—there was no more time to waste. My intention was to forward the interview statements to the CHRC as soon as I received them. It would be another two weeks, minimum, before I would receive Bernard's signed letter in the mail. I was not prepared to wait around for another two weeks, and I really did not trust Bernard to mail the letter as he had proven to be unreliable.

I made copies of all the letters granting me permission for the RCMP to release the interview statements to me and included them in my submission to the Commission; I was saving the originals to be sent to the RCMP, as they required original signatures before they would release any information to me. As soon as I received Skerrrett's original letter through the post, I mailed off my request to the RCMP. The five people who gave their consent were Captain Pamela Evelyn, Sergeant Bernard Skerrett, Carlene Harris (a friend), Ovid Nobel (my adopted uncle), and Lennox Green (one of my brothers).

A few days later, in mid-October 2001, I sent my 323-page submission to the CHRC. In it, I made it clear that my security file with the RCMP was clear. In other words, I was not a security risk. I focused on how I had experienced racism and discrimination while training with the Canadian Armed Forces. I outlined how the RCMP had exercised what appeared to be racist policies to exclude me from their enlistment process; and, I included documents to support my claims.

In case you think that 323 pages is a lot of material to send, here is an outline of the package that I sent to the Commission:

1. Cover Letter to Andrew Sunstrum reminding him of our conversation on June 27, 2001, and the contents of the submission (page 1);
2. Table of Contents (page 2);
3. Overview of my Application Process with the RCMP and the Racism [I faced] in the Canadian Armed Forces (pages 3-20);
4. Response to the RCMP and the Canadian Armed Forces' Discriminatory Practises—Rick Morris' *Investigator's Comments* and Bob Joseph's *issues* (pages 21-29),
5. Appendices (excerpts from the RCMP file and other files, publications, letters, etc.), (pages 30-70);
6. Copies of letters from some of the people interviewed by the RCMP (pages 71-75);
7. Letter from the Privacy Commissioner with Privacy Act attached (76-81);
8. A copy of my censored RCMP file (pages 82-323).

Late December 2001

In response to the letters of consent and a letter attached to them that I mailed to the RCMP in November, asking that interview statements be released to me, I received a letter from the RCMP with six pages attached to it. Except for the difference in number of pages, this package was no different from the larger file that the RCMP had sent to me in May 2001—some pages had a few words on them and letters from A to W indicating the number of people interviewed regarding my application for employment with the RCMP. *See Appendix 3.*

Of the twenty-three individuals the RCMP interviewed regarding my application, only three names appeared in the file they sent to me: Carlene Harris, Lennox Green, and Ovid Nobel. The letter that the RCMP included informed me that, ". . . we were able to locate only three of the five statements requested." How convenient that the RCMP *lost* Captain Evelyn's and Master Corporal (Sergeant) Skerrett's interviews. I thought, *"It scares me to think that these people are there to uphold the law; yet, the more I deal with them, the more they expose their lawlessness and commonness."* If I were to guess why the RCMP ". . . was able to find only three of the five statements [I] requested," I would conclude that both Constable Rick Morris and Constable Bob Joseph left that information out of my file. In the words of Rick Morris, referring to my not putting my under-aged children on a security check form reserved for adults, "[This] leaves much to ponder. Why were they not [included]?" He uses his own corrupt mentality to judge me in stating, *"Leaving her two children off her 330-60 form leaves much to ponder. Why were they not mentioned?"* Part E of the 330-360 Personal Security Clearance Questionnaire form clearly notes, "List particulars of all your immediate relatives over 18 years of age. . . ." In July 1999, when I returned my second application package to RCMP Recruiting, my daughter was seventeen years old; and my son was sixteen. In efforts to make me reflect his true character, Rick twisted and turned this situation. Now I started to comprehend why he thought me to be ruthlessly deceptive; this ruthlessly deceptive mind-set is apparently a common thread amongst the RCMP members as well as members of the Canadian Armed Forces. Once more, the Bible (Proverbs 23:7) proves to be true: "As a man thinketh, so is he." As Rick and Joseph thought, so were they. It occurred to me that, perhaps, deep in their hearts they probably believed all the things of which they accused me; they believed their lies because that is what they and their colleagues would have done—scary thought.

Notice that the letter states, ". . . we were able to locate only three of the five statements requested"; it does not state that they had *no record* of such statements. Furthermore, because only three names of the twenty-three people interviewed were not blotted out, I have no way of knowing if Master Corporal Bernard Skerrett's or Captain Pamela Evelyn's name was ever listed among those blotted out. Rick Morris officially interviewed Bernard Skerrett. Pamela Evelyn called Bob Joseph and gave her statement to him. I requested both statements. Why were their names not on the list that shows twenty-three people were interviewed? Therefore, it was up to anyone's interpretation to determine when those statements were *lost*.

I could not overlook a sentence in Ovid Noble's statement, where Rick Morris notes: "Green talked about being a *policeman* for a long time but never mentioned why she wanted that career." Ovid Noble was a university-educated accountant. I believe he knew the difference between a *policeman, policewoman* and *police officer.* Furthermore, I believe Ovid Noble knew me to be a woman not only by appearance, but he was aware that I gave *birth* to two children. I must conclude that this was Rick's way of trying to make either Ovid or me look ignorant. If not, then we see Rick's ignorance and lack of intelligence shining through his dark eyeglasses once more.

I searched through the empty pages and thought, *"Luckily, I had gone ahead and made my submission to the Canadian Human Rights Commission without waiting around for the statements I had requested from the RCMP."*

January 2002

Mr. Sunstrum put together a three-page document on a Canadian Human Rights Commission Complaint Form and mailed three copies to me where I was teaching in South Korea. The letter attached to the form instructed me to sign all three copies and return two to the CHRC within 20 calendar days. *See Appendix 4.* Not only did I sign the copies and return them within the specified time, I included the additional information that the RCMP sent to me; and I included a letter informing the CHRC that the RCMP was refusing to release the statements of Master Corporal Skerrett and Captain Pamela Evelyn. *See Appendix 3.*

I noticed that the forms did not include any claim against the Canadian Armed Forces; therefore, I phoned Mr. Sunstrum. He informed me that since the Canadian Armed Forces had not denied me a job in the same manner as the RCMP—that is, based on my race and gender—my case was really against the RCMP. Furthermore, the one-year period for taking action against the Canadian Armed Forces through the CHRC had elapsed. As a result, even though I still felt that the time frame was debatable, in that, a year had not passed since members of the Canadian Armed Forces told lies about me, I did not push for an extension to have the CHRC investigate the army.

February 2002

George Kolk, Manager of Investigations for the Canadian Human Rights Commission, sent me a letter informing me that an investigator would be assigned to my case to gather evidence relating to my allegations against the RCMP. The letter further stated that the investigator's report would include a recommendation on how to proceed with my complaint. The investigator would have three options based on his or her findings:

- recommend that a conciliator be appointed if the evidence supported my claims;
- recommend that my claim be dismissed if there was no evidence to support my claims;
- recommend that a settlement be approved, if the RCMP and I could reach an agreement during the course of the investigation.

I waited for the Human Rights Commission to contact me with their findings.

March 2002

I received a letter from the CHRC stating that they would be investigating my complaint against the RCMP. Deborah Oliver was to complete the investigation.

April 2002

Ms. Oliver sent me a fifteen-page document, which consisted of the RCMP's response to my "allegations," and she instructed me to provide comments or rebuttals to their response. *See Appendix 5.*

May 2002

In May 2002, I sent her an eleven-page, single-spaced, document in which I rebutted the various points of the RCMP's response to my complaint. *See Appendix 6.*

August 2002

I received another letter from the CHRC telling me that a Richard Warman would be completing the investigation.

September 2002

I received a third letter from the CHRC telling me that a Perry Gerhard would be completing the investigation.

April 2003

Mr. Gerhard sent me a two-page document consisting of nine questions on which he wanted clarification. By the time I answered his nine questions, I was sending him another six pages.

September 2003

In 2003, I finished a second one-year teaching contract in South Korea, and I was in Toronto for the summer. Mr. Gerhard phoned me regarding mediation with the RCMP: I was hesitant, but Mr. Gerhard said, "They want to settle." I recalled the letter from Mr. Kolk back in February 2002, informing me that I had an "obligation as a complainant to mitigate potential damages arising from the complaint." Mr. Gerhard continued, "You have nothing to lose; if it does not go well, the investigation will be continued." I agreed to meet with the RCMP.

I was still in contact with Mr. Lecky from the RCMP Board. I called him to give him an update. He encouraged me to see a lawyer before meeting with the RCMP and suggested that the Black Business and Professional Association (BBPA) was a good place to contact in finding a lawyer. Mr. Lecky was correct. Through the BBPA, I was put in contact with a brilliant lawyer named Kim Bernhardt. Ms. Bernhardt instructed me to calculate how my relationship with the RCMP had affected me financially, considering job opportunities that I missed while waiting for the RCMP to make a decision regarding hiring me. She said that other forms of general damage would be calculated separately. To be ready to represent me in the mediation, Kim reviewed my submission to the Commission. Like the human rights officer, Andrew Sunstrum, Kim felt that going after the army was a "long shot." The defamation of character aspect would not stick because the army did not publish what they told the RCMP about me. She felt that the strongest evidence was in Rick Morris' comments.

October 2003

On Tuesday, October 14, 2003, Captain Pamela Evelyn, Kim Bernhardt, and I met at 180 Dundas Street West to begin the mediation process.

We were meeting with Constable Robert (Bob) Joseph and his boss, Inspector Lindsey Brine from the RCMP, and a White female mediator who had been appointed by the CHRC. The mediator started by explaining the process.

Immediately, Joseph looked scared. When Kim started to speak, Inspector Brine interrupted her by saying, "We wanna hear what Deneace has to say." I started to discuss what Joseph referred to as his "issues with my file." Inspector Brine responded by saying, "Rick is no longer working for the RCMP." Both men paused and looked at me as though they expected me to jump on top of the table and start dancing or doing back flips. Joseph tried to soothe me, but only insulted me, by telling me that the statements made my Rick Morris did not affect my application to the RCMP. My response was, "Then, why were they such an issue?"

Pam whispered to me, "Don't show so much emotion." I wanted to take her advice; however, I just could not let them pat me on the head like a good dog and walk away, as if to say, "You're making too much of this; just forget it." I blasted him with, "You did not even bother to interview any of the people in the army who could corroborate the racism that I encountered." Again, Pam tried to discretely soothe me.

Inspector Brine spoke up to defend Joseph and threatened to walk out of the meeting. After that, Joseph looked a lot more relaxed; obviously, the boss was going to back him up in whatever he did. Kim waited for Brine to finish and then said, "That was well delivered!" in a tone that said she was well aware of their intent to intimidate.

Things could have gotten out of hand at that point, but the mediator reminded us that the purpose of mediation was not to lay blame; rather, it was to come to an agreement that would be satisfactory to both sides—while mitigating any hardship.

It was clear that neither of the officers nor I was giving much thought to what the mediator had said, because Inspector Brine and I had already started a psychological combat. As he continued to speak, I could no longer hear anything he was saying; but I saw his lips moving while he stared me down with the sole purpose of intimidating me; and I was staring him down to show him that he did not intimidate me. The hatred between us was undeniable. Neither of us blinked, for what seemed to me to be a solid three minutes. His eyes were like ice. I suppose he saw fire coming out of mine.

Kim broke the tension by introducing the calculations for a settlement. We all relaxed somewhat, as Kim gave her reasoning . . . to officers with body language that was not at all receptive. Then, the mediator dismissed us for a lunch break. Kim, Pam, and I had lunch in a restaurant on the first floor of the building, during which we discussed the case.

After lunch, neither Kim nor the mediator had returned to the mediating room where Pam and I were discussing e-mails I had received from some Korean placement agencies for English-teachers. Pam could not believe what she was reading. The responses were clearly stating that the employers would not hire Black people. The two police officers had returned. They were listening to what she was saying and wanted to know what she was reading. When she shared the information with them, they looked as though they were appalled. It appeared that they had forgotten why we were meeting. Ironic, isn't it, that Brine and Joseph would see themselves above such blatant racism?

Kim and the mediator returned to the room. Apparently they had been talking. Kim took her seat while the mediator asked the two officers to go with her to another room. After about twenty minutes, Pam stated, "They have been in there a while." Kim responded, "She is trying to get them to settle." Pam nodded her head in the affirmative. Kim spoke, "Do you realize how this looks? Pam answered, "Three Black women with a gripe." I thought, "*Was I supposed to hire a White person to represent me because of how things look?"*

When the officers returned to the room, that was the end of the meeting. They said they were going to "think things over and get in touch with the mediator." There was no settlement.

As we got up to leave the room, we all shook hands. Forgetting whose hands I was shaking, I shook without malice. I actually gave the two officers a genuine handshake, although I believe I hurt Joseph's hand when I shook it; he responded as most people do when I shake their hand. Sometimes I grip too hard; I saw his face contort briefly.

I do not believe Joseph and Brine intended to settle. I believe they wanted either to buy time to frustrate me so I would go away or to tell me that Rick was no longer working with the RCMP and that I should just move on. The *buying of time*, by the RCMP, in this manner, was a caution given to me by a current Black RCMP officer who was himself fighting a case of racism within the RCMP.

December 2003

I received a letter from the CHRC informing me that, "As mediation has not led to a resolution of your complaint against the Royal Canadian Mounted Police, Ms. Sita Ramanujam has been designated to finalize the investigation of your complaint." This letter also stated a concern regarding the timeliness of my complaint.

The concern was that although the RCMP had sent me a rejection letter in December 2000, I had not signed the CHRC Complaint Form until January 14, 2002. The Commission pointed out that the date of signing the complaint form had exceeded the one-year time period by "approximately one month" for making a complaint to the Commission, as stipulated by section 41 (1) (e) of the *Canadian Human Rights Act*.

I first made contact with Andrew Sunstrum, at the CHRC, in June 2001 and submitted my written complaint in October 2001, well within the one-year period allowed by the Act. Therefore, even if the RCMP had raised this issue, the Commission should not have dignified it in a letter to me. By raising it in a letter to me, the Commission gave it a sense of legitimacy. I looked at the name (Ramanujam) of the latest CHRC investigator assigned to my file, and I immediately felt a sense of uneasiness.

As I constructed a response to Ms. Ramanujam, I once more saw myself sitting in one of Professor de Lannoy's *Social Change* lectures at the University of Toronto. The professor was lecturing on the pariah capitalist role that East Indians played in the European Expansionism in South Africa and the Caribbean, where they acted as the "middleman" between the White people and the *black*. I identified with what the professor was saying because as a young child in Jamaica, I did not interact with White people—I had only a glimpse or two of a few North American missionaries who came to save the *blacks* from hell. However, I saw enough East Indians and Chinese people to wonder why they had nicer houses, owned all the businesses of any substance, and drove new automobiles while the Blacks who made up the bulk of the population were always subservient to them. From a first-year university philosophy class, I had a sense of the role the *coloureds* (of East Indian descent) played in South Africa. Although the Whites sat at the top of each hierarchy (racial, social, political, and economical), I understood that the *coloureds* administered the direct subjugation of the *blacks;* but it was my third-year Social Change class that really put the hierarchy into perspective for me. *More about the South African Apartheid mentality and the obliteration of "the blacks" can be found in my second book, My Thoughts, My Life: The Life of a Black Woman Living in a White World, "The Break," True Expressions.*

I thought of the interaction between Whites, Blacks, and East Indians within Canadian society. Growing up in Toronto, particularly in elementary and junior high school, I saw the repulsion Whites felt when dealing with East Indians—as Whites referred to cockroaches in East Indians' turbans—a scorn they never quite displayed when referring to Blacks as Niggers. Yet, East Indians displayed a sense of racial supremacy when dealing with Blacks.

Even today, Indians face more than their fair share of racism from White people. They do not even get the admiration that Blacks get for their musical and athletic abilities; yet, they believe themselves closer to Whites than to Blacks and treat *blacks* accordingly.

Why was the issue of *time* never raised before this East Indian woman took over my case towards the end of the process? Her conclusion and her reasoning for her conclusion speak for themselves.

February 2004

Ms. Ramanujam sent me a letter in early February informing me that her investigation into my complaint was completed and that she had prepared and forwarded a report to the Ottawa CHRC office along with files relating to my complaint. What she neglected to include was that she had advised the Commission to dismiss my complaint.

In late February 2004, I received a letter from Mr. Chamberlain, Manager of Investigations with the CHRC, informing me that the investigation was completed. *See Appendix 7.* Attached to the letter was the Investigator's Report, which included Sita Ramanujam's recommendations. *See Appendix 7, page 11, Recommendation, where Ms. Ramanujam writes the following:*

> *63. It is recommended, pursuant to subsection 41 (1) of the Canadian Human Rights Act, that the Commission deal with the complaint because the complainant contacted the Commission within the one year of the alleged act.*

> *64. It is recommended, pursuant to subsections 44 (3)(b) of the Canadian Human Rights Act, that the Commission dismiss the complaint because the evidence does not support the complainant's allegations that she was denied enrollment because of colour, sex and family status.*

Although Ms. Ramanujam cited the Canadian Human Rights Act in her dismissal letter, the woman clearly missed the purpose of the Act, section 2, which dictates the following:

> *All individuals should have an opportunity equal with other individuals to make for themselves the lives that they are able and wish to have and to have their needs accommodated, consistent with their duties and obligations as members of society, without being hindered in or prevented from doing so by discriminatory practices based on race, national or ethnic origin, colour, religion, age, sex, sexual orientation, marital status, family status, disability or conviction for an offence for which a pardon has been granted.*

Furthermore, it appears she never read the Canadian Charter of Rights and Freedoms in its entirety; otherwise, she most likely would have vaguely remembered to consider my Equality Rights, under section 15, subsection (1), which dictates thus:

> *Every individual is equal before and under the law and has the right to the equal protection and equal benefit of the law without discrimination and, in particular, without discrimination based on race, national or ethnic origin, colour, religion, sex, age or mental or physical disability.*

Ultimately, like the two RCMP officers with whom I had the meeting regarding settlement, Ramanujam felt Rick Morris' findings of why I was "unsuitable" to be hired by the RCMP had no bearing. Since she so blindly overlooked his variations of bold discrimination against me, I would have to conclude that she never even considered the RCMP's less blatant discrimination in what is meant by " . . . applicants that are deemed to be more suitable" for hiring.

The RCMP wrote Mr. Chamberlain a letter dated March 12, 2004, stating that, "The RCMP concurs fully with the analysis and recommendations made by the investigator [Ms. Ramanujam], and will await the Commission's decision." The fact that the RCMP was stating that they "fully concur" with the investigator's analysis and recommendations told me that the investigator was not impartial in her analysis; she might as well have been paid by the RCMP.

Mr. Chamberlin included an invitation for me to respond to the Investigator's Report. I submitted my rebuttals to the Commission, as though the Commission did not already have all the information they required to establish that I had experienced discrimination from the RCMP. The letter advised me not to include documents that were already considered during the investigation, but I failed to see how I could respond to the Investigator's Report without reiterating information I had already provided.

March 2004

Late in March of 2004, I moved to Calgary. Mr. Chamberlin sent me a letter informing me that all relevant documents had been submitted to the Commission;

and that in the near future, I would be advised of the Commission's decision.

June 2004

Early in June 2004, I received a letter from the CHRC informing me that the Commission had dismissed my complaint. In part, it read as follows:

> *The Commission further decided, pursuant to paragraph 44 (3)(b) of the Canadian Human Rights Act, to dismiss the complaint because the evidence does not support the complainant's allegations that she was denied enrollment because of her colour, sex and family status.*

The letter further informed me that if I was not satisfied with the Commission's decision, I could contact the Federal Court, Trial Division, "to review the decision under subsection 18.1 of the *Federal Court Act.*"

I was ready to contact the Federal Court; however, after speaking with my lawyer, Kim Berndardt, and a man named Sylvester Iheanacho, who has wisdom far beyond his years, I decided to write about my experience rather than risk more years of carrying this burden. Kim said, "Deneace, if they [the RCMP] are forced to take you, they will make your life a living hell. Your idea to write is good, but get someone to check the use of names before publishing anything."

Employment with RCMP was no longer a desire for me. I had dealt with them long enough to know that I would not want to be associated with them. What I wanted was acknowledgment that what they did to me was wrong. Acknowledgment comes only with a conscience, and that stare I received from Inspector Lindsey Brine at the mediation showed me that he lacked a soul. Bob Joseph, in his total disregard for the truth, gave me a complete view of his lack of integrity.

Sylvester's advice was, "Honey, just forget it. They are White demons, and it's their world." I decided not to pursue it any further, but I wanted to know how the Commission made its decision. Other than the letter of rejection from the RCMP in December 2000, stating, in part, that, "This decision was made as a result of the findings of our background investigation into your overall suitability. Currently, there are a limited number of positions available and we have a sufficient number of applicants that are deemed to be more suitable," no one ever really told me why the RCMP rejected me: an issue that apparently did not concern the Canadian Human Rights Investigator when making her analysis and recommendations.

On June 9, 2004, I wrote to the Commission asking them to inform me of how they came to their decision. Lucie Viellette, Secretary to the Commission, called me and then wrote me a letter informing me that, *"The decision is rendered on the basis of the information submitted. There is no detailed analysis of how the Commission renders its decision. I am sorry I cannot assist you further in the matter."*

Perhaps if I were not so tired at the time from all the other life situations I was enduring, including my battle with Coca Cola Bottling Ltd., I would have continued the fight through the Federal Court. However, by not settling with the RCMP (as in the case with Coca Cola Bottling Ltd., which was forced to compensate me, albeit little), and by the CHRC disregarding the racism and discrimination that I endured, I felt free and obligated to tell anyone who would listen about the daily racism and discrimination that is perpetuated within Canadian society.

An Update on Institutionalized Racism

One can argue that the racism I faced with the Canadian Armed Forces, the Royal Canadian Mounted Police and the Canadian Human Rights Commission occurred some time ago, and is, therefore, no longer relevant. On this day, April 24, 2010, I would argue that institutionalized racism has become even more visible. I intend to write about my experiences with Correctional Service Canada and Canada Border Services, as well as my observation of the all-White, newly graduated Calgary Police Service recruits displayed on the local news. However, for now, I want to give the reader an idea of the insignificance of my case: of my attaining the RCMP's unrealistic requirements for membership and, on my achieving it, their changing the rules with impunity.

I am referencing the case of Barack Obama, because no other individual's case is as visible. It really is the ultimate case. That is, Barack Obama cleared the unrealistic bar set for him—by virtue of his skin colour—to become president of the United States of America . . . to sit in the chair reserved for *the president of the world.* Now that a Black man had surpassed the unrealistic goal set for obtaining the job, White racists are ready to change the rules.

On Tuesday, January 20, 2009, the world witnessed Barack Obama inaugurated as the 44th president of the United States of America; they watched the peaceful transfer of power from George W. Bush to Barack Hussein Obama. Yet, a year and four months later, racist White people refused to accept him as a legitimate president. What is their issue? The say his birth certificate was faked; he was not born in the United States of America.

A racist will use any baseless notion to rationalize his position. A classic case is one I observed on April 22, 2010. I watched Anderson Cooper, on his CNN news program, interview a racist. The racist was Arizona State Representative Cecil Ash, a Republican and a Birther. Although there is no official definition for Birthers, based on television interviews of members and Internet news articles, the common belief amongst members is this: *Birthers are a group of White people who refuse to accept that a Black man could be democratically elected president of the United States of America; and as a result, in efforts to discredit his presidential legitimacy, the Birthers are fueling the lie that President-Elect Barack Obama was not born in the United States of America; therefore, he is not eligible to be their president; in other words, only a White person is acceptable as their president.*

Like Rick Morris, a main gatekeeper in denying me access into the RCMP, Cecil Ash argued that he was not convinced Obama's birth certificate was legitimate because he had not *personally* investigated it. He held this belief despite the fact that an official copy of Obama's birth certificate had been posted on the Hawaii State Legislature's website since June 2007. The stupidity of his argument caused Anderson Cooper to use the analogy of the moon and cheese, saying, "There are some people who believe the moon is made out of cheese; but I don't believe you would have to *personally* investigate it [the moon] to say the moon is not made out of cheese." Ash agreed that he would say the moon is not made out of cheese, without having personally investigated it. He trusted the experts and accepted that the moon is not made of cheese; nonetheless, he did not accept the Hawaii state's approval of Obama's birth certificate.

Ash further argued that, contrary to the present law requiring the Secretary of State's approval of each presidential candidate's qualifications, before that candidate's name can be placed on the ballot in Arizona, a new law ought to be passed requiring every presidential candidate to have his or her birth certificate submitted for approval by the Arizona Legislature. As a result, Ash supported just such legislation (Republican) that the Arizona Legislature passed only days before this interview. In arguing for the legislation, he stated, "The purpose of the bill is to eliminate such controversies [about the birthplace of presidential candidates] in the future." He was adamant that he was not a racist and that his decision had nothing to do with Obama. This prompted Anderson Cooper to ask him, "Where was George Bush born?" To this, he thought before he answered, "I have no idea where George Bush was born." Anderson responded, "So that was not a concern for you when he was in office?" The racist actually answered, "The issue never came up." Anderson next asked, "What about Bill Clinton? Where was he born?" Again, the racist Ash shook his head and answered, "I have no idea." Anderson concluded, "So all of a sudden you are concerned, based on calls you are getting from your constituents—who are misinformed?" The racist—so deep in his mindset to use "the will of the people" as a cover—answered,

"Actually, I did not get any calls from my constituents until after the bill was passed."

I watched Cecil Ash keep a straight face during his reasoning. I listened to his reason for voting in favour of the bill, and all I could think of was "Rick Morris of the RCMP." It was the same shallow, contrived reasoning as Rick Morris' recommendation that the RCMP not hire me: my socio-economic status; my being a single mother; my having a problem with authority, due to the racist people I tried to fight against in the Canadian Armed Forces—ultimately, because I am Black. Likewise, Ash's reasoning for this new bill had its foundation in Barack Obama's being Black. The more he (Ash) argued with Anderson Cooper—a man as White as they come—the more racist his argument became. Nevertheless, laws will be passed, and Black people will be denied jobs as a result; but White people may as well admit the obvious, "It is because you are Black."

In the same vein, Latinos in America will continue to be racially profiled and harassed because of another bill the Arizona Legislature passed, giving the police the power to approach anyone who "looks suspicious" and require that person to produce citizenship identification. Again, the White legislators might as well verbalize what everyone knows: *"This is how we are going to keep Arizona a White state."* In the same vein, as other states follow Arizona's lead in determining who gets on the presidential ballot, the Arizona legislators were saying, *"This is how we ensure all future American presidents are White."*

For the simple reason that they know they can get away with it, Rick Morris, Cecil Ash, the Royal Canadian Mounted Police, the Canadian Armed Forces, the Canadian Human Rights Commission and all the other racists can blatantly practise racism.

In my case, my only recourse was to write. In the case of the Latinos, as a group they took to the streets to protest; but more important than protesting, they began registering to vote. I pray that time will not inure them to racism, so that they forget the importance of their votes and their voices. While there is currently a Black man sitting in the chair of the president of the United States, it is his duty to ensure the door does not get slammed shut on all the young Blacks aspiring to take a seat in the same chair one day.

Now that I have told the story that the need to tell kept me going through those days in April 2004, when I desired nothing more than death, if the reader is interested, I have written extensively about my life—starting in book number two, "My Thoughts, My Life: The Life of a Black Woman Living in a White World."

Appendices

Appendix 1

Appendix 1

ROYAL CANADIAN MOUNTED POLICE

CONCEPTUAL OVERVIEW

The Royal Canadian Mounted Police is, in terms of the Canadian police community, a large, multifaceted organization which is charged with a broad mandate encompassing federal, provincial, and municipal policing responsibilities. Organizationally, the Force is divided into thirteen divisions for operational purposes with divisional boundaries being established primarily on the basis of provincial/territorial boundaries. Divisions are further divided into sub-divisions, which are specific geographic boundaries, and these are, in turn, divided into detachment areas. The Commanding Officers of divisions are directly responsible to the Commissioner of the Force, and receive functional direction from Directorate Heads and Branch Officers in Ottawa, Ontario.

In order to fulfil its mandate, the Force employs approximately 15,915 regular members, 1,962 civilian members, and 3,734 public service employees.

Regular members perform duties for which a full working level of police training and experience is deemed essential. Typically, regular member duties are broad in nature, and include such police activities as the investigation of major and or "white collar" crime both nationally and internationally, the conduct of a wide range of investigations under the provisions of various federal and provincial statutes, and the provision of a variety of policing services under contract to provinces and municipalities throughout Canada.

Civilian members perform duties which are technical or scientific in nature, and are hired for a specific purpose which is directly related to a particular area of expertise, such as forensic chemistry, computer technology and electronics engineering.

Public Service Employees perform the remaining support functions associated with the operation of a large organization, such as, typing and clerical services, and other functions.

CAREER DEVELOPMENT

Regular members and civilian members are all members of the Force, hired pursuant to the provisions of the Royal Canadian Mounted Police Act, and therefore, for the purposes of discussing career development, should be viewed as separate and distinct from public service employees who generally aspire to careers within the greater context of the Federal Public Service. Career development must be viewed in terms of the categories of employees within the Force, hence the following commentary is offered in relation to those categories:

REGULAR MEMBERS

Cadets attend Depot Division at Regina, Saskatchewan where they receive extensive instruction, and participate in a wide variety of training exercises for six months, all of which is directed toward preparing them for the role of "police officer". Only upon successful completion of the training program at Depot Division would individuals be given peace officer status and become members of the R.C.M.P. Regular members are transferred to divisions where they are posted to meet the human resource needs of those divisions. In the posting process, although organizational needs take precedence, the needs and aspirations of individual members, as well as any special qualifications or attributes they may possess are given due consideration.

As regular member constables gain experience and years of service, they are permitted to compete for promotional positions within the rank structure of the Force, which is, in ascending order:

- Constable
- Corporal
- Sergeant
- Staff Sergeant
- Corps Sergeant Major
- Inspector
- Superintendent
- Chief Superintendent
- Assistant Commissioner
- Deputy Commissioner
- Commissioner

In pursuing their careers through the rank structure, members are provided training which is, by and large, job-specific in nature, and given on a "need" basis. The Force is a strong proponent of higher education, hence members may also pursue courses at universities, community colleges, and technical institutes, on their own time, but funded by ourorganization (i.e. tuition fees are generally reimbursed).

CIVILIAN MEMBERS

Career development within the civilian member cadre of the Force is designed in terms of the "specialty" for which they are hired (i.e. serologist, chemist, computer scientist and mechanical technologist), hence it is somewhat narrow in scope.

GENERAL RECRUITMENT AND SPECIAL PROGRAMS

In terms of recruitment, the Force is attempting to increase the participation of women, visible minorities, aboriginal people (Canadian Indians and Inuit) and at the same time, strive to engage university graduates and bilingual persons. Additionally, the Force is seeking to employ more persons with disabilities in non-peace officer roles. Long range targets have been set for employment of women (20%), visible minorities (6.3%) and aboriginal peoples (5%).

These percentages are not fixed and will be adjusted as needs dictate. Present figures show that within the Force, there are 9.9% women, 1.85% visible minorities and 3.43% aboriginal peoples.

Recruitment materials (poster, pamphlets) have been revised to depict women, visible minorities and aboriginals as equal participants within the Force to encourage their interest in becoming members. Initial reaction to the Force's revised recruitment initiatives has been positive.

In 1988, the Commissioner's Advisory Committees on Visible Minorities and Aboriginal Peoples were established. They are intended to provide minority and aboriginal representatives with a vehicle through which they can be heard on issues respecting recruiting, hiring and promotional matters.

Training programs and articles for internal publication are under review and a Multicultural Advisor has been appointed to monitor Force activities and initiatives, and to provide advice to senior management with respect to multicultural issues.

Produced by: Staffing & Personnel Branch (94-02)
Revised by: "O" Division Recruiting (96-03)

ROYAL CANADIAN MOUNTED POLICE

BASIC QUALIFICATIONS

NATIONALITY:	Canadian citizenship
LANGUAGE:	Proficient in either of Canada's offical languages - English or French
AGE:	19 years of age at time of engagement
EDUCATION:	Grade 12 or equivalence from a Canadian educational institution
DRIVER'S LICENCE:	Valid Canadian driver's licence
HEALTH:	Able to meet specific medical and physical requirements * including visual acuity and hearing standards
TRAITS:	Be of good character

NOTE: A selected candidate will be enrolled as a cadet. Only upon successful completion of the Cadet Training Program will the cadet be appointed as a Regular Member and designated as a peace officer.

* Successfully complete the Physical Abilities Requirement Evaluation (P.A.R.E.

SALARY AND BENEFITS - REGULAR MEMBERS

ENGAGEMENT LEVEL	-	$31,172
FIRST LEVEL	-	$37,129
SECOND LEVEL	-	$40,119
THIRD LEVEL	-	$44,253
FOURTH LEVEL	-	$47,385
FIFTH LEVEL	-	$50,508

FULL MEDICAL AND DENTAL PLANS

GROUP LIFE INSURANCE

PENSION PLAN

20 YEARS SERVICE, CAN RETIRE WITH PENALTY
25 YEARS, FULL PENSION
35 YEARS, MAXIMUM PENSION

CLOTHING ALLOWANCE FOR PLAIN CLOTHES DUTIES

RELOCATIONS PAID BY THE FORCE

ANNUAL VACATION LEAVE	0-5 YEARS -	15 DAYS
	5-10 YEARS -	20 DAYS
	10 + YEARS	25 DAYS

MATERNITY/ADOPTION/PATERNITY LEAVE

LEAVE WITH AND/OR WITHOUT PAY

NOTE: The above salary and benefits do not apply to a Cadet undergoing training at Depot Division or the Cadet Official Language Training Program. During basic training, an allowance will be paid.

ROYAL CANADIAN MOUNTED POLICE

STEPS TO FOLLOW AS AN APPLICANT

1. YOU MUST ATTEND AN INFORMATION SESSION. CONTACT YOUR NEAREST R.C.M.P. DETACHMENT.

2. WRITTEN EXAMINATION

3. PHYSICAL ABILITIES REQUIREMENT EVALUATION (PARE)

4. IF YOU PASS THE WRITTEN EXAMINATION AND ARE SELECTED FOR FURTHER PROCESSING, AND APPLICATION PACKAGE WILL BE FORWARDED TO YOU. THE APPLICATION PACKAGE IS TO BE COMPLETED AND RETURNED WITHIN 10 DAYS.

5. INTERVIEW (SUITABILITY AND SECURITY)

6. LANGUAGE TEST (SECOND LANGUAGE EVALUATION) *

7. BACKGROUND INVESTIGATION

8. MEDICAL EXAMINATION

9. SELECTION AND ENROLMENT

* SUBJECT TO POSITIONS BEING AVAILABLE IN THE CADET OFFICIAL LANGUAGE TRAINING PROGRAM. A LANGUAGE TEST IS ALSO CONDUCTED TO DETERMINE WHETHER OR NOT A CANDIDATE IS BILINGUAL.

ROYAL CANADIAN MOUNTED POLICE

APPLICATION PROCESS FOR REGULAR MEMBER CONSTABLE

1. In order to become a Regular Member Constable you must successfully complete all requirements of the RCMP Cadet Training Program. Cadets undergo extensive academic and physical training for six months at Depot Division in Regina, Saskatchewan. During training, Cadets are sponsored civilian students and they receive a net weekly training allowance of approximately $210.00 before income tax and other deductions. Cadets do not receive any benefits during training. Upon graduation from Depot Division, a Cadet is engaged as a Regular Member Constable with salary and benefits.

2. To apply for a Regular Member Constable position, you must meet all of the following basic qualifications:

- be a Canadian citizen
- be at least 18 years of age
- have successfully completed Grade 12 or equivalent from a Canadian educational institution
- have a valid Canadian driver's licence
- be proficient in either English or French

In addition to the above, you must:

- be of good character
- be able to meet specific physical and medical requirements including visual acuity and hearing standards
- be willing to relocate anywhere in Canada

3. If you meet the basic qualifications, contact your local RCMP Detachment and make arrangements to attend an information session. This session will assist you in determining your suitability for police officer duties and you will have the opportunity to view the Physical Abilities Requirement Evaluation (PARE) video and be provided with handout material which includes details of our minimum vision standards.

4. If you feel that you are suitable, contact your local RCMP Detachment to schedule a date to write the RCMP Recruit Selection Test (RRST). (See Appendix "A"). You are to be provided with the RRST Study Guide at least 24 hours before you write the RRST. The Study Guide must be returned at the time that you write the RRST. When you attend to write the RRST you must produce:

- proof of Canadian citizenship (birth certificate, passport etc.)
- a valid Canadian driver's licence
- proof of education

.../2

5. The RRST totals 145 points and the pass mark is 84. You will receive formal notificatio of your test results, usually within 6 to 8 weeks. Your file will be closed if you do not obtai a pass mark and you will not be eligible to re-apply and re-write the RRST until one full yea has elapsed from the date you previously wrote. If you pass the RRST, your name will b placed on an Initial Ranked List (IRL) according to your RRST score, where you will compet for selection to the interview stage. All applicants are allowed to compete in tw consecutive selections. If you are selected for an interview, a letter with a selection packag consisting of numerous forms will be sent to you. At this stage, if you do not have a vali PARE Certificate you must make immediate arrangements to take the PARE test. (Se paragraph 6). YOU WILL NOT BE INTERVIEWED WITHOUT A VALID PARE CERTIFICATE If you are not able to produce a PARE Certificate at the time of your interview, you application will be placed into the next cycle where you will be subject to furthe competition with new applicants entering the process. If you are selected a second time fo an interview and you cannot pass the PARE, your file will be closed due to unsuitability an you will not be eligible to re-apply for two years.

6. CONTACT YOUR NEAREST PARE TEST SITE TO ARRANGE FOR TESTING. THE PAR CERTIFICATE IS VALID FOR 6 MONTHS. (See Appendix "B"). You must obtain medica clearance from a physician in order to take the PARE test. Some PARE sites administer test once per month or less frequently and you may not be able to be tested on short notic YOU ARE RESPONSIBLE FOR WHEN AND WHERE YOU CHOOSE TO TAKE THE PAR TEST AND YOU ARE RESPONSIBLE FOR THE FEE OF APPROXIMATELY $40.00 PLUS TA EACH TIME YOU TAKE THE PARE TEST. You are also responsible for any expense associated to PARE Certification, including fees charged by your physician to obtain medic clearance. IT IS IMPORTANT TO BE IN GOOD PHYSICAL CONDITION AT THE ONSE OF YOUR APPLICATION AND TO MAINTAIN THIS FITNESS LEVEL FOR THE DURATIO OF THE APPLICATION PROCESS. If you are considering a physical fitness programme, yo should concentrate on upper body strength and cardio-vascular conditioning.

7. A SELECTION PACKAGE WILL ONLY BE SENT TO APPLICANTS WHO ARE SELECTE FOR AN INTERVIEW. Read all instructions carefully and complete and return all form within the specified time period. Failure to complete the forms accurately will result i delays and could jeopardize your application.

8. Selected applicants are interviewed according to the Applicant Interview Guide (AIG which is a structured method of evaluation. Applicants must meet all criteria of the AIG i order to be recommended for further processing. Recommended applicants then have the names placed on the Post Interview Ranked List (PIRL) where they are subject to furthe competition.

.../3

Your combined RRST and AIG scores determine your standing on the PIRL. Selected applicants will be sent a Conditional Offer of Enrolment to acknowledge and return. Their file will then be forwarded for a background investigation to confirm their suitability. Applicants must satisfy all requirements specified in the Conditional Offer of Enrolment in order to be enrolled into the Cadet Training Program. APPLICANTS WILL BE REQUIRED TO SIGN A PRE-EMPLOYMENT CADET TRAINING AGREEMENT IMMEDIATELY PRIOR TO PROCEEDING TO DEPOT DIVISION IN REGINA. AT THAT TIME, PROOF OF THE FOLLOWING ADDITIONAL QUALIFICATIONS MUST BE PROVIDED:

- a valid First Aid Certificate issued by *St. John's Ambulance only*
- a valid Level "C" Cardio-Pulmonary Resuscitation (CPR) Certificate issued by the *Heart & Stroke Foundation or by St. John's Ambulance*
- keyboarding/typewriting skills at a minimum of 18 w.p.m. without any errors

YOU ARE RESPONSIBLE FOR ALL EXPENSES INCURRED IN OBTAINING THE ABOVE. TO DEFRAY UNNECESSARY COSTS, YOU SHOULD NOT SEEK TO OBTAIN THESE QUALIFICATIONS UNLESS YOU ARE SENT A "CONDITIONAL OFFER OF ENROLMENT".

9. If your PARE Certificate remains valid at the final stage of processing, medical examinations with RCMP designated physicians will then be scheduled. The cost for the final medical examinations will be paid for by the RCMP. If your PARE Certificate has expired, a final PARE test will be scheduled and paid for by the RCMP.

10. The RCMP endorses employment equity and continues to seek qualified visible minorities, females and aboriginals. Caucasian males continue to dominate the number of applications in "O" Division (Ontario) and the RCMP enrols those deemed suitable in fair and equitable proportions to other specified groups. All applicants must meet all standards and acceptance into the Cadet Training Program is subject to availability of positions. All applicants are afforded the same priority and method of processing and once an applicant is selected to proceed to the interview stage, the average processing time is approximately 4 months.

ROYAL CANADIAN MOUNTED POLICE

VISION REQUIREMENTS

In order to be engaged as a Regular Member Constable, Cadet applicants who wear corrective lenses MUST meet both of the following minimum vision standards:

1) **UNCORRECTED (WITHOUT EYEWEAR & WITHOUT SQUINTING):**

6/18 (20/60) in each eye OR
6/12 (20/40) in one eye and
UP TO 6/30 (20/100) in the other

2) **CORRECTED (WITH EYEWEAR):**

6/6 (20/20) in one eye and
UP TO 6/9 (20/30) in the other

3) **COLOUR VISION:**

Cadet applicants shall be tested by using any standardized Pseudo-Isochromatic plates (Ishihara, A-O, HRR, Dvorine). An applicant who correctly identifies all patterns presented in such tests will be considered colour-vision "normal". If difficulties are encountered with the tests, the applicant will be further evaluated with such devices as the Farnsworth D-15 discs. Applicants who demonstrate a colour-vision deficiency on the Farnsworth discs will NOT be considered as acceptable for the R.C.M.P.

4) The surgical procedure of Radial Keratotomy (both surgical and laser) is recognized as an acceptable measure to meet the visual acuity standards provided the following conditions are met:

- i) stable condition must be confirmed one (1) year after surgery.
- ii) side effects from the operation such as glare, contrast sensitivity and visual field defects must be absent.
- iii) all cases must be evaluated by the Health Services Officer (HSO) prior to further processing of applicants.

NOTE: Orthokeratology has not been proven to be a permanent form of corrective measure and therefore, it is NOT an accepted procedure to meet the visual standards.
FAILURE TO MEET ANY OF THE ABOVE CONDITIONS WILL BE CAUSE FOR REJECTION.
Revised: "O" Division Recruiting (96-03)

APPENDIX "A"

REGULAR MEMBER CONSTABLE

The RCMP Recruit Selection Test (RRST) consists of the following categories:

1. Observation
2. Memory
3. English Composition (grammar, spelling, vocabulary)
4. Logic
5. Judgement
6. Basic Computation
7. Perseverance

The number of positions available and your RRST score determine if you are selected to proceed to the next stage in the application process. This consists of a lengthy structured interview where you are evaluated in the following categories:

1. Knowledge/Abilities
2. Motivation/Conscientiousness
3. Personal Effectiveness
4. Interpersonal Skills
5. Common Sense/Judgement
6. Leadership Skills
7. Integrity/Honesty/Impartiality
8. Sensitivity/Acceptance
9. Adaptability/Flexibility
10. Oral Communication Skills

Revised: "O" Division Recruiting (96-11)

APPENDIX "B"

PHYSICAL ABILITIES REQUIREMENT EVALUATION (PARE)

The PARE is a job related physical ability test which is a condition of employment as a Regular Member with the RCMP.

A person cannot take the PARE test without first obtaining medical clearance. The "Physical Activity Readiness - Medical Clearance Form" is completed by a Physician and must be presented at the time of PARE testing. The following excerpts from the above form provide general information about the PARE test:

" PARE is designed to simulate a critical incident where a police officer chases, controls and apprehends a suspect. The test was developed by exercise scientists and is based on extensive research, including a thorough job analysis ".

" PARE is a circuit-type test where the applicant must first run six laps of an obstacle course - a distance of about 350 metres. During this run, the applicant must climb stairs, turn sharply left and right, jump over low obstacles and vault over a three foot rail and fall alternately on the back or stomach. After negotiating the six lap course, the applicant must first pull and then push a 70 pound (32 Kg) weight for six repetitions. Four controlled falls must be executed between the push and pull activity. This ends the timed portion of the test. The applicant is allowed a maximum of 4 minutes and 45 seconds to complete this phase of the PARE. Finally, the applicant must lift and carry an 80 pound (45 Kg) weight for 15 metres. A person failing any one of the items fails the overall test" .

" During the pull and push activities, the applicant grasps a large rope simulating the size of a wrist, to which a 70 pound (32 Kg) weight is attached. The applicant then pulls the weight off the floor and shuffles through an arc with a radius of 1 to 2 metres, 6 times, always keeping the weight off the floor. This activity requires upper body strength and muscular endurance. Between the pull and push activity, the applicant must fall to the floor and stand up 4 times. This activity demands power, coordination and flexibility in the trunk and leg areas. Immediately after completing the fourth fall, the applicant starts the push activity. The applicant must push the 70 pound (32 Kg) weight off the floor, again shuffling 6 times in a radius of 1 to 2 metres. The weight must be kept off the floor at all times ".

THE PARE VIDEO DEMONSTRATES THIS TEST. POTENTIAL APPLICANTS CAN VIEW THIS VIDEO AT THE GENERAL INFORMATION SESSION.

Revised: "O" Division Recruiting (96-11)

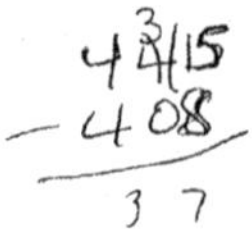

PHYSICAL ABILITIES REQUIREMENT EVALUATION (PARE)

GUIDELINES FOR APPLICANTS

As an applicant for employment in the Royal Canadian Mounted Police you will undergo a number of screening tests to help determine your suitability for police work. One of these tests, the Physical Abilities Requirement Evaluation or PARE, will be administered on several occasions to assess your capacity to meet the physical demands typically encountered in police duties.

These guidelines are provided to help you prepare for taking the PARE. Please read them so that you will have a clearer understanding of why your PARE performance is an important selection criterion as well as what you can do to improve your chances of meeting the selection standard.

WHAT IS THE PARE?

The PARE is a physical abilities test that measures the capacity to perform physical tasks often encountered in police work, namely:

* *walking*
* *running*
* *jumping*
* *vaulting*
* *carrying*
* *pushing*
* *pulling*
* *climbing (stairs, hills)*
* *lifting*

The test simulates a scenario where a police officer must:

* *get to the site of a problem or incident,*
* *physically resolve the problem, and*
* *remove a person or material from the problem site.*

These three components are represented in the PARE in the form of a six-lap obstacle course, a pushing and pulling task and the carrying of a 36 kilogram (80 pound) torso bag over a 15 meter distance.

PHYSICAL ABILITIES REQUIREMENT EVALUATION (PARE)

WHAT IS THE PARE STANDARD?

Applicants must complete the obstacle course and the pushing and pulling task within a 4 minute and 45 second time period to be eligible for selection. To graduate from the RCMP Depot Division, the minimum PARE Standard will be lowered to 4 minutes.

The torso bag carry requires you to execute a controlled carry of the bag without resting or setting it down over the 15 meter distance. This will be untimed and scored on a PASS/NO PASS basis. To graduate from Depot Division, the torso bag weight will increase from 36 kg (80 lbs.) to 45.5 kg (100 lbs.).

WHAT IS THE PARE LIKE?

The four stations of the PARE are illustrated in the diagram at Appendix "A". The test begins with a six lap obstacle course that involves running and direction changes; jumping across a six foot distance; ascending and descending steps; jumping over knee high obstacles; vaulting over a three foot barrier; and falling to one's front and back and getting back up.

The second and third stations involve pushing and pulling tasks and requires that a 32 kg (70 lb) weight, (36.4 kg or 80 lb. for Depot graduates) be pushed or pulled through six, 180 degree arcs without it dropping. Between the push and pull tasks, four controlled falls must be performed - two to your front and two to your back. The fourth and final station - the torso bag carry is then attempted after a 30 second rest.

PREPARING TO TAKE THE PARE

There are several administrative requirements that must be met before you can take the PARE at a PARE Testing Centre.

1. Obtain the location of the nearest PARE Testing Centre from your recruiting office.

2. You must have a Medical Clearance Form signed and dated by a physician. This clearance is valid for six months unless there has been a known change in your medical status.

PHYSICAL ABILITIES REQUIREMENT EVALUATION (PARE)

3. You must complete an Informed Consent form at the test site.

4. You must pay a fee of approximately $45.00 for your first PARE. If the PARE standard is met, the cost for subsequent PARE tests will be paid by the RCMP. If the PARE standard is not met on the first occasion, the cost of subsequent tests will be your responsibility until the standard is met.

In addition to the above, you are encouraged to strive for an above average level of fitness prior to taking the PARE. As PARE is physically demanding, you should be able to answer yes to the following six statements before presenting yourself for testing:

YES	NO	
___	___	I am able to perform at least five continuous minutes of moderately vigorous physical activity without feeling exhausted or over-stressed
___	___	I can lift and carry an 80 lb. weight with control over a distance of 50 feet (15 meters)
___	___	I can broad jump at least 6 feet (2 meters)
___	___	I can perform 15 - 20 push-ups (full length, pivoting from the toes) without stopping
___	___	I can vault (using my hands and feet for assistance) over a 3 foot (1 meter) high barrier
___	___	I participate in moderate to vigorous physical acitivity at least two to three times a week

1 1/2 mile in 12 min.

While answering "yes" or "no" to any of these statements will not predict your success or failure on the PARE, it will help you to decide whether some pre-PARE conditioning should be undertaken. If you are doubtful about your ability at this point, consider a minimum three to six week conditioning program before scheduling your PARE. If you need assistance, please consult with a physical activity professional in your community for sensible training tips and guidance.

TIPS FOR TAKING THE PARE

The following suggestions may be helpful:

1. Wear comfortable activity clothing that will not restrict your freedom to move or "weigh you down". Wear running shoes with soles that grip well so that slippage on the push and pull task is minimized.

2. Warm-up for the PARE by doing five to ten minutes of stretching and other large muscle activity.

3. Familiarize yourself with the apparatus used for the PARE. Experiment with the jump and vault obstacles as well as the push and pull station. Do your learning before the test.

4. Pace yourself. A moderate jogging speed is adequate for a six-lap obstacle course. Avoid going too fast. A pace of 25 seconds per lap is adequate.

5. Think positive. PARE is demanding, but it is reasonable. Most people will be tired, BUT NOT EXHAUSTED, at the end of the test. Put yourself in a positive state of mind that will give you the inner motivation to be successful.

BEYOND PARE: THE BIGGER PICTURE

Because physical ability to meet the demands of police work is ongoing, you will be required to meet the PARE standard throughout your career with the RCMP.

Although current members of the RCMP do not have to meet the PARE standard, they will be exposed to the PARE and other health promotion efforts designed to maintain or enhance their "fitness for work".

The RCMP believes in employing fit and able officers. Achieving and maintaining the PARE standard reflects your personal fitness and commitment to personal health management. Your health and fitness is a valuable resource in both your personal life as well as your future career as a member of the RCMP.

GOOD LUCK ON THE PARE !

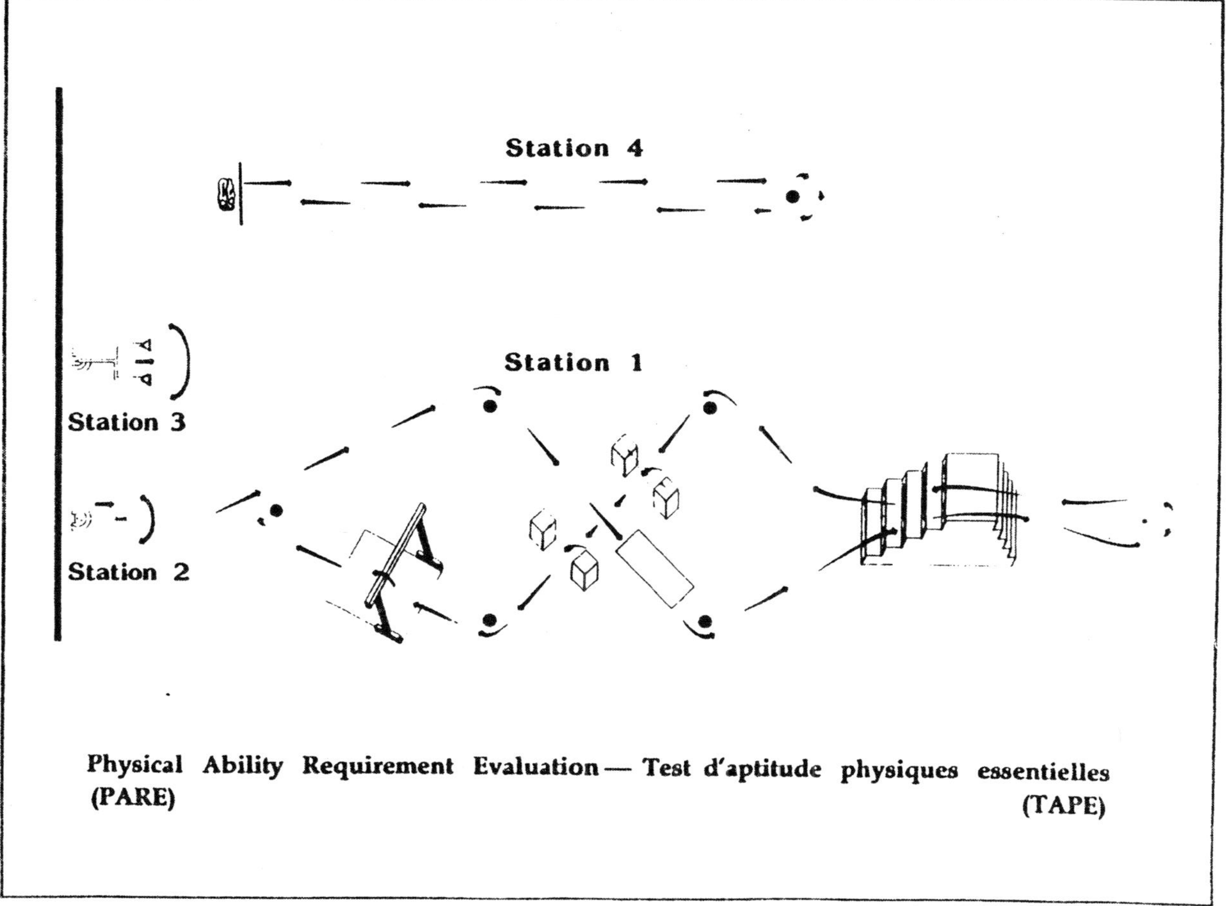
Station 4
Station 3
Station 1
Station 2
Physical Ability Requirement Evaluation — Test d'aptitude physiques essentielles
(PARE)
(TAPE)

FIGURE 1

Appendix 2

Response to the RCMP's Discriminatory Practises

Response to Investigator's Comments
I means Investigator's Comments (Rick Morris)
R means my Response

I: Green has no long-term employment.

R: I graduated from university in 1996, and I started working in 1995—a year before I graduated. Most companies, particularly government agencies, are hiring only on contract. Besides, long-term employment is not a criterion for the position of police constable.

I: She demonstrates that she is a project kind of employee who bores easily as suggested by source (J).

R: I admit that if I am not challenged, I get bored easily; police work is very challenging.

I: Green's education should have enabled her to get a better paying job in the last two years.

R: Money has never been my primary objective for working, and I hope I never get to that stage. Is Mr. Morris admitting that I really became employable within the last two years? Please note that I applied to the RCMP more than two years before this statement was written. Had the RCMP dealt with my application in a timely manner (approximately eight months), I would have been earning more money. As a new graduate without work experience, I found it virtually impossible to get employment in my field of study. Therefore, I had to take customer service jobs until better came along. Better offers did come along; however, Karen Cleary of the RCMP told me that if I left the country, "Your file will be closed. We need to be able to reach you." As a result, I rejected multiple teaching opportunities in Japan and South Korea. In addition, most of the people who are currently working in call centres as customer service representatives are university graduates and postgraduates. Some are lawyers, accountants and teachers: this is a reflection of the Canadian labour market.

Some people get hired onto police forces directly off welfare.

Some people change jobs twelve times in one year before getting hired as a police officer—example, the husband of the woman who wrote the book, Cops Don't Cry.

Long-term employment is not a criterion for employment as an RCMP officer: Appendix 8, Basic Qualifications.

I: It should be noted that at the time of the undated security interview, Green had assets of $10, 000 and liability from eye surgery of $4,400. This amount of savings would have paid over half of the debt that Green escaped from. I see this bankruptcy as an ethical problem of escaping her educational debts and still ending up with her educational credentials.

R: I cannot predict what will happen tomorrow, moreover six months from now. I declared bankruptcy in January 1997. I secured paid employment in seven months later, after doing five volunteer jobs to gain work experience. If Mr. Morris and the reader can recall, there was an economic recession in 1997. Graduates were declaring bankruptcy at an unprecedented rate. Moreover, my intention was to consolidate my loans. My Trustee in Bankruptcy advised me that I was not able to consolidate my loans because I was bankrupt. Mr. Morris, himself, stated that, "Green's income at the time in the telemarketing jobs could not pay off the bills." Please see Appendix 10. My bills were primarily my student loan.

Regarding my eye surgery, in order to be considered for employment with the RCMP, it is necessary to meet a specific vision standard. Without eye surgery, I would not have been eligible to apply for a position as a police officer. Appendix 8B, Vision requirements. I had eye surgery to become employable.

I: Now just two short years later, she has accumulated personal assets of $10,000. I think this confirms an ethical problem.

R: Here, Mr. Morris ridicules me for being able to save $10,000 in "two short years." In Appendix 11, Mr. Morris states, "Green's bankruptcy demonstrates that she is not responsible with money." Furthermore, he writes about my being able to get better paying jobs. As the reader can decipher, I must have been extremely responsible with money to be able to save $10,000 out of my "low paying jobs." Apparently Mr. Morris interprets the situation to suit his purpose. If my intentions were to not repay my student loan, I would have borrowed much more money and then declare bankruptcy. I took minimal amounts of student loans because I intended to pay back every cent.

I: Green is still living in subsidized housing with her daughter who moved back in. How will she survive without income during the RCMP training period?

R: Based on Mr. Morris' statement regarding my $10,000 in savings and my living in subsidized housing, income during the training period should not be an issue. Additionally, the RCMP provides a loan program for its candidates.

I see Mr. Morris' statement as discrimination in the purest sense, discrimination based on my socio-economic status: my living in subsidized housing and being a single mother. According to the Canadian Human Rights Commission Act: "It is against the law for an employer or provider of service that falls within the federal jurisdiction to make unlawful distinctions based on the following grounds: race, marital status...family status." Race will be discussed when I discuss the input of the Canadian Armed Forces.
Regarding my marital status, it is clear that Mr. Morris is penalizing me for being a mother, "single mother." Is it legal for the RCMP to penalize me for not having a husband to support me while I am in basic training? Is it legal for the RCMP to penalize me for being a mother? Let me point out that the child in question is nineteen years old and has a job. With subsidized housing, she would have been able to support herself while I was in basic training. How are people to break their cycle of poverty when their state of poverty prevents them from getting a job for which they qualify? Clearly Mr. Morris is using my marital status, my family status, and my economic status to deny me a job. Middle class people would not have this problem.

I: Will she quit the RCMP after a short period of time as another lark?

R: After I graduated from university, my first job of substance was with the Ontario Network of Employment Skills Training Projects (ONESTEP). I was with that organization for more than a year, and I most likely would still be working there if my position had not become redundant due to restructuring.

I have had an interest in policing since 1988. My studies in law enforcement, sociology and political science are evidence that I have a strong interest in policing. Furthermore, Mr. Morris blames me for leaving what he considers undesirable jobs, "better paying employment." Now, it seems he is saying I should have stayed in those jobs.

I: There is not indication of her ability to sustain employment for longer than two years.
R: Mr. Morris, himself, implied that I really became gainfully employed within the last two years: "Green's education should have enabled her to get better paying employment in the last two years." I am not ashamed of working as a customer service representative. A lot of good, educated people work in call centres. If they were not educated, they would not have been hired.

I: Green has proved that she can learn but seems to have no ability to apply what she has learned.

R: I find this statement personally and racially offensive, considering that the premise of slavery in America was black people represented only three-fifth of a human being. In her book, How to Be (page 158), Harriette Cole reminds us, "People fought against the premise of slavery that eventually stated in the Constitution that our ancestors represent only three-fifth of a man." Animals can be trained to do certain tricks; however, animals cannot train anyone. I find it racially offensive for anyone to say, "She can learn but seems to have no ability to apply what she learned." Even animals can do that. Mr. Morris' statement echoes the treatment I received in the Canadian Armed Forces. It is people like Mr. Morris who chose not to hire me without work experience. He is perpetuating the statement I often hear: "You have a lot of education, but no work experience." How am I to get work experience if no one hires me? In order to apply what I have learned, I need to first obtain a job in my field of training.

I: Leaving her two children off her 330-60 form leaves much to ponder. Why were they not mentioned?

R: My children's birth certificates were submitted along with both of my applications; therefore, this should not be an issue. How could I hide my children? Why would I hide them?

I: Green's exposure to military discipline did not seem to be a good situation for her. She appeared not to be suited to the military and job surroundings that had an expectation to perform like everyone else does to make the team work.

R: I must agree with Mr. Morris that the military was not a good experience for me. The military in and of itself is not a bad experience. However, the racism that I experienced in the military is not something I will soon forget. Never have I seen such blatant expression of discrimination against black people. For example, a white sergeant (Mahood) yelling at a black private (Dalel) that she should have hair like his: while stroking his hair, during inspection drill, the man said, "You should have hair like mine." Is this racism? What makes his hair better than hers? This same private was referred to as a monkey by another private (Stone). Nothing was done to support Dalel; instead, she was attacked for taking offence to the remark. Master Corporal Gardner frequently reminded the unit that they were not black guys down in the Caribbean; therefore, they should be careful not to tip their barrettes to the side of their heads. Sergeant Chernaiwski would often say to me, especially after giving me an unnecessary chit, "It is not easy being green." Considering that I have never seen a green person, I interpreted the statement as it was intended, "It is not easy being black."

Incidentally, shortly after basic training, Private Dalel left the army to attend medical school. She informed me that I kept her going in the army; whenever things were going rough, she would "Look at Green and keep going." If this is not an expression of my leadership skills, I do not know what is.

I: Not being able to take discipline and blaming discrimination against blacks as the reason she was being disciplined shows that she cannot stand up and take responsibility for her own actions.

R: Contrary to Mr. Morris' statement, I do take responsibility for my actions. The letter dated October 25, 1998 (Appendix 4), shows that I do accept responsibility for my actions. I have no problem taking my share of responsibility for the bullet that was accidentally fired. My issue is, four people misfired: two black women, one white male, and one Asian male. Why were only the two black people charged? Master Corporal Skerrett explained to Mr. Morris that I was not upset about the charge. I was unsettled because four people misfired and two went on with their lives as though nothing happened while two were brought up on charges. Oddly enough, during SHARP (sexual harassment) training, I later observed a video on sexual harassment within the military that duplicated the exact scenario of my misfire: a male soldier berated a female soldier while she was aiming at her target; she missed the target. In my case, I misfired. Therefore, the military is well aware of the effects of harassment. In the video, the person being harassed was a white female. She could have brought charges on the grounds that she is a female. I am a black female. I chose to interpret the discrimination of two people of four being charged as discrimination against blacks. Is it a coincidence? It is highly unlikely.

In the words of Colonel Sutherland (the Commanding Officer replaced by Lieutenant Colonel Von Bulow), "I commend you for seeing this through. Some people would drop their gear and walk away, but you chose to stay through the trial. For that you should be commended." How is that for standing up and taking responsibility for my actions? Additionally, Captain Chamberlinlain told Captain Pamela Evelyn that he commends me for addressing the situation. In fact, Captain Chaimberlain told Captain Pamela Evelyn, "It is people like her we need in the army."

I: Green was unsuited for the military. I believe she will ultimately be found equally unsuitable by the Force. I strongly feel that Green would be an unsuitable candidate to the RCMP.

R: Mr. Morris is further perpetuating the racism that I faced in the army. Master Corporal Bernard Skerrett told him that I was not angry at the charges themselves, but of the situation surrounding the charges. Captain

Pamela Evelyn called Constable Bob Joseph to explain her knowledge of the situation; she offered to meet with him to discuss the matter. He agreed to meet with her, but never did. I gave Joseph names of people in the army who would attest to the racism that I faced. Therefore, Mr. Morris and other members of the RCMP are fully aware that the racism I faced was not a figment of my imagination. Yet, they choose to ignore the racism and blame me for expressing my disdain of the discrimination the other blacks and I faced in the military. Ultimately, the RCMP denied me a job based on the lies that they knowing accepted from self-serving members of the army. All of my law enforcement professors recommended me for the position of police constable. Please see Appendix 12. These professors taught me for two years, and they are current police officers, retired police officers or lawyers—some of them are former RCMP officers. Mr. Morris and other members of the RCMP gave no thought to their recommendations. Who is better able to judge my abilities a police officer, a few power hungry young (age 21, some younger) people in the army or seasoned police officers? My law enforcement studies directly parallel policing college and police work. There is no question that I will do well in a policing environment. The military is not the same as police work. Moreover, military service is not a requirement for being a RCMP officer.

At the time I wrote the letter dated September 25, 1999, Appendix A, to Colonel Von Bulow, I stated that the charges were not dismissed for my benefit; they were dismissed for the benefit of Sergeant Michaud and other members of the army. I later found out that Sergeant Michaud was being processed for the Metropolitan Police Force. Therefore, the Colonel and Michaud did not want the record of discrimination on Michaud's file.

It is imperative to note that not all investigating RCMP officers share Mr. Morris' degrading attitude towards me. In the words of the original investigating officer, M. J. Carey, "Throughout the course of this investigation, nothing of a derogatory nature surfaced on the applicant. The writer had an opportunity to conduct an employment check on behalf of Milton Detaclent." Please see Appendix 13. At this point, I believe my file was returned to the RCMP's recruiting department without anyone in the Canadian Armed Forces being interviewed. If my service in the military were of primary importance to the RCMP, would the military not be one of the first sources to check? Instead, it was checked as an afterthought: almost one year after the other employers.

Additionally, another RCMP officer who disagrees with Mr. Morris is Sergeant PMP Ohare. He writes, "It should be noted that all the associates interviewed support the applicant and feel that she will be an asset to the RCMP if hired." Please see Appendix 14.

Conclusion

In conclusion, I am bringing my case to the Canadian Human Rights Commission because I have been discriminated against based on my race, my socio-economic status, and my family status.

I am requesting permission to bring the Canadian Armed Forces to the attention of the Canadian Human Rights Commission because their racist discrimination, libel and slander directly affected my gaining employment with the RCMP. My last official contact with the military was May 2000 when I was mailed my honourable discharge certificate. However, it was in September 2000 that members of the military purposely gave the RCMP false information about me. As a result, I am requesting that the Canadian Human Rights Commission grant me an extension of the one year time limit to take action. I would like this situation to be dealt with so that it does not further destroy my future.

The RCMP discriminated against me in the following ways:

- socio-economic status, that is, subsidizes housing and employment as a customer service representative (low-paying job);
- being a single mother;
- racism through the military;
- bankruptcy;
- the RCMP took three times the average length of time to process my application.

The RCMP's literature does not state that I need to be financially secured to become a member. It does not state that I need to be married. It does not state that I cannot be a single mother. The RCMP encourages minorities to apply and then discriminates against them based on race. If I had known that I had to be a wealthy minority, I would have waited until I was financially secured and married. The courts and my creditors have forgiven me for my bankruptcy, why cannot the RCMP? How many people have they hired who have declared bankruptcy? The RCMP knew of my bankruptcy situation since October 1999, why wait one year (November 2000) to make such an issue of it? Why make me a job offer knowing about my bankruptcy and then reject me based on it? Please see Appendix 2.

Like the RCMP, the Canadian Armed Forces discriminated against me in the following ways:

- race;
- gender;
- libel;
- slander.

The Canadian Human Rights Act states the following:

Every individual should have an equal opportunity with other individuals to make for him or herself the life that he or she is able and wishes to have, consistent with his or her duties and obligations as a member of society.
I believe the RCMP and the Canadian Armed Forces through discrimination have prevented me from having the life that I am able and wish to have, and for those reasons, I am bringing my situation to the knowledge of the Canadian Human Rights Commission.

Appendix 3

Royal Canadian Mounted Police | Gendarmerie royale du Canada

Security Classification / Designation
Classification / Désignation sécuritaire

December 19, 2001

Appendix 3

Your file Votre référence

Ms. Deneace Green
733 Banghak 3 Dong
Dobong-Ku, Seoul
Korea, 132-855
Seoul

Our file Notre référence

01ATIP-56718

Dear Ms. Green:

This is in response to your request under the Privacy Act received on December 12, 2001, seeking access to statements pertaining to your security check.

Enclosed is a copy of all the information to which you are entitled. Please note that we were able to locate only 3 of the 5 statements requested.

Note that you have the right to bring a complaint before the Privacy Commissioner concerning any aspect of our processing of your request. Notice of complaint should be addressed to:

Privacy Commissioner
Tower "B", Place de Ville
112 Kent Street
Ottawa, Ontario
K1A 1H3

Should you wish to discuss your request, contact Cpl. V. Laflamme at (613) 993-8761.

Yours truly,

R. Lebel, Sgt.
Office of the Departmental Privacy and ATI Coordinator

1200 Vanier Parkway
Ottawa, Ontario
K1A 0R2

attach.

Canada

Royal Canadian Mounted Police | Gendarmerie royale du Canada

Security Classification / Designation
Classification / Désignation sécuritai

December 19, 2001

Appendix 3

Your file | Votre référence

Ms. Deneace Green
733 Banghak 3 Dong
Dobong-Ku, Seoul
Korea, 132-855
Seoul

Our file | Notre référence

01ATIP-56718

Dear Ms. Green:

This is in response to your request under the Privacy Act received on December 12, 2001, seekin access to statements pertaining to your security check.

Enclosed is a copy of all the information to which you are entitled. Please note that we were able locate only 3 of the 5 statements requested.

Note that you have the right to bring a complaint before the Privacy Commissioner concerning ar aspect of our processing of your request. Notice of complaint should be addressed to:

Privacy Commissioner
Tower "B", Place de Ville
112 Kent Street
Ottawa, Ontario
K1A 1H3

Should you wish to discuss your request, contact Cpl. V. Laflamme at (613) 993-8761.

Yours truly,

R. Lebel, Sgt.
Office of the Departmental Privacy and ATI Coordinator

1200 Vanier Parkway
Ottawa, Ontario
KIA 0R2

attach.

Canada

INVESTIGATION REPORT RAPPORT D'ENQUÊTE

SECURITY CLASSIFICATION / DESIGNATION
CLASSIFICATION/DÉSIGNATION SÉCURITAIRE

OTHER FILE REFERENCES AUTRES CONSULTATIONS DE FICHIERS	DIVISION	DATE	RCMP FILE REFERENCES CONSULTATION DE FICHIERS DE LA G.R.C.
	O	2000-09-26	1999-2678
	SUB-DIVISION - SOUS-DIVISION		
	DETACHMENT - DÈTACHEMENT		

RE - OBJET
GREEN, DENEACE (DOB 66-04-01)
RM APPLICANT
SECURITY/SUITABILITY

REFERENCES:

4. Source (N) of unknown reliability was interviewed with respect to Green's use of the Source as a reference. Source (N) has known Green since 1989. The Source said that he used to see a lot of Green in 1990 & 1991 when Green was going with the Source's nephew. After that they saw her about three times a year but have not seen here in the last year. Their relationship is like uncle and niece. The Source feels Green is mature because she brought up her children and they are good children. He has not seen the children in over a year. The relationship the Source and his wife have with Green is at their house. Green has a good reputation with them. The Source feels that Green is responsible as she was on welfare and went back to school. He did not know if Green is financially responsible or how she paid for her schooling. Green has never mentioned any radical political opinions or disenchantment with the Canadian government. Green is not a loner in the Source's opinion. Green does not drink, as she is a Pentecostal. There is no knowledge if Green does drugs. The Source said that if there is anything that will get Green into trouble it will be that she "can go a little overboard about religion". The Source says that his family's main involvement with Green is that they talk about the book (Bible). The Source does not know anything about Green's kids. Green has talked about being a policeman for a long time but never mentioned why she wanted that career. She also mentioned at one time that she wanted to get into the military.

\~/

EFERENCES:

10. Source (I) of unknown reliability was interviewed reference associate status with Green. The Source & Green met when they both worked at Coca Cola in 1996. Green left that employment after developing Tunnel Carpal Syndrome but their relationship continued. The source says that Green is intelligent, intuitive, honest, straight forward, dependable, a hard worker and has a keen sense of responsibility. In discussions she will listen to the other side of an argument but is strong willed as to opinion. Stated that she understood that the children had left Green's residence to live with fewer rules. She understands that the son does not have much contact but understands he is doing well & the daughter is living with one of Green's brothers and that Green is divorced.

11. Source (J) of unknown reliability was interviewed reference Green's children's status. Source said Green's daughter is living in their basement apartment and moved there because the grandmother asked if he would take her in. Source stated that the daughter moved out of Green's apartment to escape all of the maternal rules for living in the apartment. The Source stated that he believed that Green's son was "going down the wrong road" but there did not seem to be much that could be done and that he is living with the

father. Source said that Green has been talking about working for the RCMP for a number of years. Source wished Green well but said that she gets bored easily and believes she is the type that "going to get the position is the challenge and if not challenged during the job gets bored".

EDUCATION:

INVESTIGATOR'S COMMENTS:

Green's file has large gaps in secure long term employment and has references that have not had any dealings with her for years. Green may be happy and confident but she does not seem to be a stable potential candidate.

Submitted by:

Rick Morris

0114

0114

SOURCE:

(A)

(B)

(C)

(D)

(E)

(F)

(G)

(H)

(I) Carlene Harris (associate)

(J) Lennox Marcelas Green (brother)

(K)

(L)

0113

SOURCE:

(M)

(N) Ovid NOBLE (reference)

(O)

(P)

(Q)

(R)

(S)

(T)

0118

0118

(U)

(V)

(W)

0117

011

Appendix 4

Ontario Regional Office — *Bureau régional de l'Ontario*

January 2, 2002
File Number: 20011934

Ms. Deneace Green
#733 Banghak 3 Dong
Dobongu-ku, Seoul
South Korea, 132-855

Dear Ms. Green:

Enclosed are three copies of the revised complaint form prepared in response to your allegations of discrimination on the ground of colour and sex against the RCMP. Two copies are to be completed and returned to this office; the other is to be retained for your records. It is important that you read the form carefully before signing it. Complaint forms, which are legal documents, are the property of the Canadian Human Rights Commission and cannot, once signed, be withdrawn without its approval.

If the form does not accurately reflect your allegations, please do not sign it. Instead, telephone me as soon as possible so that we can discuss the matter. If the form does not require revision, please sign and date each page, and return two copies to me. If you have additional comments to make, I would ask you to write them on a separate sheet of paper, and not on the form itself.

Once we have received the signed and dated forms, an investigator will be assigned to your complaint, and the RCMP will be officially notified. May I take this opportunity to remind you of your obligation as a complainant to mitigate potential damages arising from your complaint/minimize the effect, financially or otherwise, that the alleged actions could have.

If we do not receive your signed complaint forms within twenty (20) calendar days of the date of this letter, we will assume that you do not wish to proceed further and your file will be closed. Should you wish to raise this matter again in the future, you should be aware that under section 41 of the Canadian Human Rights Act, the Commission may refuse to deal with complaints which are filed more than one year after the alleged discriminatory act(s).

Please include in your response to the Commission, a contact to assist us in reaching you should we have difficulty doing so. We would also need to know whether you are willing to take part in the Commission's mediation service, and if so, when you are planning on returning to Canada. Mediation will not be possible without your attendance in Canada.

1002 - 175 Bloor Street East, Toronto, Ontario M4W 3R8
1002 - 175, rue Bloor est, Toronto (Ontario) M4W 3R8
Tel./tél. (416) 973-5527 or/ou 1-800-999-6899, Fax/téléc. (416) 973-6184
www.chrc-ccdp.ca

Should you have any questions or concerns, please call me at (416) 973-5577.

Yours sincerely,

Andrew Sunstrum
Human Rights Officer

CANADIAN HUMAN RIGHTS COMMISSION
COMPLAINT FORM

FIRST NAME & INITIAL	SURNAME OF COMPLAINANT	FILE NUMBER
Deneace	Green	20011934

NAME & ADDRESS OF RESPONDENT	DATE OF ALLEGED CONDUCT
Royal Canadian Mounted Police Leomont Building 155 McArthur Rd. Room 160 Vanier, Ontario K1A 0R4	May 1998 - 11 December 2000.

ADDRESS WHERE INCIDENT OCCURRED (If different from above)
Toronto, Ontario

ALLEGATION

I Deneace Green, allege that the Royal Canadian Mounted Police discriminated against me in employment by refusing to hire me on the ground of colour (black), sex (female) and family status (single mother) in contravention of section 7 of the *Canadian Human Rights Act*.

PARTICULARS

In August 1998, I began the respondent's application process to become a Police Officer by completing the screening exam. A passing grade is 84/145.

In October 1998, I received a letter informing me that I had received a score of 99/145.

In July 1999, I received an application package from the respondent.

On 18 September 1999, I took the respondent's physical aptitude test (PARE) and passed. I was the only female of six to pass the test. I was also the only black person of the eighteen people to take the test with me.

On 04 November 1999, I was interviewed for six hours by a Sergeant Crowder.

In mid-December 1999, I received a conditional offer of employment. The letter stated that I should be expecting to enroll within the next two to twelve months.

In January 2000, the respondent checked my references, and I did my psychological testing.

In mid-February 2000, I had my medical and dental examinations.

On 26 February 2000, I took my final physical aptitude test. Of the approximately eighteen candidates, I was the only female, and the only black candidate.

In late February 2000, Ms. Karen Cleary, one of the respondent's recruiters, informed me that I had passed the medical. She also stated that the background investigation is due back by 20 March 2000. "You most likely will be enrolled by April 2000," she said.

On 31 March 2000, I called the respondent's recruiting office regarding the status of my application. Ms. Cleary told me that my file was now due back at the end of April 2000.

I have read (or have had read to me) the above allegation and to the best of my knowledge it is true and correct.

I consent to the release to the CHRC of all information and documents concerning me that the CHRC considers necessary for its investigation, such as personnel records, documents, data, medical or hospital records which relate to the complaint. I also authorize the CHRC to have such information examined by any person it retains to provide advice and assistance in dealing with my complaint.

Signature : Deneace Green ***Date :*** Jan. 14/02

CE DOCUMENT EST AUSSI DISPONIBLE EN FRANÇAIS

On 30 May, I received a call from one of the respondent's recruiters, Mr. Rick Morris. I returned the call the following day. Mr. Morris wanted to know the names and date of birth of my children - information that is listed on my application. Also, he wanted updated information on my employment - again, information that was already on my file.

On 4 July 2000, I was told by Ms. Cleary that my background check had not been finished. The candidates with whom I did the physical fitness test in September 1999 had went off to basic training in April 2000.

On 12 September 2000, I received a call from Ms. Cleary stating that my file was back in London, and that she required additional information: two additional references, my children's date of birth, and my updated employment information. Ms. Cleary said that my references need to be people who I have known for at least five years, but the respondent application material mentions nothing about the five year rule. I had already provided the information regarding my children and my employment on two separate occasions.
The respondent's literature states that once an applicant is selected to proceed to the interview stage, the average processing time is approximately four months. Ten months later, I was still waiting. Nonetheless, I provided Ms. Cleary the required information.

On 14 September 2000, I spoke to Constable Bob Joseph, a recruiter, who informed me that I would have to redo the physical fitness exam in October 2000, as the previous test that I had passed was to expire, and I was told that the additional interviews would take approximately two weeks to complete.

Throughout this whole ordeal, I passed up other employment opportunities waiting to be enrolled in basic training. The candidates with whom I had completed the physical fitness test were now getting ready to graduate from the respondent's police academy, and I was still waiting.

On 25 October 2000, I left a message for Mr. Joseph, as I had yet to hear from him. He called back the same day, and told me that there were problems with my background check. Mr. Joseph asked me if my decisions would be influenced by the fact that two of my brothers had criminal records. He also told me that I had personality conflicts with co-workers in previous positions, and that I left the army to avoid charges, that I had shortcomings in the army, that I left my weapon unsecured, that I was late for training or did not show up for training. Many of these allegations were false, or taken out of context. For example, the charge of misfiring was dismissed by Lieutenant-Colonel Von Bulow. The misfiring charge was dismissed because another black recruit and myself were charged, while two white recruits who also misfired were not charged. Also, whatever problems or "shortcomings" that I may have had in the military did not prevent me from successfully completing my basic training, and from being honourably discharged on 25 January 2000. Mr. Joseph told me that he would continue his investigation, but that if I was unable to deal with the army environment, he would not recommend me for training. I provided Mr. Joseph with names of officers who could corroborate the information that I had provided for him. Captain Pamela Evelyn, my assisting officer, Master Corporal Andrea Dennis, and Corporal Sophia Miller. After the conversation, I called Ms. Evelyn to inform her of the blatant misinformation given to the respondent's investigating officer. She immediately called Mr. Joseph to explain what really happened.

On 26 October 2000, I faxed Mr. Joseph further details regarding the investigation into my background. As of this date, it has been two years and two months since I wrote my exam.

On 11 December 2000, I received a letter from the respondent rejecting my application. The letter stated that the decision was made as a result of findings in the background investigation into my overall suitability. The letter stated, "currently, there are a limited number of positions available and we have a sufficient number of applicants who are deemed more suitable." Neither Captain Pamela Evelyn, Master Corporal Dennis, nor Corporal Sophia Miller were contacted prior to the decision to reject me. I met all the requirements for the position.

In May 2001, I received a copy of the investigator's report. The investigator, Mr. Morris, mentioned that I lived

---

I have read (or have had read to me) the above allegation and to the best of my knowledge it is true and correct.

I consent to the release to the CHRC of all information and documents concerning me that the CHRC considers necessary for its investigation, such as personnel records, documents, data, medical or hospital records which relate to the complaint. I also authorize the CHRC to have such information examined by any person it retains to provide advice and assistance in dealing with my complaint.

Signature : Dennace Green ***Date :*** Jan. 14/02

CE DOCUMENT EST AUSSI DISPONIBLE EN FRANÇAIS

in subsidized housing with my daughter. He asks in his report, "how will she survive without income during the [respondent] training period?" I do not believe that being a single mother in subsidized housing should have impacted my application to the respondent.

I believe that I was denied the position because of my colour, sex and family status.

I have read (or have had read to me) the above allegation and to the best of my knowledge it is true and correct.

I consent to the release to the CHRC of all information and documents concerning me that the CHRC considers necessary for its investigation, such as personnel records, documents, data, medical or hospital records which relate to the complaint. I also authorize the CHRC to have such information examined by any person it retains to provide advice and assistance in dealing with my complaint.

Signature : Deneace Green ***Date :*** Jan. 14/01

CE DOCUMENT EST AUSSI DISPONIBLE EN FRANÇAIS

Appendix 5

CANADIAN HUMAN RIGHTS COMMISSION — COMMISSION CANADIENNE DES DROITS DE LA PERSONNE

Investigations Branch — Direction des enquêtes

APR 19 2002

200111934

Ms. Deneace Green
#733 Banghak 3 Dong
Dobong-ku, Seoul
South Korea 132-855

Appendix 5

Dear Ms. Green:

Further to your complaint of discrimination against the Royal Canadian Mounted Police (RCMP), I wish to inform you that the RCMP has now provided a response to your allegations. The next step in the complaints process allows you the opportunity to provide your comments/rebuttal to this response. I have prepared a summary of the respondent's position. Please review this summary and provide your comments along with any information you believe is relevant to the investigation of your complaint.

Statement #1

In August 1998, I began the respondent's application process to become a Police Officer by completing the screening exam. A passing grade is 84/145.

Respondent's Defence

You wrote the RRST on 16 July 1997. On 03 September 1997, a letter was sent to you advising you of your score of 89/145. On 06 October 1997, a Priority Post letter was forwarded to you advising the you had been selected from the Initial Rank List. On 12 January 1998, another letter was forwarded to you advising that you had not provided the London Recruiting Office with the PARE certificate. You were advised that your application had been carried over to the next cycle. On 06 May 1998, a letter was forwarded to you advising that you had not been successful in the 01 April 1998 selection and that your application file was now closed. On 12 August 1998, you re-wrote the RRST at the Newmarket Detachment in order to qualify for another selection.

Your Rebuttal #1

344 Slater Street, Ottawa, Ontario K1A 1E1
344, rue Slater, Ottawa (Ontario) K1A 1E1
Toll-free / Sans frais 1-888-214-1090, TTY / ATS 1-888-643-3304, Fax / téléc. (613) 947-7279
www.chrc-ccdp.ca

Statement #2

In October 1998, I received a letter informing me that I had received a score of 99/145.

Respondent's Defence

On 20 October 1998, a letter was sent to you advising of your score, 99/145. The letter indicated to you that your score qualified you for the April 1999 selection. However, there was no selection in April 1999 as "Depot" was closed.

Your Rebuttal #2

Statement #3

In July 1999, I received an application package from the respondent.

Respondent's Defence

On 03 August 1999, you were forwarded a Priority Post letter, advising that you had been selected and that a PARE certificate had to be provided in order to be interviewed. The application package was also included.

Your Rebuttal #3

Statement #4

On 18 September 1999, I took the respondent's physical aptitude test (PARE) anc passed. I was the only female of six to pass the test. I was also the only black person of the eighteen people to take the test with me.

Respondent's Defence

On 21 September 1999, a PARE statistics form was forwarded by fax to the London Recruiting office advising that you had successfully completed the PARE. We do not keep any statistics on the number of applicants attending the PARE sites at any given time.

Your Rebuttal #4

Statement #5

On 14 November 1999, I was interviewed for six hours by a Sergeant Crowder.

Respondent's Defence

You were interviewed by Sgt. Crowder on 04 November 1999. The RMSIG did not take six (6) hours. However, the Security/Reliability was completed after a one hour lunch break following the RMSIG. Sgt. Crowder did not keep record of the duration of the interview.

Your Rebuttal #5

Statement #6

In mid-December 1999, I received a conditional offer of employment. The letter stated that I should be expecting to enroll within the next two to twelve months.

Respondent's Defence

On 15 December 1999 a letter was mailed to you. The letter indicated "While the Conditional Offer merely indicates that you may expect to be enrolled before the end of September 2000, you should be prepared to be enrolled anytime within the next two to twelve months." The Conditional Offer of Enrolment stated in the first paragraph that the RCMP is now prepared to offer you enrolment as a Cadet, subject to the following conditions:

- *your field investigation confirms that you meet the RCMP's requirements for suitability and must remain suitable until enrolled;*

- *you obtain the "TOP SECRET" level of security clearance.*

You did not obtain a security clearance with the RCMP as you were not found suitable.

Your Rebuttal #6

Statement #7

In January 2000, the respondent checked my references, and I did my psychological testing.

Respondent's Defence

A letter dated 07 December 1999, was forwarded to you advising you that a psychological assessment had been scheduled for 05 January 2000. The background investigation had also been started at that time.

Your Rebuttal #7

Statement #8

In mid-February 2000, I had my medical and dental examinations.

Respondent's Defence

It is possible that you had your medical and dental examinations during that time period.

Your Rebuttal #8

Statement #9

On 26 February 2000, I took my final physical aptitude test. Of the approximately eighteen candidates, I was the only female, and the only black candidate.

Respondent's Defence

You did, in fact, take the PARE on that date. We do not have any statistics as to the number of applicants tested on that day therefore we have no record on the number of males, females or visible minorities. You did meet the standard of the PARE evaluation.

Your Rebuttal #9

Statement #10

In late February 2000, Ms. Karen Cleary, one of the respondent's recruiters, informed me that I had passed the medical. She also stated that the background investigation is due back by 20 March 2000. "You most likely will be enrolled by April 2000," she said.

Respondent's Defence

Your medical clearance was received on 16 February 2000. At the time, a diary date had probably been set for March 2000, however, the background investigation was not completed by that date. You quoted Karen Cleary, "You most likely will be enrolled by April 2000." Karen Cleary, Recruiting Clerk, advised that she never made that statement. Ms. Cleary further stated that she never indicates to applicants when they will be going to Regina, as this is the recruiters responsibility.

Your Rebuttal #10

Statement #11

On 31 March 2000, I called the respondent's recruiting office regarding the status of my application. Ms. Cleary told me that my file was now due back at the end of April 2000.

Respondent's Defence

We do not keep record of all the conversations the recruiting clerks have with the applicants. Obviously, the background investigation was not completed at that time and the diary date was postponed to a later date. The background investigation was controlled by Departmental Security Section. Due to heavy detachments workload at the time, background investigations were taking longer to complete.

Your Rebuttal #11

Statement #12

On 30 May, I received a call from one of the respondent's recruiters, Mr. Rick Morris. I returned the call the following day. Mr. Morris wanted to know the names and date of birth of my children - information that is listed on my application. Also, he wanted updated information on my employment - again, information that was already on my file.

Respondent's Defence

The background investigation was not completed and on 12 May 2000, the investigation was forwarded to Rick Morris, retired member of the RCMP hired as a contract investigator. The information concerning your children was never provided by you when filling out the form TBS330-60, nor was it provided before the background investigation was started by Rick Morris since information concerning children under the age of 18 is not required. Initially, you did not have to provide information when you completed the form since your children were under the age of 18. However, your oldest child had reached the age of eighteen by the time Rick Morris requested the information. Rick Morris also requested updated information of employment as some of the places of employment given by you could not provide information. For example, TigerTel indicated that they had no record of you working for them, Sitel Corp. Canada, had no record of you working between January 1999 and December 1999. The background investigator does not get a copy of the entire file but copies of the forms necessary to complete the background investigation.

Your Rebuttal #12

Statement #13

On 4 July 2000, I was told by Ms. Cleary that my background check had not been finished. The candidates with whom I did the physical fitness test in September 1999 had went off to basic training in April 2000.

Respondent's Defence

The background investigation was not completed at that time. As for your comment, "the candidates with whom I did the physical fitness in September 1999 had went off to basic training in April 2000", in April 2000, seven males were sent to "Depot", three were visible minority applicants, one was an Aboriginal applicant and three were Caucasian applicants. Unless you can provide the names of the applicants that you believe were sent to the Cadet Training Program in April 2000, there is a strong possibility that some of these people might have been sent later than April 2000 or not at a ll.

Your Rebuttal #13

Statement #14

On 12 September 2000, I received a call from Ms. Cleary stating that my file was back in London, and that she required additional information: two additional references, my children's date of birth, and my updated employment information. Ms. Cleary said that my references need to be people who I have known for at least five years, but the respondent application material mentions nothing about the five year rule. I had already provided the information regarding my children and my employment on two separate occasions. The respondent's literature states that once an applicant is selected to proceed to the interview stage, the average processing time is approximately four months. Ten months later, I was still waiting. Nonetheless, I provided Ms. Cleary the required information.

Respondent's Defence

On 08 September 2000, I finished reviewing your file and the background investigation. I forwarded a message to Karen Cleary, Recruiting Clerk, to contact you and asked that you provide two more character references, because one of the references was a university professor at the University of

Toronto, he had not seen or heard from you since 1995 and the other character reference had a close relationship for a period of one year and had no real involvement with you for the last two years. The guide to completion of personnel security clearance questionnaire (form TBS330-60) had been provided to you and indicates under part M that, "...references are not to include relatives. The three character references should be persons whose combined knowledge of you covers the screening period (10 or 20 years) and references must be persons residing in Canada."

Karen Cleary was also asked to seek clarification from you on your marital status, as you had indicated being separated but did not provide a date on the form. We also required information which was not mention on form TBS330-60 concerning your daughter who had now reached the age of 18 and information on your employment from January 2000 to the present.

We also sent a message to the Departmental Security Section with the following:

- Request that another credit check be conducted on the applicant;
- Informing that the applicant would be providing two more character references;
- Informing that one of your associates, Anette Grandison, was never interviewed;
- Inquiry with the Army Reserve was never done;
- The applicant's current address check was not done and if it was, it is not on the report;
- The following places of employment were not checked:
  - Coca Cola bottling (96-02 to 97-02)
  - S & P Data (95-12 to 96-02)
- Local indices with Metro Toronto Police and York Police were not done; and,
- Criminal Record check on family as well as daughter could have been done but we did not have the information.

Regarding the comment about "once an applicant is selected to proceed to the interview stage, the average processing time is approximately four months", the RCMP national web site under the recruiting information indicates that the entire process may take six to eighteen months. The process can even take longer when issues arise.

Your Rebuttal #14

Statement #15

On 14 September 2000, I spoke to Constable Bob Joseph, a recruiter, who informed me that I would have to redo the physical fitness exam in October 2000, as the previous test that I had passed was to expire, and I was told that the additional interviews would take approximately two weeks to complete.

Respondent's Defence

By that time the PARE certificate had expired, however, you were not scheduled to take another PARE. We do not recall telling you that you would have to re-do you PARE in October 2000. You were told that it would take at least two weeks before additional interviews would be completed.

Your Rebuttal #15

Statement #16

Throughout this whole ordeal, I passed up other employment opportunities waiting to be enrolled in basic training. The candidates with whom I had completed the physical fitness test were now getting ready to graduate from the respondent's police academy, and I was still waiting.

Respondent's Defence

You have never indicated to the "O" Division Recruiting Section that you were passing up other employment opportunities. Regarding the comment that, "the candidates with whom I had completed the physical fitness test were now getting ready to graduate from the respondent's police academy, and I was still waiting." Again, unless you can provide the names of the candidates that attended the PARE evaluation, you could not be aware of their status.

Your Rebuttal #16

Statement #17

On 25 October 2000, I left a message for Mr. Joseph, as I had yet to hear from him. He called back the same day, and told me that there were problems with my background check. Mr. Joseph asked me if my decisions would be influenced by the fact that two of my brothers had criminal records. He also told me that I had personality conflicts with co-workers in previous positions, and that I left the army to avoid charges, that I had shortcomings in the army, that I left my weapon unsecured, that I was late for training or did not show up for training. Many of these allegations were false, or taken out of context. For example, the charge of misfiring was dismissed by Lieutenant-Colonel Von Bulow. The misfiring charge was dismissed because another black recruit and myself were charged, while two white recruits who also misfired were not charged. Also, whatever problems or "shortcomings" that I may have had in the military did not prevent me from successfully completing my basic training, and from being honourably discharged on 25 January 2000. Mr. Joseph told me that he would continue his investigation, but that if I was unable to deal with the army environment, he would not recommend me for training. I provided Mr. Joseph with names of officers who could corroborate the information that I had provided for him. Captain Pamela Evelyn, my assisting officer, Master Corporal Andrea Dennis, and Corporal Sophia Miller. After the conversation, I called Ms. Evelyn to inform her of the blatant misinformation given to the respondent's investigating officer. She immediately called Mr. Joseph to explain what really happened.

Respondent's Defence

Cst. Robert Joseph did have a phone conversation with you during which he asked you questions about your relationship with family, in particular, your relationship with your brothers Dorman and Robin Green. Both have extensive criminal convictions and Dorman was incarcerated at that time. He did ask you if you could be influenced by your brothers and you answered that you were not influenced by your brothers.

Cst. Joseph also asked you about your employment with the Jewish Vocational Services of Metropolitan Toronto where you worked from April 1999 to November 1999. The background investigation indicated that you left because of frustrations with computers as well as personality conflicts with co-workers.

*Cst. Joseph questioned you about your Military Service. During the Security/Reliability interview, in answering question 31, "Have you ever been the subject of disciplinary action by a previous employer?" You replied that an incident occurred where you had discharged your weapon on the range. You further commented that this incident had been investigated and deemed "**unfounded**". The review of your file, security interview and background investigation revealed however, that due to a few delays they had decided not to proceed since you had requested a discharge from the Military. Although you indicated that all military charges were dropped, during your telephone conversation with Cst. Joseph, you said you had stated during your interview with Sgt. Crowder the charges had been dismissed and not **unfounded**. The C.O. Lieutenant Colonel Von Bulow decided not to proceed with the charges. She indicated that two other people had discharged their weapons on the range and were not charged. Sgt. Michaud was talking to you while directions were given and you heard fire and discharged your weapon. You did not want to say who told you, but wrote a letter through proper channels. You did provide the name of Captain Evelyn, Andrea Dennis and Cpl. Sophia Miller who witnessed what had occurred on the range.*

The Military further added that you would not show up on time or not show up at all. To this you indicated that you were late a few times since you worked downtown and had to go home to get your uniform. You indicated that you had been late about three times. There had also been another incident for which you were also charged, where a corporal left you to secure weapons in barracks and you decided to leave your post as well. Your explanation was that you were on the phone, that you could still see the room and that you had received permission from the corporal. The Military states that your attitude towards authority was poor following this incident.

Cst. Joseph asked you why you had joined the reserve. You replied that you wrote the test for the Army and also had another job. You were accepted by the reserve. You did say that you did not give 100% to the Army and could have left after basic training. Immediately after the conversation with you, Cst. Joseph had a conversation with Captain Pamela Evelyn. She was acting as the defendant's officer in the discharge of the firearm incident. Captain Evelyn indicated that the Military dropped the charges as the documentation was not sufficient. Captain Evelyn said she had concerns and wondered if it might not have been legitimate. Captain Evelyn said that she investigated the occurrence and found that more that one person had discharged their firearm and that only two were charged. Two witnesses came forward to corroborate what you had said.

Cst. Joseph advised you that he would continue his investigation regarding your file and that further inquiries with the Military would be conducted.

Your Rebuttal #17

Statement #18

On 26 October 2000, I faxed Mr. Joseph further details regarding the investigation into my background. As of this date, it has been two years and two months since I wrote my exam.

Respondent's Defence

On 25 October 2000, Cst. Joseph received faxed documentation from you which included a letter from Lieutenant Colonel Commanding Officer P. Von Bulow, a Canadian Forces Certificate of Service and a four page letter written by you addressed to Lieutenant Colonel Von Bulow, explaining your concerns regarding information in your file and justification of the following incidences on your QL2 Course:

- *Displayed poor attitude and tardiness;*
- *Left my weapon unsecured;*
- *Dressed improperly;*

- *Failed my C7 Performance Check; and,*
- *Failed my C9 Performance Check.*

As for the period of two years and two months elapsing since you wrote the test, you had been selected in August 1999. ***Nothing needed to be done until you were selected****. A total of 250 applicants were selected at the same time. You took your PARE evaluation on 18 September 1999 and was interviewed by Sgt. Crowder in London on 04 November 1999. In December 1999, the background investigation on you was initiated. Due to the heavy workload, background investigations on applicants were delayed. In May 2000, this Division hired under contract retired member of the RCMP to conduct background investigations on applicants. On 12 May 2000, the outstanding inquiries were given to Rick Morris. On 13 June 2000, Rick Morris completed his part of the investigation. Cst. Joseph reviewed your file and background investigation in early September 2000. On 08 September 2000, he forwarded messages to Karen Cleary, Recruiting Clerk for the "O" Division Recruiting Section and Adele Zeversenuke of the "O" Division Departmental Security Section requesting you provide more information and conduct further inquiries on your background (see response to statement #14). On 13 September 2000, Rick Morris received more enquiries to conduct. On 26 September 2000, Rick Morris completed the report and forwarded it to the London Headquarters. On 25 October 2000, Cst. Joseph re-interviewed you over the phone (see response to statement #17).*

On 26 October 2000, Cst. Joseph forwarded a fax to the Chief Clerk of G.1., Sgt. Castonguay, LFCA G.1. Record looking for information on Ms. Green employment with the Military. Attached with the first page was the RCMP Personnel Screening Request and Authorization form signed by you. On 01 November 2000, Cst, Joseph attended the Military Headquarters in Toronto to review your Military file. On 24 November 2000, Cst. Joseph completed the report in order not to recommend you for further consideration in the application process. The report was provided to Cpl. Heikkila, NCO i/c of the Recruiting Section and finally to Inspector Greg Johnson, OIC Staffing and Personnel "O" Division. Both concurred with Cst. Joseph findings. A letter dated 27 November 2000 signed by Inspector Greg Johnson was mailed to you informing you that the RCMP was unable to offer you enrolment, that the Conditional Offer of Enrolment for a Regular Member position was hereby revoked and that your application file would be closed.

Your Rebuttal #18

Statement #19

On 11 December 2000, I received a letter from the respondent rejecting my application. The letter stated that the decision was made as a result of findings in the background investigation into my overall suitability. The letter stated, "currently, there are a limited number of positions available and we have a sufficient number of applicants who are deemed more suitable." Neither Captain Pamela Evelyn, Master Corporal Dennis, nor Corporal Sophia Miller were contacted prior to the decision to reject me. I met all the requirements for the position.

Respondent's Defence

Captain Pamela Evelyn was, in fact, interviewed on two occasions by Cst. K.A. Chapman, Federal Enforcement Section, Toronto East Detachment possibly in January 2000 and by Cst. Joseph on 25 October 2000. You provided the name of Captain Pamela Evelyn as a Friend and Associate, and was also her business partner and she is listed as a Senior Accounts Manager in a registered company called "Total Events Management Services". Master Corporal Dennis and Corporal Sophia Miller were not interviewed. However, Lieutenant Colonel Peter Von Bulow, Commanding Officer 25 Medical Regiment, Army Reserves Moss Park Armoury, Regimental Sergeant Major Mike McFarlane, Sergeant Dave Michaud, Private Virginia Dacosta and Master Corporal Bernard Skerret were all interviewed. Prior to rejecting your application, a review of your military file was conducted.

Cst. Joseph prepared the following report and sent it to Cpl. Heikkila and Inspector Greg Johnson.

I have completed a comprehensive review of the applicant's file. During this review, several areas of concern have arisen which needs to be addressed in order to assess the overall suitability of this applicant. I will attempt to summarize these issues in the next few paragraphs.

BACKGROUND

Ms. Green began her application on 12 August 1998. On 06 May 1998, the applicant received a letter from the recruiting office advising that her file was not closed as she had not completed the PARE test and had not been selected for her second selection as her score did not meet the cut off score. On 03 August 1999, the applicant was selected for the August 1999 selection. The applicant was interviewed by Sgt. Crowder on 04 November 1999. The final part of the background investigation was concluded on 11 November 2000.

EMPLOYMENT

1. *Ms. Green was enrolled in the Army Reserve from September 1997*

until January 2000. During training she was given a number of notices of shortcomings identified by her instructors. The applicant was unwilling to accept the shortcomings listed at the end of the course. Any shortcoming she received she made excuses for and felt she should not get them in the first place. The applicant did not take criticism well and had problems with military authority. The applicant was formerly counselled for a safety violation on a live fire rifle range. Because of the incident, the applicant was disciplined and given the task of guarding a room that contained 30 automatic rifles. The applicant was found outside the room by her Sergeant and was reprimanded for this as well.

The applicant was re-interviewed by myself over the phone on 25 October 2000. The applicant indicated that she was talking on the phone and could see the door of the room. The applicant advised she was wrong in firing a bullet, but blamed the Sergeant giving instructions to her when the discharge of the weapon occurred. The applicant indicated that she received shortcomings while in the reserve but all the charges were dealt with at the same time since the military decided not to proceed with them.

2. On 01 November 2000, I attended the Military Headquarters in Toronto to review the applicant's military file. The investigation revealed Ms. Green was given shortcomings as well as being formally counselled for standard performance, which included: poor attitude; tardiness; being improperly dressed; leaving weapon insecure; failing C7 performance check; and, safety violation on a live rifle range. The applicant wrote a complaint on 08 June 1998 to have the comments that were put on her training report removed. On 06 July 1998, the Captain Adjutant stated "the nine incidents during training reveal a pattern of poor attitude, an unwillingness to accept military authority and only marginal performance. I can not support your request to have comments struck from your course report."

3. The background investigation revealed that Ms. Green believed she was not treated fairly while in the Reserves. All sources interviewed indicated that she was not treated unfairly. Even during the interview with me, the applicant gave a reason for every shortcoming received, did not take responsibility for her actions. The only responsibility she would take was for the negligent discharge, but not to the actions leading to the incident, for which she blamed the Sergeant. It should be pointed out

that during the interview with Sgt. Crowder, the applicant only indicated she had been investigated for misfire on range, which was deemed unfounded. All other information was revealed during the background investigation. The applicant admitted during the phone interview she did not give one hundred percent to the military.

The applicant omitted to provide, during the Security/Suitability interview, that she had received several shortcomings as well as being verbally counselled for standard performances while in the Army Reserves. The investigation with the Military revealed that the applicant could not take military authority and demonstrated a poor attitude towards her superiors. Based on the information provided in this report, the applicant does not meet the requirement in the competency of "Integrity and Honesty" and is found not suitable to become a member of the RCMP. It is recommended that the recruiting process for this applicant be terminated immediately as we have a number of suitable candidates to select from.

Your Rebuttal #19

Statement #20

In May 2001, I received a copy of the investigator's report. The investigator, Mr. Morris, mentioned that I lived in subsidized housing with my daughter. He asks in his report, "how will she survive without income during the [respondent] training period?" I do not believe that being a single mother in subsidized housing should have impacted my application to the respondent.

Respondent's Defence

Mr. Morris provided a separate Personal attachment with his report which was kept separate from the security file. Mr. Morris did, in fact, make the comment that you state in your complaint, however, the personal comments made by Rick Morris were not taken into consideration in order to reject you from the recruiting selection process.

Your Rebuttal #20

Allegation #1

I believe that I was denied the position because of my colour, sex and family status.

Respondent's Defence

You were selected in August 1999, amongst 250 applicants.

Male (Visible Minority)	*57*
Female (Visible Minority)	*10*
Male (Aboriginal)	*11*
Female (Aboriginal)	*1*
Female	*93*
Male	*78*

Family Status information is not entered on the HRMIS system for RCMP applicants.

The total allotment for the period covering April 2000 to March 2001 was 86 candidates. 21 positions were not filled as applicants were not fully processed. 65 candidates were enrolled and sent to "Depot" in Regina for the Cadet Training Program. The breakdown is as follows:

Visible Minorities (male and female)	*11*
Aboriginals (male and female)	*3*
Females	*17*
Males	*34*

Your Rebuttal #1

After I receive your comments, I will draft a report. Please bear in mind the information provided by you and the RCMP will be used in this report. The report will then be reviewed and a decision will be made as to whether there is sufficient information to submit this matter to the Commission for decision at this stage or whether further investigation is required.

Please provide your comments, in the same numerical order as above, by **31 May 2002**. Thank you for your cooperation.

Yours Sincerely,

Deborah M. Olver
Investigator
Investigations Branch

Appendix 6

Deneace Green
Toronto, Ontario
Canada, M1P 3T7

May 18, 2002 #200111934

Ms. Olver, Investigator
Canadian Human Rights Commission
344 Slater Street
Ottawa, Ontario
Canada, K1A 1E1

Dear Ms. Olver:

Thank you for addressing my situation. I have attached the rebuttals to this and other pages due to the limited spaces on the original document. The answers to most of the rebuttals are written in my file. The rebuttals can be found in the following documents: (1) *An Overview Chart of My Process with the RCMP and Racism in the Canadian Armed Forces* (2) *Response to the RCMP's and the Canadian Armed Forces Discriminatory Practices* (3) *Conclusion*. In other words, pages 3 to 27 cover my rebuttals in detail. Therefore, please review the stated pages in my file before proceeding. Thank you.

Rebuttals

Rebuttal #1

In response to the January 1998 letter (page 250 in my file), through Claire Shaw, the person who administered the PARE, the RCMP was aware of the result of my November 1997 PARE. Therefore, I was waiting to re-do the PARE before submitting a PARE certificate.

My response to the May 06, 1998 letter can be found on page 3, item #7, of the information that I mailed to the Canadian Human Rights Commission in October 2001. What happened to the "General Recruitment and Special Programs?" Please see Appendix 1B and 1C of my file.

Rebuttal #2

Why was I not informed that the Depot was closed and that there would be no selection during April 1999? Why was I not considered for the October 1998 selection? I wrote the exam in August 1998 and a score was available for me during the October 1998 selection.

Rebuttal #3

I immediately made an appointment to take the PARE.

Rebuttal #4

It is an incorrect statement to say, "We do not keep any statistics on the number of applicants attending the PARE sites at any given time." Corporal Karen Cleary told me and Claire Shaw confirmed that "the RCMP usually select four to six female for each PARE and only one or two are expected to pass."

Rebuttal #5

I was required to be at the RCMP recruiting office at 8:30 A.M. The first half of the interview and processing took about three hours. I was then given an hour lunch break. After the lunch break, I was interviewed for another two and one half hours. I left the recruiting office at about 2:35 P.M. I was engaged at the recruiting office for about six hours.

Rebuttal #6

Exactly what does "Security Clearance" mean? The reasons cited for rejection are as follows:

-socio-economic status i.e., subsidized housing and low-paying jobs;

-family status i.e., single mother;

-racism based on my gender and race through the military;

-bankruptcy.

Why was my file missing for almost one year?

Rebuttal #7

My background investigation started in December 1999. Why was my file missing and investigation seized until the file was given to Constable Rick Morris on May 12, 2000? Please note that July 4, 2000, when I phoned RCMP Recruiting in London, Ontario, Corporal Karen Cleary told me that, "Your background investigation is <u>not</u> complete." Meaning that the file was not back in the recruiting department. Immediately after speaking with Constable Cleary, I called Constable Morris. He told me that, "I am not going to explain it! Your file is back in London!" I wanted to call the recruiting office again, but I chose not to because I did not want to upset my prospective employers. Please see page 6, #30, in my file.

Rebuttal #8

Late February 2000, Karen Cleary, RCMP Recruiting, told me that, "Your medical is back and everything is fine. Your background investigation is due back March 20, 2000. You most likely will be enrolled by April 2000." This is in keeping with the RCMP's four months processing time, after the interview.

Rebuttal #9

The RCMP does have statistics on the number of applicants tested on that day because Claire Shaw (the person who does the PARE testing) faxed the list of candidates' names to the RCMP Recruiting. The list distinguishes the candidates who passed and those who failed.

Rebuttal #10

If Constable Cleary did not make this statement, then one of us is lying and it certainly is not me. Did I just happened to guess that the file would be completed on March 20, 2000? I am requesting that a copy of the RCMP's diary for that date be presented in court.

Rebuttal #11

What proof does the RCMP have that anything was being done with my file? Can they prove that my file was not just thrown aside?

Rebuttal #12

Rick Morris may be "a contract investigator"; however, he nonetheless enjoys the status of RCMP Constable Rick Morris.

Where was my file between January and May 2000?

Constable Rick Morris accused me of being under-handed when I left my children off the TBS330-60 form: "Leaving her children off of her 330-60 form leaves much to ponder about." Appendix 9, page 65. Now the RCMP is admitting that the information was not required. Had the RCMP processed my file in a timely manner, this would never have been an issue. Furthermore, the information that Constable Morris requested was my children's date of birth which the RCMP had since 1997. If my younger child was still not an issue, why was he placed on the TBS330-60 form for investigation?

Regarding employment with Tiger Tel and Sitel, copies of the fax can be found in my file on pages 133, 134, 226 and 227.

Rebuttal #13

Claire Shaw provided the RCMP with a list of the people who did the PARE with me. It is easy to compare the names of the people who went to Depot in April 2000 with the names of the people who did the Final PARE in February 2000.

Rebuttal #14

The fax I sent to the RCMP Recruiting December 15, 1999, (p. 127), clearly states that His Worship Steven L. Walsberg, Justice of the Peace, signed my affidavit for divorce on December 09, 1999.

As stated, I faxed the stated employment information to RCMP Recruiting on March 16, 2000, and I called to confirm that it was received. May 31, 2000, I provided Constable Rick Morris with the same information. September 12, 2000, Constable Rick Morris requested that Constable Cleary call me again for the same information.

Why was another credit check being done?

I provided the name of Dawna Davis who was already on my file. I had known her for over twenty-three years. Also, I provided the name of Ovid Noble whom I had known for over eleven years.

Why was Annette Grandison not interviewed in January 2000, along with the other references listed on my TBS/SCT 330-60 form?

My file was sent out for background investigation prior to December 07, 1999. September 2000, it is apparent that nothing was done with my file. Why? It is clear that no issue had arisen to delay my file. Perhaps the RCMP has extended its processing time; however, when I started the process, the average processing time after the interview was four months—it is written in their literature; and based on the diary date of April 2000, my file could have been processed within their stipulated time frame.

Rebuttal #15

Not only did Constable Bob Joseph tell me that I would need to re-do the PARE, but Constable Cleary told me that the RCMP would pay for it. Please see page 6, #30.

Please note that when I asked Constable Joseph when I can expect to be enrolled, he answered, "Maybe one month; maybe two months. One or two troops will be leaving in December and again in January. We shut down in December, and November is fully booked." This conversation took place on September 14, 2000, exactly ten months after my interview. Why was I not booked for the October or the November class? I am quite certain that all or most of the candidates in the October and November classes started their application process after I did. This can be easily checked by the CHRC. It is clear that the only issue with my file was that it was not being processed. Why?

Rebuttal #16

Prior to my interview, I discussed a job offer in Seoul, Korea with Constable Cleary, Recruiting RCMP. Constable Cleary informed me that, "If you leave the country, your file will be closed. You need to be accessible." This conversation came up again with Sergeant Crowder, during my interview on September 04, 1999. At that time Sergeant Crowder informed me that the RCMP loses a lot of people due to the long processing time--from the time it takes to write the basic test to the four months after the interview to be selected for basic training. I am aware that these interviews are usually video taped. If there is a tape, I am requesting that it be presented as evidence in this matter.

Rebuttal #17

I never had a problem with the computers at JVS. In fact, I was often praised for my computer abilities. My problem was with the three different databases. Prior to my accepting the job, it was clear that a single database (MIS) would be up and running with a month. Six months later I was still doing three times the work because all the information had to be entered into three different databases. Not to mention that if I wanted to simply copy a diskette, I had to travel to another location located at the opposite end of the city. A year after I left JVS, the MIS was still not in operation. Please see page 15 of my file.

Annette Grandison was an employee of JVS who during her interview with Constable Rick Morris confirmed the conflict within the organization over the three different computer bases. Also, Annette confirmed that another reason for my leaving the company was because of a change in the location of my job which would require me to commute longer each day.

Regarding the military delays, who caused the delays? How many times did I show up with my witnesses and assisting officer only to have the Colonel not show up? At least three times, three delays before situation was dealt with.

My letter to Colonel Von Bulow is evidence that I had no intention of leaving the army until the matter was settled. Colonel Von Bullow's reason for not proceeding with the trial is a very poor one: "...due to a few delays they had decided not to proceed since you had requested a discharge from the military." A letter to Colonel Von Bulow clearly states that the charge was not dismissed for my benefit; it was dismissed for the benefit of Sergeant Michaud and other immediate supervisors. Please see Appendix 5A, page 4.

During my telephone interview with Constable Joseph, which was more of an interrogation than an interview, I told Constable Joseph that "unfounded" was not my word. When I sought clarification from Constable Joseph as to the meaning of "unfounded," he said, "Unfounded means the incident never occurred." Why would I say the incident never occurred when I am the one who brought it up during the interview?

After the interview with Constable Joseph, I consulted the Oxford Dictionary for the definition of "unfounded." According to the Oxford Dictionary, "*unfounded* means unsubstantiated; without substance." I do not see how I downplayed the incident during my interview with Sergeant Crowder. I made it clear that I was charged; I prepared for trial by going through the Queen's R and Os; I was appointed an assisting officer (Captain Pamela Evelyn); I went to trial, and the case was dismissed. Please see page 12. The interview may be on video. Why did Colonel Von Bulow dismiss the charges? In my letter to Colonel Von Bulow, I made it clear that I wanted to go to trial and that the charge was not dismissed for my benefit. It was dismissed specifically for the benefit of Sergeant Michaud (and other immediate superiors) who is clearly racist and power hungry.

Some of the people in the army have a way of grossly exaggerating: "The military further added that you did not show up on time or not show up at all." I was late for training three times or less. Once I did not show up on a Friday night because I was ill. I left a message on the army's voice mail stating that I was ill. Sergeant Chernaiwski called my home the same night and I told him that I would try to attend next morning. I showed up the following Saturday morning. When a similar incident occurred with Number 1 Candidate, it was not an issue. Please see page 44. Why is it OK for one person and not for the other? Was I suppose to just turn a blind eye?

In response to the statement, "There had also been another incident for which you were also charged, where a corporal left you to secure weapons in barracks and you decided to leave your post as well." It was not a corporal who assigned me picket duties. It was Sergeant Michaud through a corporal. The other black female who misfired told me that Sergeant Michaud assigned us picket duties because we misfired. To my knowledge, a person cannot be punished twice for the same offence. Since I was already charged and scheduled to go to court for misfiring, Sergeant Michaud had no authority to take the place of the judge by assigning me picket duties for misfiring while he went drinking. Nonetheless, I accepted my picketing duties without complaint. **Approximately two Hours into my picketing duties, Corporal Crumb <u>dismissed</u> the mentioned corporal and me from picketing duties.** Therefore, when Sergeant Michaud returned, I was not required to be in the area. Nonetheless, I was in the area on the phone. After yelling at me at the top of his alcohol breath, he chose to charge me. He did not care to hear any explanation from me. **He later decided to dismiss this charge prior to going to court because he knew there was no basis for it.** Please see page 13, #7. The morning after the incident, Corporal Adofo witnessed Sergeant Michaud laughing while telling another immediate superior how he "bawled out Green last night." If this is not harassment, I don't know what is.

My attitude was poor towards which military authority? Am I required to smile and say "master" while someone degrades me based on my race and gender? Anyone who feels the need to degrade a subordinate to make himself feel better does not think highly of himself. Did Constable Rick Morris bother to find out about my attitude towards immediate supervisors Corporal Andrea Dennis, Corporal Sophia Miller, Corporal Bernard Skerrett, Corporal DeGroot and others whose names I cannot recall? To say my "attitude became poor towards military authority" is maliciously exaggerating my attitude towards military authority. I have no problem with military authority. I have a problem with individuals in the Army who use their power to perpetuate racism and gender discrimination.

I may not have given 100% to the Army; however, considering the number of people who failed and who quit before completing basic training (less than 1/3 graduated), I am satisfied with the percentage of effort that I gave.

Constable Rick Morris wrote in his report that I took the racist treatment "as a personal attack rather than for what it was meant." Please see Appendix 10. Would he have been able to maintain a positive attitude towards his oppressors?

Attached is an article entitled, "**Forces Deterring Enlistment.**" The stated discrimination practices do not get better once a candidate is recruited; they get worse. Would Constable Morris and Constable Joseph expect these minorities to maintain a positive attitude while they were being degraded?

Rebuttal #18

In response to "On November 01, 2000, Constable Joseph attended the Military Headquarters in Toronto to review your file. On 24 November 2000, Constable Joseph completed his report in order not to recommend you for further consideration in the application process.": This is clearly stating that the RCMP rejected me for employment based on my military record. During the orientation in July 1997, a prospective applicant asked Constable Wanda Jackson whether military service gave added points for employment with the RCMP. Constable Jackson replied, "No." Then, why is my military service such an issue? Also, as Constable Morris stated in his report when referring to my shortcomings, "These mean nothing if you pass the course in training situations. They are not recorded anywhere to cause you grief." Appendix 10, page 66. On the contrary, these recorded statements have caused me nothing but grief. In fact, they are the primary reasons for my not getting employed by the RCMP.

Obviously Constable Joseph chooses to interpret the harassment and racism that I faced in the army as my "justification" for my performance. The fact is, some of my immediate supervisors were racist and biased. Unfortunately, these people were put in a position of power; and they used that power to discriminate against me every chance they got.

Rebuttal #19

Apparently Captain Pamela Evelyn's interview did not carry any weight because she is considered my "friend, associate and business partner." I would like to point out that Captain Evelyn and I met when she was appointed my assisting officer by Captain Chamberlain. Yes, we developed a friendship which is evidence that I have no difficulty relating to military authority.

Sergeant Major Mike McFarlane and I never had a conversation. I don't think he even knows who I am because I certainly do not know who he is.

Sergeant Michaud was not on my basic training course (QL2). I met him one training weekend and it is a weekend that I will never forget because of the sergeant's racist treatment towards me. Private Virgania Dacosta and I went through basic training together. She is the girlfriend of Sergeant Michaud (maybe wife by now). Considering the history between Sergeant Michaud and me, it is highly unlikely that Private DaCosta would give an impartial evaluation of me. The RCMP embraced her statements even though she is the spouse of my major oppressor; however, they basically rejected the statements of Captain Evelyn because she is my "friend."

Master Corporal Skerrett was my direct supervisor while working on base. He told Constable Morris that I was not against being charged for misfiring. **I was opposed to the fact that four people misfired: the two female, black people were charged while the two male non-black people went on with their lives as though nothing happened. I find it amazing that the RCMP finds nothing wrong with this**. Master Corporal Skerrett recommended me for employment with the RCMP; however, his recommendation was disregarded. I say Master Corporal Skerrett's statements were disregarded because Constable Joseph **accused me** of leaving the army to avoid charges after Master Corporal Skerrett stated otherwise in his interview. Please see page 9.

Corporal Sophia Miller and Corporal Andrea Dennis were my direct supervisors on my QL2 course. Why were they not interviewed? The RCMP was perfectly biased in their interviewing; they interviewed people who would tell then what they wanted to hear--information to reject my application for employment. I am inclined to believe that the situation with the army is an excuse to reject my application for employment; if it were not the army, it would have been something else considering that my background investigation started in December 1999 and then thrown aside until May 2000.

Response to Background

Is it legal to arbitrarily raise the score? Please see page 3, #7.

"The final part of the background investigation was concluded on 11 November 2000." The final part of the background investigation took place one year after my interview. Why?

In response to "...The applicant was found outside the room by her sergeant and reprimanded for this as well." I was not even required to be in the area because I was dismissed from picketing duties. If Corporal Sophia Miller was interviewed, she would have properly informed the interviewer; however, the interviewer was not interested in the truth. Common sense should have told the interviewer that if power hungry Sergeant Michaud dropped this charge prior to going to trial, obviously he should not have charged me in the first place. Even when it was confirmed that I had permission to leave, Sergeant Michaud never apologized for "reprimanding" me.

The sergeant dropped this charge before going to court because he should not have charged me in the first place. However, according to the RCMP, I should not feel that I did not deserve the charge.

In response to "All sources interviewed indicated that she was not treated unfairly." Did the interviewer expect the people who treated me unfairly to say they were biased and racist?

In response to "The applicant omitted to provide, during the Security/Suitability interview, that she had received several shortcomings as well as being verbally counselled for standard performances while in the Army Reserves." Question 31was, 'Have you ever been the subject of disciplinary action by a previous employer?'" Except for the charge of misfiring, where were there other disciplinary actions? Who did not have shortcomings? Who was not counselled for standard performance? No charge was laid for my performance nor shortcomings. During my interview with Sergeant Crowder, I did not put much emphasis on my employment with the military because it was not a requirement for employment with the RCMP. Since when do prospective employees go to interviews to focus on discussing their shortcomings?

In response to "Based on the information provided in this report, the applicant does not meet the requirement in the competency of 'Integrity and Honesty' and is found not suitable to become a member of the RCMP." I find this statement to be libelous and slanderous against me. I would like to remind Constable Joseph that Captain Chamberlain told Captain Pamela Evelyn that it is people with my characteristics that the army needs. Furthermore, Colonel Sutherland, in the presence of Master Corporal Skerrett, said to me, "I commend you for seeing this through. Most people would drop their gear and walk away, but you did not do that and for that you should be commended." How is that for integrity? I still do not see an issue of honesty; where have I lied?

The RCMP interviewers have nerves questioning my integrity and honesty when they are blatantly lying about not discussing my job offers in Korea; they are blatantly lying about giving me a date of March 20, 2000 for the return of my file from the background investigation; and they are blatantly lying about re-doing my PARE and paying for it in October 2000. Furthermore, they focus on petty issues. They interviewed people who harassed and discriminated against and then accepted their lies as gospel while ignoring the people who told the truth. Moreover, the RCMP deliberately blotted out the positives in my file. They refuse to release Master Corporal Skerrett's interview even though he gave me written permission to have a copy. I did not hide anything during my interview because I have nothing to hide; my life is an open book.

My law enforcement professors at Seneca College are all police officers or retired police officers. They all recommended me for employment with the RCMP. Obviously they do not feel that I have a problem with a policing environment. However, their opinions mean nothing to Constables Bob Joseph and Rick Morris. I should also add that the two people who were interviewed from my Member of Parliament's Office recommended me for the position.

Leaving the army was my decision. I can return if I choose to do so. Would the RCMP have rejected me if I were still in the army?

Rebuttal #20

In response to "...the personal comments made by Rick Morris were not taken into consideration in order to reject you from the recruitment selection process." Really? I would not expect the RCMP to say otherwise. Please see Appendix 9, 10 and 11.

Response to Allegation #1

Allegation: "I believe I was denied the position because of my colour, sex and family status."

In this report, the RCMP chose to focus on the issues in the military as the primary reason for denying me employment. The RCMP has a deliberate inaccurate perception of my service in the army.

The RCMP chose to downplay Constable Rick Morris' comments of my family status i.e., single mother living in subsidized housing. If it were not an issue, why include it?

What about the focus on my low-paying jobs and my bankruptcy issue where Constable Morris referred to me as being unethical? "I see this bankruptcy as an ethical problem of escaping her educational debts and still ending up with her educational credentials."

Constable Morris further wrote, "Green has proved that she can learn but seems to have no ability to apply what she learned." I find this statement degrading. In fact, I find it racist. It reminds me of how Sergeant Michaud and some other immediate supervisors treated me while I was in the Canadian Armed Forces. Please read Appendix 9, page 65. In Constable Morris' writing, I sense a strong tone of hostility towards me.

Regarding the RCMP statistics: a total of 11 visible minorities (male and female) were sent to Depot covering the period of April 2000 to March 2001. How many of those 11 minorities were black female? According to RCMP's rejection letter dated November 27, 2000, "Currently there are a limited number of positions available and we have a sufficient number of applicants who are deemed to be more suitable." What happened to the RCMP's quota? Please see page 53.

I maintain that the RCMP discriminated against me based on the following:

-racism (through the military);

-my family status (single mother);

-my gender (female/mother)

-bankruptcy;

-delayed my application without cause while hoping I would lose interest;

-my socio-economic status (low-paying jobs).

I was not denied employment with the RCMP based on my inability to be a good police officer; I was denied employment due to discrimination, primarily based on my race, my gender, and my family status.

Sincerely,

Deneace Green

Appendix 7

Investigations Branch Direction des enquêtes

Appendix 7

File 20011034

February 20, 2004

PROTECTED **BY EMAIL AND PRIORITY POST**

Ms Deneace Green
7/2 Ban 516-8 San Yong 1 Dong
Dong Du Chon City
Kyung ki Do - 483-031
South Korea

Dear Ms Green:

The investigation into your complaint against the Royal Canadian Mounted Police has been completed. A copy of the investigation report is enclosed for your review.

If you would like to submit comments on the report, you can do so by writing to me at the address below, fax or email. **Your submission must be no more than 10 pages in length (including any attachments), and must not include documents which have been provided and reviewed during the course of the investigation, or any information related to confidential settlement discussions in the course of mediation or conciliation. Any such documents or information will not be placed before the Commission.** Your submission may be disclosed to the other party.

You can provide your submission on or before March 15, 2004. In order to avoid delay in the handling of this matter, extensions to this period will not be granted, except in extraordinary circumstances. This may be your last opportunity to provide comments to the Commission on the merits of the complaint.

The complaint, along with the investigation report and submissions which we receive from the parties, will be submitted to the Commission at one of its upcoming meetings. After reviewing these documents, the Commission will make a decision on the disposition of the case. The Commission can accept or reject the recommendation in the report. You will be advised of the Commission's decision as soon as it is rendered.

Yours sincerely,

John J. Chamberlin
Manager, Investigations

Att.

344 Slater Street, Ottawa, Ontario K1A 1E1
344, rue Slater, Ottawa (Ontario) K1A 1E1
Toll-free / Sans frais 1-888-214-1090, TTY / ATS 1-888-643-3304, Fax / téléc. (613) 947-7279
www.chrc-ccdp.ca

CANADIAN HUMAN RIGHTS COMMISSION
COMMISSION CANADIENNE DES DROITS DE LA PERSONNE

Investigator's Report

Complaint Information

File Number(s): 20011934

Date of Complaint(s): January 14, 2002

Complainant: Deneace Green

Respondent(s): Royal Canadian Mounted Police

Section(s) of the Act: Section 7

Ground(s): Colour, Sex and Family Status

Referred to Mediation: Yes

Parties Participated in Mediation: Yes

Recommendation

It is recommended, pursuant to subsection 41(1) of the *Canadian Human Rights Act,* that the Commission deal with the complaint.

It is recommended, pursuant to subsections 44(3)(b) of the *Canadian Human Rights Act,* that the Commission dismiss the complaint.

Signature

S Ramanujam — Feb. 03. 2004.

Investigator: Sita Ramanujam — ***Date***

Summary of Complaint and Respondent's Defence

1. The Complainant, Ms. Deneace Green alleges that the Respondent, Royal Canadian Mounted Police discriminated against her in employment by refusing to hire her on the grounds of colour (Black), sex (female) and family status (single mother) in contravention of section 7 of the *Canadian Human Rights Act.*

2. The Complainant alleges that in August 1998, she began the respondent's application process including physical aptitude test, was interviewed and was offered a conditional offer in December 1999. She continued the process in 2000 for the second time and she was ultimately denied employment in December 2000.

3. The Complainant alleges that in 1999 when she took the physical aptitude test she was the only Black out of the 18 candidates. In February 2000 when she took the final physical aptitude test she was the only Black candidate to pass the test.

4. The Complainant alleges that the respondent's recruiter asked her for the names and dates of birth of her children which she had previously provided in the application form. Further, the recruiter in his report made derogatory comments about her single mother and financial status.

5. The Respondent and its representatives deny the allegations that the Complainant's application was rejected because of her colour, sex and family status. The conditional offer was made on the basis that she pass the "Top Secret" level of security. The complainant did not obtain this security clearance because she was found unsuitable. The Complainant's application was rejected based on applicant's background investigation.

6. The Respondent and its representatives state that of the 65 successful candidates, 11 were Visible Minorities (male and female), 17 were females, 3 were Aboriginals (male and female) and 34 were males. The Respondent states the applicant's family status is not entered into their computer system when they are enrolled. The Respondent states that the contract investigator who did the background check and who made the derogatory remarks in his report was reprimanded.

Background

7. The Respondent, Royal Canadian Mounted Police is a national police force.

8. All documentation pertinent to the complaint was reviewed. The Respondent's representatives, Cst.Robert Joseph, Sgt. Crowder, Ms. Karen Cleary and the Contract Investigator, Mr. Rick Morris were interviewed. The Complainant's witnesses, Capt. Pamela Evelyn, and Master Corporal Andrea Dennis and Corporal. Sophia Miller(from the Military Reserve) were interviewed.. Master Corporal. Bernard Skerrett also from the Military Reserve, did not respond to the voice mail message and a letter sent to him to contact this Investigator.

Reasons for Delay in Filing Complaint

9. The Complainant's application was rejected on December 11, 2000. At her request, the Complainant received a copy of the RCMP investigator's report on her background check in May 2001. The Complainant contacted the Commission in June 2001. The complaint was signed on

January 11, 2002. The one month delay is due to the Commission's administrative process as the complaint needed revisions.

Prejudice to the Respondent

10. The respondent has not raised an objection to the delay in filing and provided its defence. Witness were available.

Recommendation on Timeliness

11. It is recommended, pursuant to subsection 41(1) of the *Canadian Human Rights Act,* that the Commission deal with the complaint.

(Allegation 1) The Complainant was denied employment by the Respondent because of her colour, sex and family status.

12. The Complainant states that in August 1998, she began the Respondent's application process to become a Police Officer by completing the screening exam and in October 1998, she received a letter informing her that she received a score of 99/145. The passing grade was 84/145.

13. The Respondent states that Ms.Green wrote the "RRST" (screening test) on July 16, 1997. On September 3, 1997, a letter was sent to her by the Respondent advising her of her score of 89/145. On October 6, 1997 she was advised by Priority Mail letter that she had been selected from the initial Rank List. On January 12, 1998, another letter was forwarded to her advising her that she had not provided the London Recruiting Office with the "PARE" (Physical Aptitude Test) certificate. She was advised that her application was carried over to the next cycle. On May 6. 1998, a letter was sent to Ms. Green advising her that she was had not been successful in the April 1, 1998 selection and that her application file was closed. On August 12, 1998, she rewrote RRST at the Newmarket Detachment in order to qualify for another selection. On October 20, 1998, she was advised by letter that she scored 99/145 in the screening exam and that her score qualified her for the April 1999 selection. However, there was no selection in April 1999 as "Depot" (The Cadet Training Centre in Regina) was closed.

14. Ms. Green rebuts that the RCMP was aware of her November 1997 PARE results; therefore, she was waiting to re-do the PARE before submitting a PARE certificate. She states that she was not informed that the Depot was closed.

15. Ms. Green states that she received an application package and on September 18, 1999, she took the PARE test which she passed. Of the eighteen people that took this test she was the only Black candidate. Of the six females who took this test she is the only one who passed the test. On November 14, 1999, she was interviewed by Sgt. Crowder for six hours and in December 1999, she received a conditional offer which stated that she should be expecting to enroll within the next two to twelve months.

16. The respondent states that on August 3, 1999, a priority letter was forwarded to Ms. Green advising her that she has been selected and that a PARE certificate had to be provided in order to be interviewed. The application package was included. On September 21, 1999, a PARE statistics form was forwarded by fax to the London Recruitment office advising that she had successfully completed the PARE. The Respondent does not keep any statistics on the number of applicants attending the PARE sites at any given time therefore it cannot provide any statistics on how many males, females and visible minorities took the PARE test on that day. The Respondent and Sgt. Crowder confirm that on November 4, 1999, Ms. Green was interviewed by Sgt.

→ • The certificate has a form that gives a description ~~of~~ each person.
• The RCMP sends people to the PARE. If they don't know who is at what stage of the recruiting process, how do the know if they are actually doing anything to improve the number of minorities on the force? How do they measure their target of ... listed in their recruitment package? Please see pages 146 & 147. The RCMP ~~[illegible]~~ states that it "cannot provide any statistics on ..." Yet, the form that accompanies the PARE certificate is called Pare statistics. The upper left corner of the form tells where to send the statistics [illegible]

Crowder and that the RMSIG interview did not take six hours. However, the Security/Reliability interview was completed after a one hour lunch break following the RMSIG. There was indeed a one hour lunch break. However, I started the interview at AM. and finished at 2: PM. The number of hours add up to

17. Ms. Green rebuts that Corporal Karen Cleary told her that the RCMP usually select four to six females for each PARE and only one or two are expected to pass. She maintains that she was at the recruiting office for six hours for the interviews.

18. The Respondent states that on December 15, 1999 a letter was mailed to Ms. Green. The letter indicated "while the conditional offer merely indicates that you may expect to be enrolled before the end of September 2000, you should be prepared to be enrolled anytime within the next two to twelve months." The conditional offer states "RCMP is prepared to offer you enrolment as a cadet, subject to the following conditions: "Your field investigation confirms that you meet the RCMP requirements for suitability and must remain suitable until enrolled; that you obtain the "Top Secret" level of security clearance." Ms. Green did not obtain a security clearance as Ms. Green was found unsuitable. The recruitment clerk, Ms. Cleary denies having made the comments attributed to her.

19. Ms. Green rebuts that between January 2000 and February 26, 2000, RCMP did the reference checks on her and she completed her psychological testing, medical and dental examinations. She took her final PARE test on February 26, 2000 and of the 18 she was the only female and the only Black candidate. She states that Ms. Karen Cleary informed her that "she would most likely be enrolled by April 2000." On March 31, 2000 Ms. Cleary told her that her file was due back by the end of April 2000.

20. The Respondent states that a letter dated December 7, 1999 was sent to Ms. Green informing her that a psychological assessment had been scheduled for January 5, 2000. The background investigation had also been started at that time. The respondent confirms that Ms. Green took the PARE test but it does not have any statistics on the applicants that took PARE on that particular day and therefore, any record of how many males, females and visible minorities took the PARE test that day. Same as before

21. The recruiting clerk, Ms. Karen Cleary, denies having made the comments attributed to her. Further, she does not indicate to the applicants when they would be going to Regina as this is the recruiters' responsibility.

22. Ms. Green rebuts that Ms. Cleary did make the comments that she made to her. If she did not, then one of them is lying and it is not she. She contends that the RCMP lost her file. Her background investigation was not completed because her file was back in the London office. Otherwise, based on the comments made by Ms. Cleary she would have been most likely enrolled by April 2000, after four months processing time, after the interview on November 14, 1999. She also reiterates that she was the only Black candidate when she took PARE tests on September 18, 1999 and February 26, 2000.

23. Ms Green states that in connection with her background check, on May 30, 2000, the RCMP recruiter, Mr. Rick Morris contacted her and requested information pertaining to her employment and the dates of birth of her children which information she had provided earlier. She states that on July 4, 2000, she was informed by Ms. Cleary that the background check on her was not completed. The candidates who took the PARE test in September 1999, went off to basic training (to Regina) in April 2000. She states that Ms. Cleary also called her on September 12, 2000 and requested two additional references, her children's' dates of birth and updated employment information. On September 14, she spoke to the recruiter Cst. Robert Joseph who informed her that she would have to redo the PARE test in October 2000 as the last one she did was about to expire. She was also told that the additional interviews would take only two weeks. Ms. Green states that the candidates who had passed the PARE test with her were getting ready to graduate (in Regina) while she was waiting for her application process to be completed.

24. The Respondent and its representative, Const. Joseph and Mr. Morris state that the background investigation was controlled by Department Security Section. Due to the detachment's heavy workload at that time, background investigations were taking a longer to complete. Mr. Rick Morris who was a retired member of the RCMP was hired as a contract investigator. The background investigator does not have a copy of the candidate's entire file rather only the necessary forms to complete the background information on the candidate. The information concerning Ms. Green's children was not provided when filling out the TBS330-60 form, nor was it provided prior to Mr. Morris starting the background information because information on children under the age of 18 was not required. Ms. Green's children initially were under 18 years of age. However, her oldest child had reached the age of 18, hence the date of birth was requested. Mr. Morris also requested updated information of employment as some of the places of employment provided by Ms. Green could not provide information on her. The company TigerTe indicated that they had no record of Ms. Green working for them. Sitel Corporation Canada, had no record of Ms. Green working for it between January 1999 and December 1999.

25. The Respondent and Cst. Joseph state in April 2000 or later, seven males were sent to Depot (Regina.) Of these, three were visible minority applicants, one was Aboriginal and three were Caucasian applicants. On September 8, 2000, Const. Joseph reviewed Ms. Green's file and the background information. He requested the recruiting clerk, Ms. Cleary to contact Ms. Green and request two more character references, because one of the references was a University Professor at the University of Toronto, who had not seen or heard from Ms. Green since 1995. The other character reference had a close relationship with Ms. Green for a period of one year and had not had any involvement with her in the previous two years. Moreover, Part M of the guide to completion of personnel security clearance provided to all candidates including Ms. Green states; "References are not to include relatives. The three character references should be persons whose combined knowledge of you covers the screening period (10 or 20 years) and reference must be persons residing in Canada."

26. The Respondent and Cst. Joseph state that Ms. Cleary was also asked to seek clarification from Ms. Green on her marital status, as she had indicated being separated but had not provided a date on the form. They also required information which was not mentioned on form TBS330-60 concerning Ms. Green's daughter who had reached the age of 18 and information on Ms. Green's employment from January 2000 to date. They also sent a message to the Departmental Security Section with the following:

"* Request that another credit check be conducted on the applicant.
* Informing that the applicant would be providing two more character references;
* Informing that one of her associates, Anette Grandison was never interviewed;
* Inquiry with Army Reserve was never done;
* The applicant's current address check ws not done and if it was done, it was not on the report;
* The following places of employment were not checked: Coco-Cola Bottling.('96-02 to 97-02) and S&P Data ('95-12 to 96-02)
* Local indices with Metro Toronto Police and York Police were not done; and
* Criminal Record check on family as well as daughter could have been done but they did not have the information at that time."

27. The Respondent states that it takes well over four months to process an application. The RCMP national web site under the recruiting information indicates that the entire process may take six to eighteen months. The process can take longer when issues arise. Cst. Joseph states that Ms. Green's PARE certificate had expired. He did not inform her that she had to redo the PARE test in October 2000. He informed Ms. Green that it would take at least two weeks before additional interviews would be completed.

28. Ms. Green rebuts that when she started the application process, the average time for processing an application was four months. Had the Respondent processed her application and done a background check in a timely fashion, she would have been able to proceed to the Cadet

Training program by April 2000. She states that she provided her children's dates of birth in 1997. However, Mr. Rick Morris accused her of leaving her children off the TBS330-60 form and commented in his report "Leaving her children off her TBS330-60 form leaves much to ponder." She states that she faxed a copy of her divorce certificate to the Respondent on December 15, 1999; therefore, it was aware of her marital/family status. With respect to her previous employer TigerTel and Sitel, she faxed an update to Sgt. Crowder on March 19. 2000 that she no longer worked there as of January 2000 and that she was working elsewhere through Quantum Agency. She states Cst. Joseph in his conversation with her on September 14, 2000 told her that she would have to redo the PARE test and Ms. Cleary told her that the Respondent would pay for the test.

29. Ms. Green states that throughout this ordeal, she passed up other employment opportunities waiting to be enrolled in basic training. The candidates with whom she had completed PARE test were now (September 2000) getting ready to graduate.

30. The Respondent and Cst. Joseph state that Ms. Green had never indicated to the "O" Division recruiting section that she was passing up other employment opportunities. Unless Ms. Green provides the names of the candidates whom she thinks graduated from the Training College, the Respondent will not be able to verify this information.

31. Ms. Green rebuts that prior to her interview she discussed a job offer in Seoul, Korea with Ms. Cleary who informed her that she had to be accessible and if she left the country, her file would be closed. She states that during her interview with Sgt. Crowder on September 4, 1999, this matter came up and Sgt. Crowder informed her that RCMP loses a lot of people due to the long processing time from the time of the application to the interview and selection for the basic training program.

32. Ms. Green states that on October 25, 2000, she spoke to Cst. Joseph. He told her that there were problems with her background check. 1. He asked her if her decisions would be influenced by the fact that two of her brothers had records. 2. She had conflicts with her co-workers in her previous positions. 3. She left the Army (Military Reserve) to avoid charges. 4. She had short comings in the Army and she left her weapon unsecured. 5. She was late for training in the Army and did not show up for training. She states that she informed Cst. Joseph that these were taken out of context. For example, the charge of misfiring a weapon was dismissed by the Commanding Officer, Lt. Col. Von Bulow, because another Black recruit and she were charged whereas two white recruits who misfired were not charged. Whatever shortcomings she had in the Military, she successfully completed her basic training and she was honourably discharged on January 25, 2000. She states that Cst. Joseph advised her that he would continue the investigation and if she was unable to deal with the Army, he would not recommend her for RCMP training. She states that she provided the names of her colleagues in the Military. Capt. Pamela Evelyn, Master Corporal Andrea Dennis and Corporal Sophia Miller as references to clarify the alleged problems in the Military.

33. Cst. Joseph states that he did have a conversation with Ms. Green on October 25, 2000 in which he asked her questions about her relationship with her family and in particular with her two brothers, Dorman and Robin Green, both of whom had extensive criminal convictions and Dorman was incarcerated at that time. In this context, he did ask Ms. Green whether she would be influenced by her brothers and she replied that she would not.

34. Cst. Joseph states that the background investigation indicated that Ms. Green had personality conflicts with her coworkers at Jewish Vocational Services Toronto where she was employed between April and November 1999 and she left because of her frustrations with computers.

35. Cst. Joseph states that he asked her whether she had ever been the subject of disciplinary action by a previous employer. Ms. Green indicated that an incident occurred in the Military where she had discharged a weapon on the range which incident was investigated and was

deemed "unfounded." The review of her file, security interview and background investigation revealed, however, that due to a few delays, the Military decided not to proceed with the charge and also because Ms. Green had asked for a discharge. In her interview with Sgt. Crowder of RCMP, Ms. Green indicated that the charges were "dismissed." With respect to the discharge of a firearm, Ms. Green indicated that she heard the word "fire" while Sgt. Michaud was talking to her and she discharged the weapon. Two others who discharged their weapons were not charged. Cst. Joseph confirms that Ms. Green provided him with the names of the three individuals who witnessed what had occurred on the range.

36. Cst. Joseph states that the Military had also advised that Ms. Green would show up late or would not show up at all for training. Ms. Green admitted that she was late about three times and the delay was due to going home from work to change into her uniform. The Military had also indicated that Ms. Green was also charged in the Military for leaving weapons unsecured in the Guard room. A Corporal left Ms. Green to secure weapons (in the barracks) and Ms. Green decided to leave the post as well. Ms. Green responded that she was on the phone and she could still see the room and she had permission from the Corporal to leave the barracks. The Military stated that her attitude towards authority following this incident was poor.

37. Cst. Joseph states that he asked Ms. Green why she had joined the reserve and Ms. Green responded that she wrote the test (to join the Army) and she had another job. She was accepted by the Reserve. Ms. Green stated that she did not give 100% to the Army and could have left after basic training. Immediately after the conversation with Ms. Green he spoke to Cpt. Pamela Evelyn, the assisting officer in the weapon's discharge charge. Cpt. Evelyn stated that the Military had dropped the charges due to insufficient documentation. Cpt. Evelyn said that she had concerns and wondered whether it (the charge) might not have been legitimate. Cpt. Evelyn also said that she investigated the occurrence and found that more than one person had discharged their firearm and only two were charged. Two witnesses came forward to corroborate what Ms. Green had said about discharging the weapon. Cst. Joseph informed Ms. Green that he would continue his investigation regarding her file and further inquiries with the Military would be conducted.

38. Ms. Green rebuts that she never had a problem with the computers at JVC Toronto. The problem was with three different data bases. Ms. Green states that Lt. Col. Von Bulow dismissed the charges not for her benefit but for the benefit of Sgt. Michaud, the instructor who is a racist and power hungry and for the benefit of other immediate supervisors. The Military Representatives are grossly exaggerating when they state that she showed up late or did not show up at all. When she was sick, she left a message on the Military voice mail and Sgt. Chernaiwski called her at home. As a result, she went to work the next morning. With respect to not securing the weapons, she states that she was on picketing duty (guard duty of weapons room) and Corporal Crumb dismissed her from her picketing duties. When Sgt. Michaud returned, she was not required to be in the area. However, she was in the area and on the phone. She states that it is gross exaggeration to say that her attitude towards the Military authority was poor. She has problems with individuals in the Army who use power to perpetuate racism and gender discrimination. She also states that she may not have given 100% to the Army; however, considering the number of people who failed and who quit before completing basic training (less than one third graduated), she was satisfied with the percentage of effort she gave to the Army.

39. Ms. Green states that on October 26, 2000 she faxed further details regarding the investigation into her background. As of that date it had been two years and two months since she first wrote her exam with RCMP. On December 11, 2000, she received a letter from the respondent rejecting her application although she met all the requirements. The letter stated that "the decision was made as a result of the findings of our background investigation into your overall suitability. Currently, there are limited number of positions available and we have sufficient number of applicants who are deemed to be more suitable." She states that her witnesses, Capt. Pamela Evelyn, Master Corporal Andrea Dennis and Corporal Sophia Miller were not contacted prior to making the decision to reject her.

40. Cst. Joseph states that on October 25, 2000, Ms. Green faxed documentation of her previous correspondence with Lt. Col. Von Bulow, with respect to the various incidents in the Army and a copy of Canadian Forces Certificate of Service. They state that Ms. Green's application was processed as discussed in the preceding paragraphs of this report. On October 26, 2000, Cst. Joseph contacted the Military for further information on Ms. Green. On November 1, 2000, Cst. Joseph attended the Military Head Quarters and interviewed Lt. Col. Von Bulow, Sgt. Dave Michaud, Private Virginia Dacosta and Master Corporal Bernard Skerrett and reviewed Ms. Green's Military Personnel file. There were several disciplinary incidents documented besides the discharge of a weapon on the Range and leaving the barracks (Guard Room) with weapons unsecured that were documented. It was also documented that the incidents revealed a pattern of poor attitude, an unwillingness to accept military authority and only marginally acceptable performance. Ms. Green was on non effective strength from October 23, 1999 to January 20, 2000 and she was released from Military on January 25, 2000.

41. On November 24, 2000, Cst. Joseph completed his report. Based on all the information that was gathered, Cst. Joseph's report did not recommend Ms. Green for further consideration in the application process. The report was provided to Cpl.Heikkila, NCO i/c of the Recruiting Section and finally to Inspector Greg Johnson, OIC Staffing and Personnel "O" Division who concurred with Const. Joseph's findings. On November 27, 2000, Ms. Green was informed by a letter from Inspector Greg Johnson that RCMP was unable to offer her enrollment, that the conditional offer of Enrollment for a Regular Member position was hereby revoked and her application would be closed. It also indicated "the decision was made as a result of the findings of our background investigation into your overall suitability. Currently, there are limited number of positions available and we have sufficient number of applicants who are deemed to be more suitable."

42. Cst. Joseph states that Capt. Pamela Evelyn was interviewed by Cst. K.A. Chapman, Federal Enforcement Section, Toronto East Detachment possibly in January 2000 and by Cst. Joseph on October 25, 2000. Master Corporal Andrea Dennis and Corporal Sophia Miller were not interviewed. However, the Commanding Officer, Lt. Col. Von Bulow and other Military personnel were interviewed as stated in paragraph 38.

43. Ms. Green disputes the information provided by the Military Reserve with respect to her performance and attitude towards authority. She maintains that her explanations with respect to her performance and the incidents were not taken into consideration by Cst. Joseph. Her witnesses were not interviewed and/or the information given by Capt. Evelyn was disregarded by Cst. Joseph. She states that Master Corporal Bernard Skerrett recommended her for the RCMP position. She states that she faced racism and discrimination while she was in the Military Reserve and she left the Military Reserve on her own accord.

44. Capt. Pamela Evelyn who was interviewed states that she was in the Air Force Reserve and Ms. Green was in the Army Reserve. As such she cannot comment on Ms. Green's performance in the Army. Capt. Evelyn was also a Range Officer. She confirms that she was the Assisting Officer to assist Ms. Green in the charge of discharging a firearm on the range. She states that the Instructor used the word "fire" often while instructing the recruits and Ms. Green discharged the firearm when she heard the word "fire". Three others had also discharged their firearms but only two of them (Ms. Green and Ms. Piere) who were both Black were charged. The Commanding Officer, Lt. Col. Von Bulow did not proceed further with the charges against any of them due to insufficient information. Ms. Green requested her release from the Army and she was released. Capt. Evelyn confirms that she was interviewed by Cst. Joseph but did not think that Cst. Chapman interviewed her.

45. Master Corporal Andrea Dennis who was interviewed confirms that she was in the Army Reserve with Ms. Green between 1997 and January 2000 when Ms. Green left the Army. They went on weekend training sessions with parades on Thursdays. She states that she did not have any problems with Ms. Green while she was in the Army. Ms. Green always showed up for

parades and was never late. Ms. Green was always polite and courteous at all times and she followed orders at all times. Ms. Dennis was not a witness to the weapon's discharge on the Range incident.

46.Corporal Sofia Miller confirms that she was on the range at the time of "misfire" incidents. She did not witness Ms. Green "misfiring" her weapon however, she witnessed Private Lo who misfired his weapon during the practice rounds.She states that Ms. Green, Corporal Piere, Private Lo(Asian) and a Caucasian officer had misfired. Ms. Green and Corporal Piere who are both Black were charged and assigned to picketing duties to secure and guard the weapons room. The other two were not charged. Ms. Miller confirms that the charges were dropped due to insufficient evidence. Ms. Miller states that Ms. Green and she were in different units therefore, she cannot comment on Ms. Miller's performance in the Army. Ms. Miller confirms that Ms. Green resigned from the Army.

47. Master Corporal Bernard Skerrett was contacted by the Investigator. He did not respond to the voice mail messages left for him or the letter requesting them to contact the Investigator.

48. Ms. Green states that in May 2001, she requested and received a copy of the RCMP Investigator, Mr. Rick Morris's report. She states that in his report, Mr. Morris mentioned that she lived in subsidizing housing with her daughter and commented " how will she survive without income during the (Respondent) training period?" She states that being a single mother in subsidized housing should not have impacted on her application to the Respondent.

49. The Respondent and Cst. Joseph state that Ms. Green requested the security reports under the Privacy Act and she was provided with three reports on December 19, 2001. They admit that Mr. Morris provided a separate personal attachment with his security report which was kept separate from the Security file. They admit the comment made by Mr. Morris however, the personal comments made by Mr. Morris were not taken into consideration in order to reject her from the recruiting selection process. They state that Mr. Morris was reprimanded for his personal comments.

50. Mr. Morris who was interviewed admits that the background check usually involves the checking of references, employers and anyone else who may have pertinent information on the applicant. Mr. Morris spoke to Ms. Green because at the time of his investigation, the references/information Ms. Green provided were over a year old. He admits that he made the alleged comment about Ms. Green in his report and commented on the fact that she had declared personal bankruptcy. He states that he was not being judgmental rather, he was reporting the facts and he was not the decision maker on whether an applicant gets hired or not.

51. Ms. Green maintains that "RCMP discriminated against her based on the following:
* racism (through the Military)
* my family status (single mother)
* my gender (female/mother)
* bankruptcy
* delayed my application without cause while hoping she would lose interest and
* my socio-economic status (low paying jobs.)"

52 The Respondent reiterates that Ms. Green was not discriminated against because of her colour, sex or family status. Ms. Green was selected in August 1999, amongst 250 applicants.
* Male (visible Minority) 57
* Female (Visible Minority) 10
* Male (Aboriginal) 11
* Female (Aboriginal) 1
*Female 93

More female than male: where are they?

*Male 78
Total: 250

Family status information is not entered into the HRMIS (Human Resources MIS) system for RCMP applicants. Mr. Morris's personal comments on Ms. Green's family status were not taken into consideration in making the decision to reject her application.

53. The Respondent also states that the total allotment for the period covering April 2000 to March 2001 was 86 candidates. 21 positions were not filled as applicants were not fully processed. 65 candidates were enrolled and sent to "Depot" in Regina for the Cadet Training Program. The breakdown is as follows;

* Visible minorities (male and female)	11
* Aboriginals (male and female)	3
* Females	17
* Males	34
Total:	65

Cst. Joseph states that in 1999-2000 three Black females were selected and one was hired. In 2000-2001 no Black females were hired. In 2001-2002, one Black female was hired. This is a prime exam of how the RCMP's the is not in keeping with their hiring practices.

54. The Respondent and Cst Joseph state that Ms. Green's application was finally rejected based on the background investigation findings and references from her previous employers including the Military. Between 1999 and 2002, two black females in Ontario were hired by the RCMP. What a grand accomplishment on both sides. The RCMP, in their 6

Analysis

55. The investigation indicates that the RCMP application and recruitment process takes six to 18 months. This information is posted on the RCMP web site. The process could take longer if issues arise during the application and recruiting process. This may be posted now. however, that was not the policy when I applied. Maybe longer does not mean two years and three months, and it certainly does not mean three and a half years. What kind of issues?

56. The investigation indicates that the Complainant commenced the application process in July 1997. Since she had not provided her PARE (Physical Aptitude Test) certificate by January 1998, her application was carried over to the next cycle. The Complainant rewrote the screening test in August 1998, and completed the PARE test and qualified for the April 1999, selection. However, since the Depot (The Cadet Training Centre in Regina) was closed in April 1999 the process continued to the next cycle.

57. The investigation shows that the Complainant continued the various steps in the next selection process in 1999 and received a conditional offer in December 1999. This offer was conditional on the results of a field investigation followed by Top Security clearance. The Complainant had to remain suitable until enrolled. The selection process continued in 2000 during which time interviews with the Complainant and a background investigation was completed by November 2000. In December 2000, the Complainant was informed that based on the findings of the background investigation including the employment history, her application was rejected. The length of time taken on this application and recruiting process was in part due to the Complainant not providing the PARE certificate in time for the first cycle of recruitment and in part due to the RCMP depot being closed in the next cycle. It was also due to issues arising from the interview and background investigation process with respect to insufficient information provided by the Complainant which necessitated further investigation and in part due to the Respondent's heavy workload in processing the applications. Issues were dealt with in weeks.

58. The investigation shows that it could not be established that of the eighteen candidates who took the PARE test on September 18, 1999 the Complainant was the only Black candidate or that of the 18 candidates who took the PARE test on February 26, 2000, she was the only Black

candidate. The RCMP does not keep statistical records of the candidates who take the PARE test on the grounds of colour, sex or family status on any given PARE test days.

59. The investigation shows that in April 2000, seven male applicants who completed the application and recruiting process were sent to the Depot in Regina. Of these three were Visible Minority applicants, one was an aboriginal applicant and three were Caucasian applicants.

60. The investigation indicates that the total allotment for the period covering April 2000 to March 2001 was 86 candidates. 21 of these positions were not filled as applicants were not fully processed. Of the 65 applicants that were selected there were 11 Visible Minority males and females, three Aboriginal males and females, 17 females and 34 males. in 1999-2000 three Black females were selected and one was hired. In 2000 no Black females were hired. In 2001-2002, one Black female was hired.

61. The investigation shows that the RCMP does not enter the applicant's family status in their HRMIS (Human Resources MIS) system. The investigation shows that the RCMP and the RCMP Contract Investigator admit that the Investigator made personal comments about the Complainant's family and financial status. However, these comments were separate from the background investigation done on the Complainant by him. Therefore, these comments were not taken into consideration when the Respondent made the decision to reject her application. The Investigator was reprimanded for making these personal comments.

This is the same as saying Canadian Human Righ does not take their investigatio comments i consideratio

62. The investigation indicates that the Respondent's decision to not accept the Complainant's application was made as a result of the findings of its background investigation into the Complainant's overall suitability. Therefore, the Conditional Offer of Enrollment for a Regular Member position was revoked and her application was closed. She was so informed on November 27, 2000 by letter which she received on December 11, 2000.

Recommendation

63. It is recommended, pursuant to subsection 41 (1) of the *Canadian Human Rights Act,* that the Commission deal with the complaint because:

> the Complainant contacted the Commission within the one year of the alleged act.

64. It is recommended, pursuant to subsections 44 (3)(b) of the *Canadian Human Rights Act,* that the Commission dismiss the complaint because:

> the evidence does not support the Complainant's allegations that she was denied enrollment because of colour, sex and family status.